To Todd,
Best

Prime Time

.

How Baby Boomers
Will Revolutionize
Retirement
and
Transform America

MARC FREEDMAN

with Photographs by
Alex Harris and Thomas Roma

PUBLIC AFFAIRS

New York

TO
John Gardner

PUBLISHED IN THE UNITED STATES BY PUBLICAFFAIRS™,
A MEMBER OF THE PERSEUS BOOKS GROUP.

BOOK DESIGN BY JENNY DOSSIN.

Library of Congress Cataloging-in-Publication Data
FREEDMAN, MARC
PRIME TIME: HOW BABY BOOMERS WILL REVOLUTIONIZE RETIREMENT AND TRANSFORM AMERICA / MARC FREEDMAN : WITH PHOTOGRAPHS BY ALEX HARRIS AND THOMAS ROMA. — 1ST ED.
P. CM.
ISBN 1-58648-120-7 (PB)
1. RETIREMENT—UNITED STATES.
2. BABY BOOM GENERATION–UNITED STATES.
I. TITLE.
HQ1063.2.U6F73 1999
306.3'8—DC21 99-26333
CIP

1 3 5 7 9 10 8 6 4 2

CONTENTS

Our enormous and rapidly growing older population—commonly portrayed as a burden to the nation and a drain on future generations—is a vast, untapped social resource. If we can engage these individuals in ways that fill urgent gaps in our society, the result would be a windfall for American civic life in the twenty-first century. We might just accomplish something else along the way: bring greater fulfillment and purpose to the postmidlife years and transform what it means to age in this country.

This is the argument of *Prime Time*. And with publication of the hardcover in spring 2000, I set out on a tour designed to communicate the book's message as widely as possible. It was a heartening experience. Many of the people I met agreed emphatically with the notion that older Americans are an overlooked national asset, and some were already at work forging "second acts" dedicated to public service.

One of the most inspiring encounters occurred early in the tour, in San Diego, where I appeared on a morning interview show at the local National Public Radio station. After talking with me about *Prime Time*, the show's host asked listeners to respond to the ideas being discussed. His invitation unleashed a procession of calls, mostly personal testimonials about finding new life in so-called retirement, underscoring the power of purpose and illustrating the wide range of possibilities for significant engagement in later life.

These tales and several more like them left me eager to hear more, and I found myself edging forward as the host agreed to take one final caller. On the line was Mary, a woman just turned sixty. However, she had not phoned to announce her own third-age civic heroics.

"I would like to disagree with everything that's been said," she began in a voice polite but quavering with emotion. I was stunned. Wasn't the notion that older adults are an important social asset obvious to all? How could anybody disagree so vehemently, especially somebody in this stage of life themselves?

To make matters worse, Mary wasn't a crank. She was simply someone who had worked hard since age sixteen, functioning as a paragon of productivity for more than forty years, opting to put on the brakes only when her boss persisted in heaping greater and greater responsibility on her. Finally she said, "That's it," and retired.

Having also, along the way, raised children on her own, she was exhausted. And though Mary was by no means yearning for the golf-course retreat of her parents' generation (her goal was to walk on the beach and to meditate), she was offended by what sounded like my exhortation to take on more duties, make more contributions, do *more work*.

In the coming weeks I heard this protest from others, interspersed among more affirmative reactions. Its recurrence forced me to a pair of realizations. The first was that I was inadequately communicating the hope for an aging America expressed in *Prime Time*. My goal was to expand opportunities and options, not obligations; it wasn't to promote an endless grindstone, or to uphold giving back as the only legitimate route to aging successfully.

Rather, what we need to do is widen the range of compelling pathways available to individuals in later life. Specifically, I believe, we need to uphold and develop the option for public service that constitutes the greatest potential "win-win" combination for individuals and society. We have long failed to do so. It is still much easier to disengage or focus on leisure in later life than it is to make a significant investment in the common good.

The second realization was that as much as I would like to dismiss the concerns of individuals such as Mary as unusual or idiosyncratic, they in fact reflect a widespread social problem in this country today. Quite simply, midlife overwork in America has reached pathological proportions. Indeed, this situation presents one of the greatest challenges to realizing the aspirations at the core of *Prime Time*.

Consider new data from the International Labor Organization (ILO) revealing that Americans now work harder than any other population in the world. According to the ILO study, we added 36 hours of annual work during the 1990s. As a result, we can claim 137 more hours of labor a year than Japanese workers and an astounding 499 hours—or twelve and a half weeks—more work than our German counterparts.

No wonder Mary, like so many others, is tired. Indeed, the new wave of Americans approaching later life might well constitute the most exhausted generation in our nation's history. So, at precisely the juncture when we need the time, talent, and experience of the older population more than ever before—given that those in the middle generation are overwhelmed with work and family responsibilities—this group is worn out from years battling the midlife time bind.

How might we resolve this dilemma, not only to realize the potential benefits of engaging the talent of older Americans but also to avert troubling concerns about the consequences of a rapidly growing, politically powerful, and socially disengaged population of aging boomers?

First, we need to be realistic. Not everyone will want to pursue public service in later life. Some will prefer to hit the links, while others will choose to do nothing at all. It is their privilege.

The good news is that studies continue to show that a significant portion of the aging population is interested in giving back. Recent AARP research reveals, for example, that half of Americans over fifty are planning to incorporate service into later life. Considering the size of this cohort in the coming decades, we are talking about a potential tidal wave of available talent.

We also need to be patient. Many of those interested in making community service, volunteering, or public interest work an important part of their postmidlife plans are not going to be ready to plunge headlong into these pursuits after leaving midlife jobs. They will want time to rest and exult in their liberation from schedules and commitments. For a while, they will likely want to do the exact opposite of everything they were doing before. However, after some months, or even years, of tending to other priorities many will likely be rested and restless—ready to explore new kinds of commitments.

This last point suggests something very important about how the concept of retirement is shifting. Increasingly, retirement has ceased to characterize a stage of life and instead describes an interlude between stages. More and more individuals are "retiring" for a period—to catch their breath—before making the transition to a new chapter in life embodying a new definition of success and a distinctive combination of learning, growth, and contribution.

Finally, realizing the potential for individual and social renewal inherent in the aging society will require considerable savvy. Significant numbers may well be receptive to engagement in volunteering, national service, and other forms of public interest work in the new chapter replacing retirement, but there is a difference between receptivity and reality. Bringing about a transformation in the actual role of older Americans will require substantial cultural and institutional change. We will need both to tell a new story about what is possible and desirable in later life and to create far more compelling opportunities for translating interest into action.

Much of *Prime Time* is dedicated to laying out how we might move forward on each of these fronts. However, a set of important developments since the first publication of the book is worth reporting.

As stated, we must revamp our message to the current and coming generation of aging Americans. To start, the challenge will be to convince these individuals that public service can be more than the kind of busywork long associated with "senior volunteering" (whose obsolescence is captured brilliantly in a recent *Fortune* article chronicling the frustration of retired executives attempting to apply their talents as volunteers in the nonprofit world—a piece titled, "Candy Striper, My Ass").

In replacing these musty notions, we will simultaneously need to do a better job of understanding what is on the minds of this new generation, what they might be looking for in new kinds of civic engagement. Some insights may be found in important social marketing research just completed by Margaret Mark, the former head of research at the advertising agency Young and Rubicam.

Mark's interviews with "retired" Americans (aged fifty-five to seventy) across the country and all along the socioeconomic spectrum confirms that these individuals love their newfound freedom and will be reluctant to trade it in for anything that smacks of punching the clock again. In focus groups and in-depth interviews, for example, they wax rhapsodic about the pleasure of no longer having to commute. Yet, when asked about their overall happiness with the retirement experience, they also express profound reservations. In particular they reveal a powerful sense of loneliness. Initially, these sentiments are puzzling, given that the men and women interviewed describe themselves as now far more available to friends and family. What they miss, it turns out, is not only a sense of purpose but the bonds they experienced at work—in Mark's words, "relationships with a purpose." Although purely social relationships have expanded in retirement, these developments cannot replace the kind of connection that came from working together with others to achieve a common goal. People not only miss these relationships but fear that they are lost forever.

None of this should be surprising for a reason closely linked to the post-work fatigue of the new retirees. Another side to the reality that Americans are spending all their time on the job is that they are accustomed to deriving an unprecedented degree of their identity and social life from the workplace. When they leave their careers, the paycheck isn't the only thing that vanishes.

In keeping with this notion, Mark argues that an important hook in prompting these men and women to try public service options may well be the chance to recapture purposeful bonds, especially if these opportunities simultaneously promise to make good use of the skills they have accumulated over the years. This last point raises another key finding of the research: although the individuals studied detest labels evoking chronological age or separation from earlier stages, they are drawn to language that emphasizes and affirms the value of what they have learned from life.

There is an adage in the marketing world that the fastest way to kill a bad product is good advertising. What if we succeeded in telling a compelling new story about the benefits of civic engagement in later life? What would individuals find waiting for them once they made the decision to come forward? Overall, the landscape of opportunities continues to be spotty, and we risk squandering the idealism of those who want to serve.

Signs of progress are to be found, however, among them a growing range of models aiming to translate the skills of aging professionals to new civic purposes—to my mind the undiscovered continent in this arena. *Prime Time* describes the work by older doctors to create free community health clinics serving the poor, and I am pleased to report not only that these medical clinics continue to proliferate but that lawyers are now getting into the act. One example, Legal Service for Children in New York, is mobilizing retired attorneys to help families of children with special education needs. At a time when only 13 percent of lawyers in firms of fifty or more attornies are over the age of fifty-five, we are witnessing a massive departure of talent in the law-firm world—an exodus that might be redirected to help nonprofit organizations and legal services.

Innovation is coming from established organizations as well. For example, through Habitat for Humanity's Care-A-Vanners, hundreds of older adults in recreational vehicles are defying the conventional notion of a Winnebago retirement. Rather than heading down the leisure road, the Care-A-Vanners travel from one Habitat site to another, building houses for the poor. In the process, a mobile community—built around "relationships with a purpose"— has taken shape.

Other noteworthy developments are evident in places both familiar and unexpected. I am encouraged by AARP's recent appointment of Bill Novelli as the organization's new leader. Novelli, a former Peace Corps staffer who retired from a highly successful marketing career in his fifties to run the Campaign for Tobacco Free Kids and other public interest operations, embodies everything that I uphold in this book. Given his background, it is little surprise that he has pledged a return to the vision of AARP's founder, Ethel Percy Andrus, who established "To Serve, Not to Be Served" as the organization's motto.

More surprising are predictions coming from leaders among the younger generation of public policy thinkers, quarters usually associated with the doom-and-gloom perspective on the aging of America emanating from groups such as Third Millennium. In a recent book, *The Radical Center*, Ted

Halsted, head of the New America Foundation, and Michael Lind, a senior fellow at the foundation, hold out the aging of America as an impending civic renaissance. "While many fret about the fiscal implications of the baby boom's mass retirement," argue Halsted and Lind, "history may show these worries to be far outweighed by all the potential economic and civic contributions of a large pool of healthy and publicly minded senior citizens."

They make a case for the presence of this potential in many ways identical to the one articulated in the coming chapters; however, they propose radically different means for getting there. To me this is an enormously encouraging development: the emergence of genuine debate about what it might take to realize the potential present in an aging America.

The most important impetus of all toward realizing a new role for older Americans in the civic life of this country may well be the events of September 11.

John Gardner, to whom this book is dedicated, recently observed that "it is a simple, easily forgotten truth that we need each other." In the aftermath of the terrorist attacks, there is much heightened awareness of the truth Gardner articulates. We can hope that this awareness will include realizing that we need the most experienced segment of the population, especially if we are to have any chance of sustaining the civic outpouring we have witnessed since the events of September 2001.

The potential payoff is not just in expanding volunteer numbers or talent. As the *New York Times* reported shortly after the attacks—in a commentary subtitled, "Younger Americans notice that experience counts in a time of crisis"—many of us were turning to older relatives, friends, and neighbors for the consolation of a longer-term perspective. It was a powerful example of how much we need the long view and other unique contributions that only this group can provide.

Ultimately, if we succeed in harnessing the social resources and distinctive perspective of older Americans, we might not only revitalize our civic life but help solve another fundamental issue in the process: the insane distribution of work and time that currently exists in this country, where midlife exhaustion is rampant while millions of older people are shoved off into the sunset. In short, we stand to create a society where both the burdens and joys of engagement are balanced across the life span, and all generations help to share the load—in other words, one that works better for everybody.

Marc Freedman
San Francisco
January 2002

CHAPTER I

The Aging Opportunity

We're living through the greatest miracle in the history of our species—the doubling of life expectancy since the Industrial Revolution—but we prefer to believe that our troubles are growing.

.

John Tierney

The Work Connection was inspired, in part, by Peter DiCicco's conviction that labor unions needed to think bigger, to range beyond the narrow objective of improving contracts for their members. They needed to become involved in strengthening the community and in standing up for the disenfranchised. The failure to do so, he was convinced, would mean marginalization. And as a vice president of the International Union of Electrical Workers (IUE) and head of its New England District Council representing workers at the Lynn, Massachusetts, General Electric plant, DiCicco was in a position to act on this conviction.

However, it was a personal experience as much as anything that sparked The Work Connection idea. DiCicco's nineteen-year-old son was in a car accident and ended up in court. At the hearing, DiCicco came forward to ask the judge for a community service sentence rather than a fine. "My son wasn't working," the union leader recalls. "He couldn't pay. So the court was fining the parents—not the boy. It isn't that I was unwilling to pay, but I was concerned because it didn't hold my son accountable for what he did." The judge agreed—but was simply too busy to get involved with creating new programs.

So DiCicco took on the idea himself, and soon the local electrical workers union was preparing to create what would become The Work Connection. In technical terms, The Work Connection was an "alternative sentencing program." Young people in trouble with the law for nonviolent crimes were given a second chance and a choice: They could avoid going to a "house of corrections" if they stayed out of trouble and compensated the victims of their crimes. In other words, they had to repay owners of all those televisions and stereos they had pilfered to get money for drugs.

The early reactions to the idea—from judges, police, community leaders—were quite favorable, yet there was also persistent concern about the ability of these young people to find and keep jobs. After all, if they failed to make their restitution payments, they would end up in jail. And these were kids who had never held steady employment, had dropped out of school, had no job skills or know-how, and could now boast a criminal record on their resumé.

For any of these kids to succeed, they would need extensive hand-holding, pragmatic advice, and new connections. They could forget about getting any of these from their probation officers, staggering under huge caseloads and generally more inclined toward scaring the boys straight than helping them get a foothold in mainstream society. They were unlikely to get that help from social workers either, for all their lofty intentions. How many social workers had ever looked for a job at an auto repair shop?

At roughly the same time DiCicco was struggling to get the program off the ground, he was required to leave town for an IUE conference in upstate New York. One of his responsibilities as an official in the international union was making the rounds to meet with various constituent groups. At one point in the proceedings, he ended up with the retirees. It was a low point of the conference.

These retired men seemed only to want to complain about what the union wasn't doing for them. As DiCicco was driving home, he continued to stew about the session. The retirees had everything going for them: excellent pensions, health benefits, years to live. Meanwhile, young guys in the union were being laid off and were facing real hardships. They were the ones with reason to complain. As DiCicco turned the session over and over in his mind, he realized it wasn't that these retirees were all that bad off materially—or had gotten such a raw deal from the union. What they lacked was purpose in their lives. They had too much time to sit around and think about what might be wrong with their situations.

Most of these men were individuals who had taken early retirement, often through incentive packages, but who were unprepared psychologically and socially to retire. For decades, the structure, human contact, and purpose in their lives had come, to a significant extent, from work. Now they found themselves in the position the great labor leader Walter Reuther years earlier had characterized as "too old to work, too young to die." They didn't consider themselves senior citizens: They weren't ready for the casino trips to Atlantic City. The local senior center had little to offer them. By default, they were spending their days staring at Phil Donahue, doing odd jobs around the house, and driving their spouses crazy.

But they were hardly washed up. In fact, they possessed exactly the kind of skills that the kids targeted by The Work Connection so desperately required. These men knew the Boston-area, blue-collar job networks—and were privy to the kind of informal information that's so often far more useful than the want ads when looking for jobs. They also knew the workplace. They knew what was expected, what you could and couldn't get away with, and how to get along in that setting. What's more, they had the time to listen to these kids, as human beings, not as professionals.

Why not solve two problems simultaneously, DiCicco thought, in a way that made obvious common sense? Get union retirees involved in mentoring kids and helping them break into the job market, and in the process, give the retirees themselves a new lease on life.

After he returned to District Council headquarters in the working-class town of Saugus (next to Lynn and the GE plant), DiCicco sent out a mailing to his own retirees, inviting them to help plan a role for themselves in The Work Connection. He received a dozen responses. For several weeks these retired electrical workers came down to the District Council headquarters every day at noon to eat sandwiches, shoot the breeze, and help devise the program.

A Stroke of Luck

arrived at The Work Connection two years later. DiCicco's program was by then flourishing. He'd raised money from foundations and from the state criminal justice system. The number of retired mentors had grown considerably. Success stories were piling up. And all of this was good news for me.

At the time, I was working for a nonprofit group in Philadelphia dedicated to helping poor children. We'd just run into unanticipated good fortune. Our director flew to California to talk to the board of a foundation newly interested in the issue of jobs for inner-city teenagers. His speech went well. So well that the trustees of the foundation decided to give him an unsolicited grant.

There would be one string attached, however. For several years, the foundation had been funding "intergenerational" projects in which young and old were brought together to enjoy each other's company. Most of the money was spent on feel-good efforts that did little harm but were not about to change the world. The board decided more serious problems needed to be tackled than underwriting field trips to the nursing home for elementary school students.

Nevertheless, a small sum remained unspent in the foundation's budget. Would we be able to use that money to write something—really, anything— about bringing the young and old together? It was time for the philanthropy to get its budget spent and to move on to bigger and better things.

We said yes, in part because we were just not inclined to turn away money. But, mostly, we had an idea. For years one issue had continued to loom larger and larger in our experience with efforts to help children. It seemed that whenever we bothered to talk to the young people about what mattered most to them, we heard little about the sophisticated curriculum or other techniques we professionals spent so much time and money concocting. Rather, these young people wanted to talk about a person, usually an adult staff member or volunteer, with whom they had developed a close relationship.

Because we were an organization full of economists and quantitative social scientists, we didn't quite know how to incorporate what the young people were telling us. These relationships couldn't be reduced to variables or shoehorned into our research equations. We hankered to return to the hardnosed business of developing "people-proof" programs—in other words, the kind we believed could be more reliably reproduced.

But as time went by, the perspectives of these young people became increasingly hard to ignore. They kept recurring, in more and more settings, with growing insistence. What these teenagers were saying—to anyone who would listen—was that they needed, more than anything else, adults who cared about them, who listened to them, who were willing to take a personal interest in their lives.

So by the time our serendipitous grant arrived, we were finally ready to take a closer look at the role mentoring might play in young lives. To satisfy the California foundation, we would restrict our focus to situations in which the mentors were older adults, and I was soon busy scouring the country for examples of members of the older generation being recruited to take young people under their wing.

Unfortunately, I couldn't find any. I found plenty of "nice" things going on: lots of arts and crafts and friendly visiting, but nothing that seemed to be taking on urgent social problems. I was beginning to understand why our benefactors in California were getting out of the "intergenerational" business—when chance intervened again. As luck would have it, in casual conversation I learned that a friend of a friend was employed at something called The Work Connection—and The Work Connection was using labor union retirees to mentor young people growing up on the wrong side of the tracks. I would at least have one project to talk about in my report to our fortuitous funder.

Tough Love

Nevertheless, driving into Saugus on a damp November day, I could feel my initial enthusiasm wane. Downsizing had arrived in the area, and the whole North Shore above Boston was showing the effects. Saugus looked like a ghost town. My destination, the New England District Council "headquarters," turned out to be little more than a drab, two-story house covered in clapboard siding, surrounded by a rusty fence and a dirt yard full of rocks and trash. Hanging over the front door was a weathered sign with the IUE logo. I parked in front of the sub shop across the street and headed inside.

As soon as I met Tom Flood—my friend's friend and contact at IUE—my spirits again began to lift. Flood's excitement about what was happening through The Work Connection was palpable. Athletic, witty, full of good humor, Flood was in his fifties. (Something about him was immediately familiar; later I realized it was his voice, indistinguishable from that of the actor Harvey Keitel.) A veteran of the antipoverty movement, Flood got his start as a youth worker in New Haven—an Irish kid working in the city's African American neighborhoods during the heyday of War on Poverty programs. He later was involved in some of the most innovative job training experiments supported by the Ford Foundation in the 1960s. Now he was helping DiCicco turn The Work Connection into a professional operation. Flood's enthusiasm was not only palpable but credible: He'd seen plenty of oversold programs and dashed expectations over the past two decades. He could tell the real thing.

After a quick trip upstairs to see the urbane DiCicco (the antithesis of the "union boss" I'd somehow anticipated), Flood took me directly to a back room in the house where a group of The Work Connection "mentors" were in the midst of their weekly meeting. It was a scene closely resembling the weekly staff meeting at any human services agency: a group of adults sitting around a conference table discussing troubled youth in concerned tones, swapping ideas for dealing with thorny issues that had arisen, providing mutual support in the face of their daunting assignments.

The main difference, of course, was that this was not a human services agency, and the individuals seated around the table were not a collection of newly minted MSWs. This was a union hall, and around the table were Nick Spaneas, Micky Petti, George Riley, Jim Brennan, and a dozen other retired Teamsters, cops, electrical workers, and firemen. (By now, the program had mushroomed beyond DiCicco's own union.)

These were Reagan Democrats, tough guys talking about the need for "tough love," in George Riley's blunt words. George, no more than five feet, six inches tall, resembled an old photograph of a professional wrestler: barrel chest, thick glasses, low center of gravity. You wouldn't want him to have you in a half nelson. (If Tom Flood reminded me of Harvey Keitel, then George was reminiscent of Marlon Brando's *Godfather*.) He had, until recently, led the Teamsters in a neighboring town.

Micky Petti was once a stand-up comic and musician who performed in Las Vegas, before alcohol ended that phase of his career. The one woman in the group, Frances Perrin, was retired from the local GE plant. Soft-spoken, Frances was part of the original group that planned the program. Her presence had a leavening effect on the men, and she defended a brand of tough love considerably more nurturing than George Riley's. "We can build any kind of relationship we want to," she explained. "You do become attached to them, and the more you do for a particular person, the more influence you can have on them."

Another member of the group, retired Salem fire chief Jim Brennan, was recruited by Frances. It took her quite some time to bring Brennan in, but she won through persistence: "Some people are a little bit leery. Their first thought is 'What good is it going to do?'" But Jim turned out to be a good recruit. He knew how to talk to kids. And the impact of having the respected former fire chief stand behind the young men when they were up for their probation hearings was significant. Jim's friendships with the police chief and other key local officials also turned out to be instrumental in building acceptance of the fledgling program.

Nobody's Kid

At one end of the table was Nick Spaneas. He commanded little attention at first. Nick wasn't funny like Micky Petti, or as imposing as George Riley. He hadn't held a vaunted position like Jim Brennan. But when Nick began talking, he commanded the rapt attention of the group.

An intense man in his late fifties, with gray-black hair, heavy eyebrows, and deep-set eyes, Nick was dressed in the official outfit of retirement—neatly pressed slacks, a blue polo shirt, and a light tan jacket open in the front. From his attire, it was not hard to imagine him leaning on his putter on the fourteenth green, gassing it up with other men of leisure.

But Nick was not a duffer. And he was hardly a member of the leisure class. "I don't have an education," he explained, "but I have an education in life . . . in real life, and that's what I teach them." All the young men attending Nick's one-on-one university of the real world had, like their mentor, dropped out of school. Most had lost interest in education years before. Some were homeless.

Nick's job was to get them a job. But he recognized that before he could tackle the issue of employment, he would have to overcome considerable wariness toward adults forged over years of stormy relationships with parents, teachers, police, probation officers, and other authority figures. "The first thing I tell them," Nick continued, "I'm not a government agent. I'm here for you. Only you. I'm here because I want to do this.'"

And despite initial resistance, Nick was getting through because he offered something these young people desperately wanted: He cared. "They need adults with patience, adults who feel about them. They don't want bluffers," he reflected. "They know. Because they can outsmart anybody. They've been out in the streets so long, they know if you're sincere or if you're faking."

Tom Flood told me years later that Nick was the one guy he'd ever met who could talk to inner-city kids and "convince them that America is a land of opportunity." It wasn't a ploy. Nick believed there was hope for change, and the young people believed Nick because his own story was so powerful. As a child in Greece during World War II, he endured the slaughter of his entire family of twenty-four. He watched his mother and sister die within two weeks. ("I was never a little boy," he recalled. "I was a man when I was seven years old.") He survived, emigrating to the United States where he started working in a leather factory. Later he was a barber, then a bus driver. For over a quarter century, he played the bouzouki in a Greek band. But there were hardships as well, the most painful a divorce that left him cut off from his only child, a daughter.

In Nick, the young men recognized an anti–role model. He didn't preach to them. There was no exhorting them to "Be like me." Rather, his message was a version of "Don't be like me, don't make the mistakes I made. You're young enough to save your own life." He reminded them that he could still remember what it was like "not to have any supervision in life, to bounce around, and feel that you are nobody's kid."

A Wiser Man

But Nick and the other retirees did more than focus on connecting with the young people and improving their attitudes. They displayed a radarlike appreciation of how these kids were likely to get derailed. They knew, for example, that the young people would probably get turned down at least three times before landing a job. In anticipation, the older men would accompany their charges to early interviews and be waiting outside to prop them up after the rejections. Knowing that the young people would oversleep on their first week of work, the older men turned themselves into human alarm clocks. In an act recalling Woody Allen's line that 90 percent of success in life is showing up, the retirees were outside the kid's house on day one of work, banging on the door at 7 a.m. to make sure he got to work on time. For weeks they would repeat the practice on Monday mornings.

Most telling, they stationed themselves outside the plant gate on payday, knowing that with a pocket full of money the young men would be easily tempted to go out and blow their paychecks. The Work Connection retirees would intercept the kids first and head with them directly to the bank to make their restitution payments. After that, how the kids spent their money was their business. (There were many variations of this kind of help. Micky Petti was so trusted by his young men that several would actually give him their paycheck when they received it in the middle of the day. Micky would pick up the checks, go to the bank and cash them by special arrangement, take restitution payments to the courts, and be waiting for the young men with the balance of the paycheck when they got off from work. This way the boys didn't have to leave work in the middle of the day or draw attention to their legal problems.)

Micky was also a master at getting the young men jobs. He knew exactly when to show up with his "boys" at the local diner to maximize the likelihood of "accidentally" running into local employers. Micky would introduce his boys to these men—most of them local contractors and small business owners—and personally vouch for them. Over time, he even managed to convince his son, the manager of several equipment rental stores, to hire exclusively from The Work Connection.

For all these success stories, the work was rarely easy. Nick, for example, spent two years trying to get through to one young man, Eddie Dillon. From the start, things were rocky. "When Eddie was feeling bad, when he was taking dope, he called me everything under the sun," Nick recalled. "He had the house upside down, clothes all over the place, broken dishes, broken glasses, his girlfriend was shaking like a leaf." For a while, Nick threatened to wash his hands of Eddie. But over time, Eddie began to turn his life around. He sobered up, started working more steadily, took greater responsibility for his children. Nick reflected, "This kid was in bad, bad shape. . . . It took me all this time, but I fought and I fought. . . . I made up my mind not to give up until he goes straight, but Jesus, finally, he woke up."

"Some of them," Nick stated, reflecting on the various young men he'd mentored, "already know [they need to change]. But they don't know how to get out of it, because they don't have any connections. The only connections they got is the same people who started them that way." He added: "Most of the families, they don't care. They've put up with so much from these kids—and these families aren't stable to begin with—they kick them out of the house." The result: "These kids have no shoes, they're hungry, they live in the streets, and they try to block everything out by getting drunk or being doped up, because nobody cares." One of Nick's "boys" was living in a refrigerator box.

The turning point with Eddie was when the drug-addicted and depressed twenty-year-old, who had never known his father, committed himself to the psychiatric ward of Massachusetts General Hospital. Nick visited him daily in the hospital, then helped him make the difficult transition back home. It cemented their relationship: "I trust him more than anybody on this earth," Eddie told me in a low voice. "He always makes me feel like someone cares . . . he's been more or less a father to me. He understands me. Maybe because he went through it himself. He's seen something that's made him a wiser man."

A Win-Win Situation

After my time with Nick and Micky and the other retirees, I was filled with a sense of optimism not only about what was happening in Saugus but also about the possibility of expanding The Work Connection idea to other communities. There were certainly plenty of union retirees and plenty of kids in Eddie's position.

One reason for my optimism was that The Work Connection retirees were such "ordinary people." They relied not on any special training or esoteric skills but on their own common sense and practical experience—their "educations in life." And they did so in the service of helping to alleviate real problems. (Jack Petropolous, one of The Work Connection staff, described the young people in the program as "the last-straw crowd.") Weren't there others out there with the same common sense, life experience, and yearning to make a difference?

The other reason I felt so encouraged sounds almost cynical: Nick and the others were not doing this work out of pure altruism. As Petropolous once remarked, these mentors were not a bunch of Mother Teresas. The men continued to show up, week in and week out, because they were getting so much out of their relationships with the youth. Reciprocity and mutual benefit were present in abundance.

As Nick once explained: "It's like being a father or a brother; I really get attached to them." Another time he revealed: "I'm hooked up with one kid—he touches some kind of spot in me." For Nick and the others, in many ways, The Work Connection offered a second chance every bit as much as it did for the kids—the chance to redeem themselves from past failings, to be the father they hadn't been before, to reaffirm the value of their own life experience. It was an opportunity for finding new purpose, for leaving the land a little better than they found it. They were doing something that mattered to themselves and to the community. In short, the success of The Work Connection program wasn't dependent on the shaky soil of idealism but rather was anchored in the much sturdier ground of enlightened self-interest.

In 1998 I reconnected with Tom Flood. We talked about The Work Connection and he told me about another retiree, one of his favorite mentors. "Mac" McElroy was a foreman at GE, a "big, raw-boned Irishman," recalled

Flood, who rode a motorcycle well into his 70s—"the kids used to think he was John Wayne." Mac had assembled a good life but in his fifties started drinking heavily: "He lost his job, he lost his house, lost everything, even his motorcycle." But somehow he managed to pull himself together, remarried, even bought another motorcycle. He turned out to be one of Flood's best mentors. He'd take kids to AA meetings, get them jobs, talk to them about the lessons he'd learned in life. In the process, he found new meaning and dignity and some peace.

Flood also told me that The Work Connection was dead. He left in the late 1980s, and funding dried up a couple years later. I was stunned to hear that this little jewel of a program, so much of a win-win situation for all involved, was unable to attract even modest support. I wondered about Nick, Micky, and the others and the vacuum that this demise must have left in their lives.

The news was also disconcerting. At a juncture when America is about to become a much older society, when warnings about coming generational warfare abound, how could we let this affirmative glimpse of a different kind of relationship between young and old slip away? At a time when our communities face a profound shortage of human beings to tend the social fabric, how is it that we continue to overlook the presence of vast and untapped human resources in the older population? Even in individuals (like Nick) who on paper might not look so impressive but who in reality possess so much that we desperately need.

A Solution Waiting to Happen

The Long Gray Wave

America today is in the midst of a demographic revolution, one that will transform the country into a much older nation. Although awareness of its proportions is growing, the revolution is hardly new. It has been building in slow motion for most of the past century, starting with the Industrial Revolution and then beginning to accelerate in the post-war decades. In 1935, the U.S. Committee on Economic Security observed that although there were 6.5 million Americans over age 65 at the time—a little over 5 percent of the population—"this percentage has been increasing quite rapidly since the turn of the century and is expected to increase for several decades."

By the early 1960s, the over-65 population had reached 17 million. Thirty years later, the number has doubled to 34 million people, nearly 13 percent of the population. There are now five times as many older adults as there were when Social Security was introduced in the mid-1930s, and ten times as many Americans over 65 as there were in 1900. The proportion of individuals in later life has tripled, overall, since 1900, to produce an end result that is truly staggering: Half of all the people who have *ever* lived to age 65 are *currently* alive.

The major force driving these numbers is the dramatic growth in longevity, alongside reductions in infant and child mortality. In 1900, the average American could anticipate living to age 47. Today the figure is 76, with continued increases into the 80s anticipated by the middle of the twenty-first century. By then centenarians will be commonplace, with over 800,000 expected (compared with approximately 40,000 today)—and these individuals will likely be far more vigorous than they are today. They are part of an overall phenomenon that some call "downaging": Today's 80-year-olds are comparable in well-being and vigor to 60-year-olds in the last generation; 60-year-olds are like 40-year-olds; and so on. As gerontologist Robert Binstock has observed, "People used to think if you were in your 60s, you were basically waiting to die, and in a rocker." Now if somebody passes away before their 80s, people feel sorry and say, "He was a young guy."

The addition of three decades to the average life span in less than a hundred years—an increase in longevity greater than the total change over the previous 5,000 years—is surely one of the great wonders of the twentieth century. That change amounts to a 62 percent increase in the number of our days. As a result, an American woman reaching age 65 today can plan on living nearly twenty more years, while men can expect more than a decade and a half of continued life—most of it in reasonably good health. Demographic expert Chulhee Lee of the University of California, Berkeley, has projected that the average man aged 20 in 1990 can anticipate spending one-third of life in retirement. In short, we've added a new stage to life, one as long in duration as childhood or the middle years.

As remarkable as these numbers are, the real revolution is yet to be felt. Beginning just after the year 2000, the first wave of 80 million baby boomers will reach their late fifties and begin transforming America into a place where, for the first time ever, there will be more older adults than children and youth. By 2030, the number of older adults will have doubled again, to 70 million. Between a fifth and a quarter of the country will consist of these seasoned citizens, a transformation that has inspired some experts to talk about the "Floridization of America." Yet if anything, this characterization understates the change: A "mere" 19 percent of Florida's population today is over 65.

Demography Is Destiny—and Despair

Awareness of the magnitude of this demographic transformation is growing, but for the most part the aging of America is portrayed as a source of impending strife—as a "shipwreck," to borrow the word Chateaubriand used to describe his own old age. We hear little about individuals like Nick, but much about a vast and selfish cohort of elders out to bankrupt posterity. The anthem for the generation, we are told, can be found on the oft-cited bumper sticker "I'm spending my children's inheritance."

To date, the implications of the aging society have been primarily arbitrated by two groups of experts. Physicians cornering one part of the debate warn us to brace for an exponential increase in dependency, disease, and dementia as the oldest of the old become society's fastest-growing group. They talk bluntly about the "failure of success," the ironic downside to our ability to prolong life. As a result, we will soon be saddled with an immense burden: to families, human services, and the health care system.

Outdoing even the doctors in their gloomy predictions is a cadre of financiers and economists who truly dominate public debate about the aging society. And where the doctors locate decay, these analysts find greed. Chief among them is investment banker and former Nixon administration commerce secretary Pete Peterson. Peterson distills the aging of America into aphorisms like "graying means paying," depicting a crisis that he calls a "demographic time bomb." Peterson and the other wealthy backers of his anti-entitlement group, the Concord Coalition, excoriate members of the older population for their self-indulgence, charging that "Americans seem to think they have an inalienable right to live the last third of their adult lives in subsidized leisure."

For Peterson, the problem is not just entitlements but an "entitlement ethic" that threatens to condemn our posterity. He paints a bleak picture of our future as "a nation of Floridas," one dominated by older adults capable of little other than recreation, consumerism, ill-health, or, of course, snapping up their ever-growing government checks. "Been to Florida lately?" he asks readers in a May 1996 *Atlantic Monthly* article, "Will America Grow Up Before It Grows Old?" "You may not realize it, but you have seen the future. . . the gray wave of senior citizens that fills the state's streets, beaches, parks, hotels, shopping malls, hospitals, Social Security offices, and senior centers." Peterson's article is accompanied by clever artwork portraying the elderly as a callous leisure class, living in age-segregated retirement communities, inured to the needs of the rest of society. One cartoon depicts an island filled with palm trees and populated by seniors sunning themselves indulgently while the rest of society—their arms flailing for help—drowns offshore.

Three years later in the 1999 book, *Gray Dawn*, Peterson returns to tell us that the aging of the population will not only sink America, but take the whole civilized world down with it. Shifting from tropical insouciance to a post-*Titanic* motif, *Gray Dawn*'s subtitle announced: "There's an iceberg dead ahead. It's called global aging, and it threatens to bankrupt the great powers. . . ." Full page advertisements for the book depict an ominous, impassable iceberg, informing potential readers that *Gray Dawn* will help them grasp just "how big the problem is."

Dating back to the mid-1980s, Peterson and his compatriots Neil Howe and Philip Longman have published a series of articles and books that hammer away at a trio of messages: (1) The elderly are selfish; (2) we can't afford entitlements; and (3) we are careening toward generational warfare. But Peterson and his Wall Street colleagues—who play a major role in financing the antientitlements campaigns, eager to reap a windfall if Social Security is privatized—are hardly alone in the backlash against the "greedy geezers."

Even the liberal economist Lester Thurow describes older Americans as a "new revolutionary class," displaying an antipathy for them that Peterson would be hard-pressed to match. For the first time in human history, he announces in apocalyptic language, we have a large group of elders who are affluent, inactive, in need of expensive social services, largely dependent on the government for their income, and intent on continually aggrandizing their position at the expense of the rest of society. According to Thurow, this new class is "bringing down the social welfare state, destroying government finances, altering the distribution of purchasing power and threatening the investments that all societies need to make to have a successful future."

In the process, these selfish seniors have us crashing headlong toward a new kind of social warfare, one between the young and the old rather than between the poor and the rich. And this prospect is not a distant worry: "In America the conflict is already clear," writes Thurow. "The elderly systematically vote against education levies when they have a chance. Better yet, they establish segregated retirement communities for themselves so that they will not have to pay for schools at all." In the arguments of Peterson, Thurow, and many other critics of the older population, these retirement communities function as the symbol of the elderly and their self-indulgence. (Thurow's *New York Times Magazine* essay, "The Birth of a Revolutionary Class," begins with the image of an elderly couple living in a Sun City–like setting, lounging about in lawn chairs perched atop plump sacks of cash.)

In his 1996 book *The Future of Capitalism*, Thurow invokes an obscure school district adjacent to a retirement community in Michigan to illustrate his case: "The most dramatic recent example of impending social conflict," he explains, "occurred in Kalhaska, Michigan, a retirement haven, where elderly voters essentially robbed the school budget to pay for other things such as snow plowing and then refused to vote the funds to allow the schools to finish the year." As a result, schools closed early and children were deprived of completing a full term.

We have met the enemy, Thurow concludes, "and he is the elderly 'us.'"

Thurow and Peterson are joined by a parade of columnists and editorial writers who envision an aging America as a land of gleaming hospitals and decaying schools. However, these dire scenarios not only overstate the crisis we face but also overlook the opportunity presented by the aging revolution.

There is no question that our entitlement programs require reevaluation and change, and to some extent these critics play a useful role in reminding us that we need to address these issues at once. However, the message they deliver is often exaggerated and confusing. For example, Social Security can be fixed without wrenching changes. As John Cassidy notes in his incisive debunking of Peterson's alarmism ("Spooking the Boomers" in *The New Yorker*): "If no reforms were to be introduced between now and 2029—an eventuality that is highly unlikely—the government would still be able to send out checks worth three-quarters of today's benefits to all retirees for the succeeding half century." Hardly a demographic time bomb. By raising the payroll tax 2.2 percent—split evenly among employers and employees—the system would be made solvent through 2070. Other changes, even more modest, would produce similarly salubrious results. Social Security can be fixed, and it will be fixed without draconian measures.

As for the issue of schools, incidents like those occurring in the Kalhaska retirement community are truly distressing. And they are happening elsewhere too. Given that 49 percent of the voting population by 2030 will be over age 55, it is worth paying close attention to how older people vote on school funding issues. However, the research to date shows that older adults do not vote monolithically in response to these bond issues. Thurow is simply wrong on this point. Rather, their vote depends on several factors: One is whether the existing tax burden is high (since older adults often own their homes but are living on a fixed income, they are especially sensitive to increases in property taxes—the traditional vehicle for funding public schools). However, research shows that the decision is by no means driven exclusively by financial concerns. Two other critical issues are how good a job older adults believe the schools are doing, and how connected they are to these institutions.

For every Kalhaska, there is a Miami. In the late 1980s, Miami began a concerted effort to get more older adults involved as volunteers in the schools. Several years later, this corps—thousands strong—served as the spearhead for a campaign to pass a billion-dollar bond issue. Over 80 percent of the older population supported the successful measure, the largest in Miami's history. This fact is all the more striking because the preponderance of these older adults—like those in Kalhaska—had grandchildren living elsewhere.

Our Only Increasing Natural Resource

The problem with so much hand-wringing about the aging of America is not only that it distorts the purported crisis but also that it is blinding us to the benefits of an aging society—as the counterexample from Miami highlights. Graying is about more than just paying, and the aging of America is about more than entitlements and the cost of supporting a much larger older population. In fact, the long gray wave that Peterson describes may be every bit as much an opportunity to be seized as a crisis to be solved—provided we can learn to capture the time, talent, and experience of the older population and apply this largely untapped resource to some of the most urgent unmet needs of society. Indeed, the purported source of our downfall may actually be our salvation.

Contrary to prevailing stereotypes, America now possesses not only the largest and fastest-growing population of older adults in our history but also the healthiest, most vigorous, and best educated. Only 5 percent of these individuals live in nursing homes, and the vast majority experience no disability whatsoever. In fact, recent research by Duke University's Center for Demographic Studies shows a 15 percent drop in disability during the period 1982–1994. There are also more college and high school graduates in the population group than ever before.

Perhaps most important, older Americans possess what everybody else in society so desperately lacks: time. First, older Americans have time to care. As the British historian Peter Laslett observes, free time was once the exclusive province of the aristocracy; today, it is the democratic possession of millions of citizens—those in later life. Retirement frees up 25 hours a week for men and 18 hours for women, according to time-diary studies conducted by the University of Maryland's Survey Research Center. And even though the trend has started to slow, many people are retiring early. In 1948, 90 percent of all men between 55 and 64 were working: nearly a half century later, only 67 percent are in the paid labor force. Overall, only one in five Americans over age 55 is on the job.

Second, older adults have more time lived. They have practical knowledge—and, often, wisdom—gained from experience. Nick and his colleagues in The Work Connection offer vivid illustration; like so many others in this age group, they've been around the block. They've held jobs, built social networks, raised families. They are also particularly civic-minded: Older adults vote at a higher rate than any other segment of the population. And because these individuals often carry with them a world lost to younger generations, they may well be our greatest practical repository of the "social capital" that many observers today fear is drying up.

Third, time left to live may give older adults a special reason to become involved in ways that both provide personal meaning and make a significant difference to others. The awareness in old age that death is closer than birth inspires many to reflect—and act—related to the legacy that we leave behind. According to the late psychologist Erik Erikson, the hallmark of successful late-life development is the capacity to be generative, to pass on to future generations what one has learned from life. For Erikson, this notion is encapsulated in the understanding "I am what survives of me."

For all these reasons, older Americans may well be our only *increasing* natural resource. Nevertheless, it is not a resource in oversupply. At precisely the juncture that this country contains so much pent-up time, talent, and experience in the older population, we are in the midst of a human resource crisis of staggering proportions, a crisis that goes well beyond Silicon Valley's never-ending search for more software engineers. It is a crisis in our communities, in the realm of civil society—where children are all too often growing up alone, where we don't have nearly enough people to care for the frail elderly, where we face a teacher shortage of nearly 200,000 over the coming decade.

In *Democracy in America*, Alexis de Tocqueville wrote that "The American heart readily leans to the side of kindness." A century and a half later, it's hard to be so sure. Observers across the political spectrum—most notably the Harvard political scientist Robert Putnam—are sounding the civic alarm, citing research indicating diminished community involvement. According to a 1996 Gallup survey conducted for Independent Sector, the proportion of adults who volunteer declined from 54 to 49 percent between 1989 and 1995. In absolute numbers, that's a decline of 5 million volunteers. And the vast majority of participating individuals gave only a few hours a week.

These numbers are hardly surprising, given the time famine afflicting so many adults in our society. As Harvard economist Juliet Schorr documents, the average American now works 162 more hours a year than twenty years ago, the equivalent of an extra month on the job. With these individuals attempting to compress thirteen months of work into the space of twelve, something has to give. As Schorr's analysis reveals, "The time squeeze has taken a toll on volunteer activities, which have fallen considerably since the rise in hours began."

Changes in the role of women are surely one of the key factors in the overall crisis in the social sector. For most of the twentieth century, through a myriad of unpaid, undervalued, often unnoticed tasks, women have served as the glue in American communities. But today, 61.7 percent of mothers with preschoolers (and half of all mothers with infants) are working at paid jobs, up from 19 percent in 1960. And two-thirds of employed mothers work full-time. Berkeley sociologist Arlie Hochschild has shown that when child rearing, housework, and paid employment are combined, women work 15 more hours a week than men do—equivalent to an extra month of 24-hour days each year. After a workweek of 80 or even 100 hours, how many people have the time and energy for a third shift laboring on behalf of the greater good? It is no wonder that even PTA membership has plummeted from 12 million to 7 million since the mid-1960s.

In *The Time Bind*, Hochschild provides a familiar example of this transformation. In her study of a community in upstate New York, she reports that while some women in the middle generation continue to make substantial contributions to volunteer work, the majority are no longer available: "Like Emily Denton, many of these mothers found themselves part of a dwindling band of volunteers at school, the Girl Scout troop, or the church Christmas pageant." The effect was not only a diminished civic workforce but diminished overall value placed on this type of engagement. "As community volunteers," Hochschild concludes, "it seemed harder these days to feel that they were doing desirable work for an appreciative community."

In the eyes of reactionaries, this vacuum is another reason for women to resume their traditional role. In a 1996 *Commentary* article, "Why Mothers Should Stay Home," Yale professor and conservative social critic David Galernter chastises the women's movement for championing equal employment instead of "a national corps of full-time mothers" serving "as the mainstay of community and civil society." But this view ignores the profound economic, psychological, and social forces propelling women to work. Even Galernter admits that a full-time mother corps is now unrealistic.

A more promising route to civic renewal resides in looking forward, not in hoping that history will suddenly begin running backward.

The Aging Opportunity

Against this backdrop of women's changing social roles, America's burgeoning older population is poised to become the new trustees of civic life in this country. These individuals have the time to care; they have the skills and experience required; they have the personal need to contribute in new ways. Society desperately needs them, and at the same time, there is considerable reason to believe that older Americans could reap tremendous mutual benefit in the process—without many of the frustrations and sacrifices middle-aged women have faced in their historical role. This match, between the untapped resources of older Americans and the needs of American communities, constitutes *the great opportunity* presented by America's aging.

Given so many appealing factors, one might expect to see an all-out clamor to engage older Americans in new roles focused on greater involvement in communities (for example, a nationwide crusade akin to Miami's mobilization of older volunteers on behalf of schools). After all, as the Gray Panthers' late founder Maggie Kuhn observed, "We don't have a single person to waste"—much less the most experienced, stable, and available portion of the population (especially at the same time we lecture single moms on welfare that they need to contribute in some way to society). However, there is no clamor to engage older adults and community contribution falls off sharply after retirement. Although the level of involvement has improved substantially since the early 1960s, older Americans still volunteer less than any other age group—even those overwhelmed Americans in the middle generation.

Although some inquiries, such as the Commonwealth Fund's "Americans Over 55 At Work" study, have correctly demonstrated that we continue to overlook certain contributions of older Americans to families, communities, and the economy, even these studies conclude that we are nowhere near where we should be. (The commission's final report is entitled *The Untapped Resource*.) In their recent book summarizing findings from the MacArthur Foundation's ten-year project on successful aging, John Rowe, president of Mt. Sinai Medical School, and Robert Kahn, a psychologist at the University of Michigan, reach similar conclusions. According to Rowe and Kahn, "Fewer than one-third of all older men and women work as volunteers and those who do spend, on average, fewer than two hours a week on the job."

If older Americans remain an untapped resource for society, then how are these individuals spending their time? To be sure, some are working, serving as volunteers, or caring for relatives. However, a closer look at time-use data suggests that critics like Peterson and Thurow are not entirely off-base when they argue that older adults have become America's most leisured population.

Indeed, MIT economist Dora Costa comes to the same verdict in her book *The Evolution of Retirement*, arguing that the "retired have become the true leisured class." She shows that, in essence, our society hoards most leisure time until the last two or three decades of life. While individuals in the middle generation are struggling to find time to tie their shoes, free time is burgeoning for older Americans. In 1995, Americans over age 65 could claim seven more hours of free time a week than their counterparts a decade earlier, and ten hours more than in 1975. The over-65 population works less than a quarter the number of hours than the 18–64 group, while the proportion of older adults' lives dedicated to leisure is 50 percent greater than the rest of the country's. Next to sleep (35 percent of time use for those over 65), recreation is the biggest single activity in later life. Nothing else is even close.

When one looks at specifics within the leisure and recreation category, it is further evident that older adults watch more television than any other age group does—a staggering half of all elders' free time. As John Robinson of the University Maryland and Geoffrey Godbey of Penn State, the nation's leading experts on time use, comment: "The lives of most seniors who fill out our time diaries seem to revolve around the television set." Housework is the next major subcategory of activity absorbing time liberated in later life. Given these findings, it is no surprise that a majority of older respondents to a recent Louis Harris poll lament the loss of usefulness after retirement.

The lack of involvement of older adults in the civic life of communities is all the more baffling for three additional reasons. First, an accumulation of research suggests that many older people *want* to be more involved. For example, another Harris poll, from the early 1990s, estimates the number of older adults not volunteering but willing and able to do so at 6 million. A survey commissioned by the federal Administration on Aging puts the number at 14 million and states that a quarter of the older adults serving say they would prefer to put in more time.

Second, these older adults' responses to the polls likely reflect a healthy dose of enlightened self-interest. Numerous studies following people over their lives link strong social ties and community engagement to prolonged physical and mental health. The aforementioned decade-long MacArthur inquiry into successful aging produces exactly these conclusions and strongly recommends more volunteer and service opportunities for older Americans.

Third, older adults are so "civic" in other ways. They vote at a higher rate than any other segment of the population, and they are the most generous with their financial contributions.

So why then is the "aging opportunity" yet to be realized? Are we to believe Peterson and Thurow that the chief culprit is Social Security or perhaps a more encompassing "entitlement ethic"? In reality, there are three principal reasons.

The first problem is in the realm of *ideas*. America today simply lacks a compelling vision for later life. F. Scott Fitzgerald proclaimed, "There are no second acts in American lives," and for the most part this dictum defines our view of age. Much of our intellectual energy goes into simply denying the prospect of aging. A visit to the local Borders or Barnes and Noble reveals shelf after shelf of books with titles like *Stop Aging Now*, *The End of Aging*, or *Ancient Secrets of the Fountain of Youth*. Face-lifts are a multibillion-dollar annual business.

Beyond outright denial, there is the "failure of success" perspective—essentially projecting later life as a "second infancy" of dependency, helplessness, and constant care. However, the predominate outlook is the "second childhood" ideal, glorifying leisure and offering up the chance for endless play—often at age-segregated playgrounds with names like "Sun City" and "Leisure World." Neither of these perspectives constitutes a compelling ideal for how we might spend the new third of life we've been granted. Despite the great gift of longevity, this third stage remains, in the words of cultural historians Harry Moody and Thomas Cole, "a season in search of a purpose."

A second problem is with our *institutions*. "Institutions" is an abstract word, but it comes down to something simple. Most people can't just walk out their door and make a difference. There needs to be someplace to go, a well-developed avenue to help channel goodwill into good deeds. As a society, we are missing the institutions that fit with an increasingly vital and well-educated older population. The pioneering gerontologist Matilda White Riley calls this phenomenon "structural lag," a situation in which the roles and opportunities of our society simply haven't caught up to the capacities and interests of today's 50- or 60- or 70-year-old—much less the aging boomers of the coming decades. We face a burgeoning mismatch between demographics and opportunities—and the demographics are way ahead.

In short, we have lots of senior centers and retirement communities, but these institutions, as they stand, are simply not going to unleash the talent or capture the imagination of the new population entering the third age. Even the volunteer programs that exist are all too often focused on keeping the "old folks" busy rather than on accomplishing work of genuine significance.

American historian and former librarian of Congress Daniel Boorstin observes that we have been ingenious over the past two centuries in inventing new institutions to develop young people—such as the system of land-grant colleges and the G.I. Bill. But our creativity in this sphere "has not been matched by any similar ingenuity in devising initiatives to employ our older population." Boorstin adds: "The most conspicuous American institution directed to senior citizens is the so-called Leisure City, a place not of creation but of recreation and vegetation."

Along with our deficiencies in concepts and roles, we confront a third problem: We are missing the *infrastructure* that could sustain and expand a new kind of aging. In other words, the vast majority of our policies related to aging are focused on the needs of older Americans. The most notable of these policies is the Older Americans Act, which supports a variety of activities including senior centers and Meals on Wheels programs. These efforts are admirable, but they are also incomplete. By comparison, our efforts in the realm of policy aimed at promoting the contribution of older Americans to society remain anemic.

This imbalance was painfully clear during the 1995 White House Conference on Aging, the first such conference in nearly two decades. The conference was primarily a *defensive* event—focused on defending the triumphs of the past without also articulating any new vision for aging in the next century. The narrow focus on entitlements at the conference was partly understandable in the context of persistent attacks on these programs. And it is essential to underscore that the presence of a solid base of income security and health care is necessary if we are going to tap the resources residing in older adults. As economist Robert Kuttner observes, a retiree "fortified by a Social Security check and a Medicare card has less need to patronize the local soup kitchen, as well as more time and self-confidence to become engaged in the community's civic life."

However, the question of what this hard-won independence might liberate older adults *to do* was ignored by the conference. Quite simply, little constituency has existed within the vast and powerful aging field for broadening the discussion to include potential opportunities provided by the dramatic growth in older Americans. It is as if some groups fear discussing these positive possibilities weakens the case for ministering to the genuine needs of frail or impoverished elders.

The Road Ahead

Transforming the aging of America will require new ideas and new policies—and a new constituency for change—but it will especially require new institutions. If we can devise creative new roles and opportunities at the community level, there is much reason to believe that people will respond. Broad surveys and ethnographic accounts alike reveal a deep hunger on the part of older Americans to live lives that matter, to use their experience and knowledge in important ways, and to continue learning and growing in the process.

I argue in this book that institutions are the key to bringing about the kind of transformation that could help revitalize our communities and inject new meaning into later life. In part my perspective draws inspiration from the accomplishments and experience of Elderhostel. Twenty-five years ago, the notion that people would spend their retirement involved in learning was exotic. School was something reserved for the younger generation. Today, hundreds of thousands of men and women over age 55 each year take Elderhostel classes in the United States and abroad. The nonprofit organization has $120 million in annual revenues. And that's just the tip of the iceberg. The success of Elderhostel has spawned an entire industry of learning in retirement, involving universities, corporations, and travel groups.

No longer exotic, late-life learning today is almost expected. Indeed, it has cachet. The key to all of this participation, argues William Berkeley, founding president of Elderhostel and leader of the organization over the past twenty years, was finding the right "package." By "package," Berkeley means a simple, straightforward, accessible, and reproducible way for older adults to become involved.

Now we must do for community contribution by older adults what Elderhostel has done for learning. And the good news—despite the barriers previously outlined—is that we don't have to start from scratch. Across the country, a growing group of social entrepreneurs is busy reinventing retirement, while taking a page from the movie *Field of Dreams*. If we build it, they are betting, many of us will come. And some have already started. Six such individuals—role models for a new retirement—reflect on their experience between the chapters of this book. Their first-person tales of new (second and third and fourth) "acts" devoted to "leaving a legacy"—through volunteer work, Peace Corps–like assignments, and paid employment in the public interest—offer a compelling refutation of Fitzgerald's outdated adage.

Their achievements are also well-timed, as millions of baby boomers prepare to graduate over the next decade into the phase of life the British call "the third age"—that period when the children are grown and most of us are nearing completion of our first career with all its anxiety about achievement and income. Now the questions that start to loom are different ones. As Carl Jung asserted, "We cannot live the afternoon of life according to the programme of life's morning." What are new and more appropriate definitions of success in this phase? What is the legacy we would like to leave to others, to our communities, to posterity? We need, in Peter Laslett's words, "a fresh map of life," one that can guide us through these still-uncharted waters and do so in a way that balances personal fulfillment with responsibility to others.

The Time for Change

There is one thing everybody seems to agree on: The boomers will not accept the old notions of later life and retirement—they will refuse to remove themselves, go away, or put up with being taken "out of use or circulation," to quote three of the dictionary's current definitions of retirement. By the time the boomers hit their sixties, Webster's will need to redefine the word or simply replace it with one more accurate. (The Yankelovich Group suggests in its marketing report *Rocking the Ages* that the boomers will "retread" rather than "retire.")

Ultimately, our best hope is in a new vision—and a new practice of later life—focused not only on continued learning and growth, but also on contribution to community and care for the future. It is a vision that some of the most compelling spokespersons for the new generation of older Americans have begun to articulate as a new ideal for the aging society. As Betty Friedan notes in *The Fountain of Age*, this concern must go beyond our personal well-being: "It is only by continuing to work on the problems confronting our society right now with whatever wisdom and generativity we have attained over our own lifetimes that we leave a legacy to our grandchildren."

Friedan is joined in this appeal by an unlikely ally: Pete Peterson. Buried deep in his 1996 *Atlantic Monthly* article (never to surface again) is the suggestion that "the maturity, wisdom, and experience of older adults" should not be lost to the country. Writes Peterson: "It is time to do elders the honor of making their phase of life one of ongoing contribution—of genuine 'generativity.'"

There may well be seeds of consensus among even such disparate voices as Friedan and Peterson. The problem, of course, is not just to reach agreement about the important contribution the older generation might make to society but also to address the practical question of how we are going to get there. As an aside, Peterson mentions that we need to create both part-time and full-time "service jobs" in child care, health care, and education. It is an idea worth considering.

Indeed, recently an array of prominent intellectuals and policymakers have called for the creation of new institutions to enable older Americans to play a more substantial role in strengthening civil society. These many calls, which include arguments for an Elder Corps, Senior Corps, Wisdom Corps, or even "a national army of winter soldiers"—are heartening. They acknowledge the opportunity present in the aging of America, help counterbalance all the gloom and doom about the changing demographics, and address the need to invent new ways to realize the many encouraging possibilities in the longevity revolution. As this last point underscores, just as the long gray wave will not inherently spell despair, neither will it automatically produce an increase in activism simply by virtue of our having more aging baby boomers.

Now is the time to take these proposals as well as other innovative approaches seriously, translating rhetoric to reality in a way that makes things happen in the real world of our communities. However, doing so will not be easy.

There are many who sense another kind of "aging opportunity," commercial interests that continue to peddle "lifestyles" and products to older Americans focused much more on self-indulgence and consumption than on social engagement and productive contribution. (Others are gearing up as well. A favorite headline of mine is from the Gannett News Service: "Aging Boomers a

Potential Boon to Funeral Industry.") Humor aside, a battle for the heart and soul of later life is under way, and the stakes are substantial. Will the aging of America primarily serve to enrich these industries and send us reeling toward the kind of intergenerational conflict many are now predicting? Or will it produce a civic windfall for American communities, one that will rejuvenate civil society and strengthen social solidarity? Much will depend on what we do over the next decade, as the first boomers cross into the third phase of life.

The first step to unleashing the vast potential present in America's aging is to understand better why this appealing, common-sense, win-win opportunity isn't already happening on a massive scale. And the best way to start is by understanding how it is that we've inherited the kind of retirement that currently prevails. The story takes us back four hundred years in American history, but it leads inexorably to the emblematic institution of the most recent phase in the history of aging in this country: the retirement community movement and the leisured lifestyle it both reflects—and has done so much to create.

PART ONE

ALEX HARRIS

Steve Weiner describes himself as "vocationally celibate." Now in his late fifties, he opted to retire early (in 1996) from a distinguished career as a college administrator and policy expert. A Ph.D. from Stanford, he was a staff member for the Kerner Commission, a professor at Stanford, dean of the School of Education at the University of California–Berkeley, provost and dean of faculty at Mills College, and director of the commission responsible for accrediting California's colleges and universities. He is married to an attorney and has two daughters—one of them a teacher, the other an actress and writer. Weiner and his wife currently volunteer recording books for the blind. In addition, he serves on the boards of the Food Bank of Alameda County and the East Bay

Conservation Corps and consults in the area of higher education. Weiner lives near Oakland, California.

·

Retirement creeps up on you. I must have started thinking about it in '90 or '91—the first time I went to see a financial planner. However, the major single event in this process was a sabbatical. My wife and I went on a six-week trip to New Zealand and we talked about retirement. When we got back, she returned to work, but I had six more weeks to think. I bought books about financial planning. I began to get more into the nuts and bolts of what we'd been spending and our resources.

A critical aspect of retirement planning is estimating how long you expect to live. I remember sitting at the kitchen table with a simple actuarial table showing "if you are a man of this age, you can expect to live this much longer." I decided to take a conservative view. According to the table, being fifty-five at the time, I estimated that I'd live another thirty years. Then I calculated what proportion of an eighty-five-year lifetime those thirty years represented.

When I realized that I had lived two-thirds of my life, I was immediately struck by two very strong feelings. On the one hand, I panicked: I had lived two-thirds of my life! But on the other hand, I had thirty years left! Assuming reasonable health during most of those years, that's an immense amount of time. I was struck with how much was over—but even more by how much was left.

In the midst of all this retirement planning, I discovered a tremendous number of books with titles like *How to Grow Rich and Retire*. Shelf after shelf on how to invest, how to be rich, how to save on insurance—but little, if any, advice about what one can do with this third of life, when earning a salary is no longer the center of things. In particular, I was looking for something recounting the experiences of other people. I found very little advice—or examples—about how people could use their new freedom to do something worthwhile.

I found few role models in my own life, either. Mostly, there've been role models of the reverse. Some of my friends and colleagues still derive great meaning from putting on their suit and tie and going into the office every day. I think that is wonderful. But in most cases what I've observed are college presidents, who, having worked sixty to eighty hours a week for years, really couldn't approach leaving the office of the presidency as anything other than going off a cliff and into a dark abyss, the depths of which could not be calculated.

So I did not find in my immediate experience many folks who said, "I'm going to now base my time on that which is going to give me a sense of contribution. A sense of involvement and of community."

Shortly after coming back from New Zealand, I went to Sacramento and had breakfast with my board chair. I told him that I had made a decision to retire in two years [at fifty-seven].

Probably the best advice came from a fellow who told me after he retired he took six months and did absolutely nothing. He said, "You probably don't realize it, but you're tired. Get some rest and relaxation at first. Don't press things."

The first feeling was of liberation. Being able to wake up without an alarm clock telling you when you should wake up. I think very shortly, though, the flip side becomes more evident—the absence of deadlines, the absence of meetings, of the sense that you must do something. I realized how deeply wired in my nervous system was forty years of meeting deadlines. It was strange to wake up in the morning and think, "I'm going to pretty much do what I feel like doing."

It's been often said, and I think it's true: One of the great virtues of growing older is that you feel the burden of ambitions, much of which proved to be unrealistic, being lifted off of your back. Perhaps feeling less than you might have, earlier in life, that you have to prove something.

I started out wanting to be the president of the United States [laughs]. That was the first ambition to go! In the years immediately preceding 1988, if you had asked me, "Steve, what is the thing you want to do professionally?" I would have said I want to be a university president. And 1988 was a turning point for me. I interviewed for several presidencies. And there were one or two that I could have had. And I remember—after interviewing at one of the campuses in Washington D.C.—my mind was in a jumble. I went for a walk. It was a very long walk. I must have walked for several hours. And on that walk I realized I had been saying two things: one, I want to be a university president; and at the very same time I was saying I want to have more control over my life. I want to have evenings and weekends to myself. I no longer want to be the property of others.

I also realized the colleges and universities where I was under consideration were places that did not stand for things that I thought were particularly important. These were places that typically said, "We are number thirty-five on the *U.S. News and World Report* ranking and we want to be number twenty-two." And we want you to work ninety hours a week for the next ten years to make that happen. And I put those two things together, and I realized I didn't want to make that sacrifice. I mean, if you say, "Yes, we are going to register and empower African Americans to vote in the South," that's worth ninety or a hundred hours a week!—but not to go from number thirty-five to number twenty-two.

I had been talking past myself, avowing goals that were directly in contradiction. And it was at that point I said to myself, "You know what, I've wanted desperately to be a college or university president for at least five years, but now that I have gotten close—I don't think I want to do it!" At least not at the places likely to ask me. That is an ambition whose disappearance I can very precisely locate. . . . The other ambitions disappeared gradually over time [laughter].

Now, I actively struggle with what it means to be successful in retirement. My entire life, my feeling has been that you have to make a difference in the world. This can be a positive, as well as a destructive, notion. Having lived as many years as I have, I realize that there are few of us who can reasonably expect to leave a significant mark on society. It's like "Oh, yeah, we remember Steve. He did a wonderful job. What's for lunch?" [laughs]

I don't feel unengaged or inactive these days. But I would like to have at least one more passionate involvement in something I care about deeply. I recognize that this probably sounds contradictory—being more of a spectator than on the field now. But that notion of a passionate involvement is still very much alive in me. As is the desire for intellectual stimulation, for feeling my mind is at work, for working with people who are lively.

A friend of mine jokes that retirement is the weekend that never ends. Actually, I've never had the experience of twiddling my thumbs or being bored out of my mind. What's been much more difficult is to employ my skills and energy as a volunteer. I thought that if a person with my experience came to an organization and told them that I was here to give them a chunk of my time, and all they have to do is make it interesting for me. . . I thought the response would be enthusiastic.

But the nonprofit world is not as permeable as I expected. I've got to assume that part of it may be a reaction to me. However, it seems that as much is the mindset of organizations, a certain reluctance, hesitation, lack of experience involving older people. I don't understand this very well. I've talked to people my age, in similar circumstances, who have much to contribute but can't even get their phone calls returned.

There are so many retired people out there who could be mobilized to do worthwhile things. I think there's an understanding that an older person can be a tutor or a mentor. What needs to be shown is what people can do more broadly. Something for people to look at and say, "Wow, that may not have changed the world—but it changed a part of it." People will say, "That's something I'd like to be involved with." It may not be the majority of people, but—given the size of the older population—even if you involve a small portion of the people around you, that's a very large potential force.

The energy is there, but it needs to be organized. The road is there, but it's rocky. It has to be paved. That can happen in the next five to ten years. My sense is we are just beginning to crawl with this issue. And so I think that the experience I'm having is probably not atypical. It's like being on the leading edge, like those who were the first in our families to arrive in college and had to explain to those back home what the experience was all about.

Ali of this does compete with the notion of the third phase of life being back to toys. How much can you consume? How much can you play? I find myself resisting this view of retirement. I want to say to my retired colleagues, "This is supposed to be fun—and worthwhile." What I hear the culture saying is "Yes, we're serious—we're seriously irresponsible."

CHAPTER 2

A Year-Round Vacation

Probably at no period and in no culture have the old been so completely rejected as in our own country, during the last generation.

·

Lewis Mumford, 1956

Wake up and live in Sun City
For an active new way of life.
Wake up and live in Sun City
Mr. Senior Citizen and wife.
Don't let retirement get you down!
Be happy in Sun City; it's a paradise-town.

·

Radio advertising jingle, Del Webb Corporation, 1960

For five months Tom Breen had been holding his boss at bay. Every time he got a nervous call from Del Webb asking "Do you know what you're doing out there?" Breen would respond calmly that all was under control. Now, on New Year's Eve 1959, hours before the opening of what would become Sun City, Breen was experiencing jitters. So along with Owen Childress, John Meeker, and Jack Ford—the other members of the Del Webb Company team developing the new community restricted to adults over age fifty—Breen headed down to Manuel's Place in the neighboring town of Peoria, Arizona, to talk over, one more time, their prospects for the New Year's Day 1960 opening.

"Everybody was quiet," Breen recalls, "We were all wondering the same thing. 'Will anybody come tomorrow?'" Then Owen Childress broke the ice, "I'm worried," he admitted to the others, "how I'm going to get a thirty-year mortgage on a guy who is sixty-five years old." Suddenly, the absurdity of an age-segregated housing development in the middle of the desert began to dawn on them—along with the unhappy consequences of a major flop the next day. The formidable Webb had put $2 million on the line at Breen's urging.

They could take some comfort in knowing that all their marketing bases were covered. Over the past months the Webb Company had conducted a national advertising campaign. And throughout the upcoming three-day weekend *The Arizona Republic* would carry a double-page ad heralding "An Active Way of Life!" offered by the new development focused exclusively on the older set. A brand-new two-bedroom, top-of-the-line house valued at $10,000 would be awarded to the visitor who named the new retirement town.

Also complete were a golf course, swimming pool, recreation center, shuffleboard courts, lawn bowling green, card rooms, and auditorium, not to mention a shopping center, motel with restaurant, and five model homes. The decision to build the recreational facilities first was not accidental—in keeping with Childress's comment, Breen was not about to sell "futures" to people in their later years. There would be no promises about facilities to come. Everything would be on display.

The goal for the weekend was 10,000 visitors, and Del Webb himself had been convinced to make an appearance. The stakes were high for Breen and the others, given Webb's apprehension from the beginning about the practicality of an age-segregated community. But Breen was not a wild dreamer. And Sun City was not an entirely new idea.

Activity, Economy, Individuality

R etirement communities first started appearing in America in the 1920s. Some fraternal organizations, religious groups, and labor unions began acquiring inexpensive land in Florida with plans to turn these plots into supportive living environments for their older members. Moosehaven was established in 1922 by the Loyal Order of Moose. However, the crash of 1929 quelled this trend, and it was not until after World War II that private developers showed any interest in establishing new towns entirely for individuals in later life. ·

Although some cities in Florida—most notably St. Petersburg—were becoming de facto retirement havens as more and more older adults from the

Snowbelt gravitated there, the first community to bar residents from the younger and middle generations was Youngtown. Developed just sixteen miles from the Del Webb Company's downtown Phoenix offices, Youngtown was created in 1954 by a bearlike Russian immigrant named "Big" Ben Schleifer. Schleifer moved to Phoenix from New York, bouncing from one real estate company to another, until he came up with the idea of a community exclusively for people over the age of sixty. Backed by several local businessmen, he purchased ranchland northwest of Phoenix and developed a small community—really just a cluster of houses and a tiny store. Sales were modest but steady.

Despite such humble beginnings, Schleifer's complex received a surprising amount of national attention. First Alistair Cooke aired a television segment about Youngtown on his *Omnibus* show in 1955, then Dave Garroway devoted part of the *Today* show to the Arizona community. Thomas Breen watched both episodes and was captivated. One of Webb's chief lieutenants and his vice president for development, Breen was a rising star in the company. He was young, handsome, an ex-Marine, and a former actor who grew up in a well-to-do Hollywood family. Breen was rumored by Sun Citeans to have been the first man to kiss Elizabeth Taylor on film (although not true, he did act alongside her in several films when both were teenagers).

Decisions at the Webb Company were based on extensive, methodical research, and Breen determined to talk with a range of experts before seriously proposing any moves along the lines of Youngtown. He hired a pricey consulting firm and sought out the opinions of gerontologists and geriatricians. The response all around was discouraging. First of all, Breen was told by the aging scholars, it would be nearly impossible to get older adults to move away from their families to come to an age-segregated community. It was also the experts' view—in keeping with the dictates of disengagement theory, which prevailed in gerontology at the time—that older adults should not overexert themselves; their best bet would be to lead a quiet life. The financial consultants saw obstacles as well, reminding Breen that the FHA (Federal Housing Administration) and its Fannie Mae program were historically reluctant to provide loans for senior citizen housing.

Sobered, Breen nevertheless decided that he would test the idea out more directly, and he concocted a somewhat less scientific scheme to determine whether a variation on the Youngtown idea might be feasible. His friend Lou Silverstein, a local radio personality, was planning a trip to Florida to help his brother set up a new radio station. Florida was already a retirement mecca and a natural place to solicit the opinions of older adults. Breen asked Silverstein if he might be willing, for gas money and some travel expenses, to extend his trip and conduct a little "research" on the side.

Silverstein returned from Florida excited about two major discoveries. Repeatedly he had heard that although older people were fond of their own children and grandchildren, they had little interest in raising "someone else's children." Furthermore, they were tired of broken promises—real estate amenities touted in marketing brochures but never delivered. These observations piqued Breen's curiosity and convinced him it was time for firsthand observation. He went immediately to Florida, where he was struck by thousands of elderly men and women "just sitting around on beaches" despite the absence of any serious physical infirmities. His conversations with these people convinced him that a more vigorous lifestyle would be welcomed—and would sell.

Breen took his own observations, integrated Silverstein's report, and produced a two-page memo thumbing its nose at gerontological conventions. It urged the Webb Company to invest in building an age-segregated retirement town organized around three principles: "activity, economy, and individuality." The centerpieces would be a golf course and recreation center—providing the focus on activity. The cost of the houses would be kept affordable, and since the facilities like the recreation center would be shared by all the residents of the community, construction would be relatively inexpensive. Part-time employment would also be made available, and the age restriction would be lowered a decade from Youngtown's sixty, to the age of fifty, to broaden the market and take into account increases in early retirement. Finally, there wouldn't be a lot of meddling from the development company: "No organizing," Breen asserted. "Let them do what they want with it."

The memo was presented to Webb in 1959 proposing a $2 million investment. It was a daring move: "Turning our backs on 80 percent of the potential housing market was a big gamble," recalled Breen twenty-five years later. Webb Company officials were willing to take it not only because of Breen's insistence, Youngtown's modest success, and Lou Silverstein's scouting in Florida, but also because their research suggested that the demographics looked promising. So did the entitlements picture: Social Security was expanding steadily, and there was a big segment of the population entering their sixties that benefited both from cheap housing loans after World War II and from a long stretch of appreciation in the real estate market. They owned homes that could be cashed in at considerable profit. Furthermore, both private banks and the FHA were beginning to evince signs of increased receptivity to lending money to older adults, in part a result of years of lobbying on the part of the homebuilding industry. As industry lobbyists pointed out, due to longevity advances the average life expectancy of a sixty-five-year-old was now greater than the average number of years (seven to eight) required for lenders to recoup their money on a mortgage.

The only additional task was finding land to build on, and it turned out to be the easiest. Breen and Webb didn't even have to look. It was widely known in the Phoenix area that the Webb Company was in an expansionist mode. One day a wealthy Arizona rancher, James Boswell, drove to the company's office and asked Webb if he might be interested in 20,000 acres of alfalfa and cotton fields bordering Grand Avenue, twelve miles northwest of Phoenix, near the town of Peoria. The land was perfect for the project, and Webb convinced Boswell to give it to him in return for a minority interest in the new development. Ever the savvy dealmaker, Webb had managed to reduce his risk and carrying cost while securing prime real estate for the new development.

If You Build It. . .

When the sun rose on New Year's Day 1960, Breen was already on the Sun City grounds, nervously awaiting the festivities. However, well before the official opening that morning, it was already clear from the vast number of people arriving that his gamble was going to be vindicated. Spectacularly. For weeks, Breen had worried that the admittedly ambitious goal of 10,000 visitors was unrealistic. By the close of the opening weekend, 100,000 people—ten times the company's most optimistic projection—had come to the site. The event produced the largest traffic jam in Arizona history. For many consecutive miles, stretching from 107th and Grand Avenue in Phoenix all the way to the development, older adults lined up to check out the new experiment in active aging. The company couldn't even bring Del Webb in on the highway as originally planned. He had to be driven over cotton fields and irrigation ditches, adding an element of drama to his entrance.

When Webb arrived and saw the prospective gold mine, he wasted no time. A brilliant salesman, he immediately went to work on prospective buyers. Sales were frantic, and they stayed that way for years. That first weekend the company sold so many houses that the staff ran out of contracts and had to buy blank receipts at the local store. Altogether, the two days netted $2.5 million in revenues, and by the end of the first month 400 houses had been purchased. By the next New Year's Day, 1,300 homes were sold, and Sun City's population was 2,500. Ten years later that number was 15,000, and a decade after that nearly 50,000—making it by 1980 the seventh-largest city in Arizona. By that time Webb had sold over 25,000 homes in Sun City and was developing a sister town—Sun City West—where another 31,000 people would come to live.

Over the next decade, not only would Sun City and its offshoots become the core business of the Webb Company, but Webb himself would become a symbol for a retirement lifestyle built around leisure. He would also become an icon at Sun City, where his appearances were treated, according to one observer, like visits from the pope.

For the sixty-one-year-old Webb, this project quickly assumed a personal significance extending beyond its (substantial) monetary value. Two years after Sun City opened, he told *Time* magazine, "When I see what we've built, it's the most satisfying thing that's ever happened to me." Soon an even more telling indication of his enthusiasm appeared: The story coming out of the company's public relations division was that Webb himself had thought up the idea. "My grandfather, Jimmy Webb, used to grouch about being old with nothing to do," Webb was quoted as saying. "Well, it's pretty grim, being old with nothing to do." Remembering his grandfather's plight was what inspired the CEO—the official company story soon ran—to assign Breen to figure out what could be done.

From "A Crown Of Gold" to "The Golden Years"

Interviewing Steve Weiner and other "pioneers" on the threshold of a new kind of aging, listening to their frustrations at trying to buck the prevailing notions of retirement as play and consumption—of being "seriously irresponsible"—I was left with a basic question: How is it that we became saddled with the reigning view of retirement as disengagement and leisure? Has it always been this way? Was there something natural, even inevitable, about the ascendancy of this outlook?

These questions eventually converged on Del Webb, Thomas Breen, and

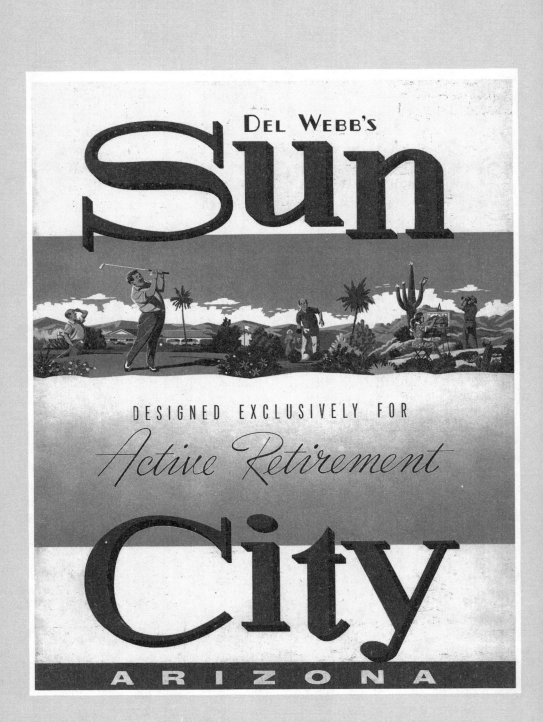

Sun City marketing brochure, circa early 1960s, courtesy of the Sun City Areas Historical Society.

"Concrete, steel and lumber can make the buildings but People make the community. Together, we can realize a Way-of-Life unprecedented in America."

Del E. Webb
President and founder of the famous construction and development organization, which bears his name, *[Also recipient of the New York Yankees]*

IN
Sun City
ARIZONA

An Active "New Way-of-Life"
is waiting for you

Reserved exclusively for those who have reached the age of fifty or more (and parents of any adult age) who are retired, semi-retired or planning retirement and are interested in actively enjoying those wonderful years ahead . . . the best years of their lives. Children of any age may, of course, visit in Sun City, but they cannot become residents until they are out of high school.

Beautiful Homes in a Country Club Setting
The velvety green fairways of the golf course wind about among the lovely neighborhoods of top-quality homes and competitive apartments which are priced with unbelievable modesty.

Recreational Facilities for Endless Activity
Championship Golf Course   Riviera-Size Swimming Pool
Shuffleboard   Lawn Bowling   Putting Green
Complete Town Hall   Casual and Riding Circle
Arts & Crafts Center   Agricultural Project

Everything You Want — Right at Home
Sun City's Shopping Center offers all the merchandise and services you want for everyday needs. Right next door is Del Webb's HiwayHome Motor Hotel with superb guest accommodations, a Coffee Shop and Restaurant.

The Nation's Most Ideal Location
Set in a sun-splashed valley of rich, green wonderland, Sun City is just 12 miles from the large, modern city of Phoenix. Here snow is a rarity, rain is infrequent, humidity readings are among the nation's lowest, and every day is blessed with a full measure of clear, invigorating air.

The Freedom to Live As You Wish
In Sun City you will enjoy complete individuality, privacy and happy, satisfying living, and most important: the right to do what you want . . . when you want . . . to live exactly as you wish. 12 Miles NW of Phoenix on Highway 60-70-80.

Master Builder, Del E. Webb, invites you to fulfill your dream in this complete and completely different community . . . Sun City, Arizona . . . where his lifelong dream first found its realization.

It was more than 50 years ago that Mr. Webb's firm had its humble beginning in Phoenix with hammers, saws and willing hands as the only tools. Since then, it has grown to a large, internationally-respected organization, the course of hospitals, schools, hotels, motels, industrial plants, military installations, office buildings, shopping centers and high-quality homes.

During those years when his company was building America from coast to coast, Mr. Webb had a never-diminishing dream: to create a community exclusively for America's retired citizens with attractive, modestly-priced homes and endless facilities for their recreational and creative activity, the whole based upon an entirely new perspective toward retirement living . . . A New, Active Way-of-Life.

Only a builder of the magnitude of Del Webb, only a faith and purpose as strong as his could have made it all come true, so perfect in concept, so complete in every detail, as he did with the January, 1960, opening of Sun City here in Arizona . . . and as he is continuing to do with his Kern City in California and the new Florida-located Sun City.

With the initial introduction of his new concept of active retirement, Mr. Webb said, "Concrete, steel and lumber can make the buildings, but People make the community. Together, we can realize a Way-of-Life unprecedented in America." And what a very special kind of People they are, those thousands of retired Americans who have been attracted by this new idea of Active retired living and together have found a new pride in living . . . a pride in the knowledge that here is a community conceived and designed exclusively for them, a pride in each other and their increasing life . . . and most important, a pride in themselves as happy, increasing people with a purpose in living.

For further information on Del Webb's California and Florida sites for Active Retirement, write:
Kern City, P.O. Box 151-HRA, Bakersfield, California . . . or at Sun City, P.O. Box 9000-HRA, Del Webb's Sun City, Florida.

The Kentworth

2 BEDROOMS, 1 BATH, PORCH & PATIO

This lovely home is perfect for two-person living and offers compact efficiency for easy care. It incorporates a spacious kitchen-dining room, big-windowed living room and king-size master bedroom and features such special details as an entrance directly from the carport, guest closet at the front door and bathroom vanity with imported marble top and large plate glass mirror.

Plan 1-C

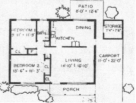

the other leisure entrepreneurs who were so spectacularly successful in transforming the culture—and practice—of later life over the past four decades. The rise of Sun City and the hundreds of other retirement communities that quickly followed its early success marked an important turning point in the history of aging in this country—one in which a leisured lifestyle gained ascendance as the ideal for success in later life, and older Americans emerged as this country's mass leisure class. Indeed, Sun City and its look-alikes became the emblematic institution of this most recent phase in America's long experience with aging.

However, it wasn't always so. At one time older Americans were a central part of the social fabric, and old age was viewed with considerable reverence. The story about how age went from being a "crown of gold" held in the highest respect to being "golden years" dedicated to bingo and shuffleboard is a story worth telling, and one that provides essential backdrop for understanding our current predicament.

A Crown of Gold

"If any man is favored with long life," wrote the eminent Puritan clergyman Increase Mather in 1716, "it is God that has lengthened his days." In short, the cause of long life was not diet, exercise, vitamin supplements, or even thinking the right thoughts, but the divine at work. Older adults were seen as chosen by and closer to God and were to be respected. According to Puritan preaching, "The fear of God and honoring the old man is commanded with the same breath." In the words of a popular saying of the day, "A hoary head is a crown of gold."

This view of long life as divine providence dominated the pulpits and popular writings of preindustrial America for over two centuries, a period during which the elderly were thoroughly integrated into the affairs of the community and upheld as a source of wisdom and higher values. They were, in particular, cast as role models for the younger generation. One drawing from the period is illustrative. Entitled "The Grandfather's Advice," it depicts a patient and sagacious—and decidedly unfrail—older man reading to a young, adoring grandson from a sacred text. They are connected by the volume—the boy rests upon it, the old man's graceful fingers drape the page, his gaze off at some distant shore. A companion drawing depicts an attractive older woman studied by a worshipful young granddaughter. Once again the holy book connects the two, as the older woman passes higher truths on to the younger generation.

Signs of this respect are easily found in other facets of early American culture. The Puritans' image of Jesus was not of the trim, youthful, long-haired figure we so often see today but rather of a wizened septuagenarian with hair "white like wool." Their angels, likewise, were depicted as old men. In this context, it is little surprise that the best seats at the front of the meetinghouse were reserved for the elderly.

More surprising, given our contemporary habits, are the ways in which early Americans worked at trying to appear older. Men powdered their wigs so that they too might have hair as white as wool. Clothes were cut to imitate the sloping shoulders of the elderly. Responses to the census were regularly adjusted upward, with individuals striving to appear two or three years older than they actually were. In our era of Rogaine, Viagra, and a face-lift industry with annual revenues in the billions, it comes as no shock that Americans today tend to overlook a few years when providing age data for the Census Bureau.

The early American reverence for age makes sense from many perspectives extending beyond the pulpit. At a time when only 2 percent of the population lived past sixty-five, and the median age was a mere sixteen, some of the Puritans' "cult of age" was likely fed by scarcity value. But there were other supports as well. According to American historian David Hackett Fischer, at a time when literacy was limited, elders were "keepers of the culture" and a bridge between generations. In an economy that changed slowly over time, the know-how and skills of the older population were immediately pertinent to the young. And in a society oriented toward tradition and traditional values, one that turned to the past for guidance and social values, older adults were "living representatives of the past, armed with ancient precedents and cloaked in the authority of ancestral ways." Fischer notes that regular recourse was made to the memory of the "oldest inhabitant" and to the judgment and experience of "ancient men" and "reverent women."

Throughout, this cultural orientation was supported by the agrarian economy. Older people particularly benefited from a landowning system that gave them control of the farm until they decided to deed it to their children or until they died. Many hung on until the end, benefiting financially from the labors of their offspring, ensuring themselves work roles, and exercising considerable control. In this context, retirement was an essentially unknown concept. People simply worked as long as health permitted. Most men continued to farm actively into their later years, and older women too played an important role in their separate sphere, functioning as midwives, overseeing dairy operation, supervising their daughters' labor, and managing myriad other "female" tasks.

Older adults enjoyed a central place in both economic and community life in preindustrial America, but it was by no means an unqualified golden age for the aged. Because agrarian early America was a poor, subsistence society, even the greater than average resources of older adults provided little security. The health of older persons, and the population at large, was terrible by contemporary standards. Because individuals couldn't afford to retire, many worked on in pain as they entered later life. When illness caused them to stop working entirely, this change brought with it the risk of lost economic standing as power passed on to the younger generation.

In part out of this fear but also out of abuse of power, some older adults clung to their control of the family farm to the bitter end, often treating their offspring poorly and engendering resentment on the part of the younger generation. In *A Word to the Aged*, for example, the Reverend William Bridge gave voice in the late seventeenth century to growing concern that the old exploited their position and could be "too covetous and tenacious for the things of the world," too convinced that they "know more than others," and, ultimately, too "hard to be pleased." Some historians have observed that, in fact, older people in early America were more often respected than loved.

Overall, however, the culture stressed the importance of reciprocity between the generations, emphasizing not only how much youth needed the wisdom of age (and should therefore honor their elders) but also how dependent older adults were on the loyalty and devotion of the younger generation—especially given the realistic prospect of declining health.

As Thomas Cole, the preeminent cultural historian of aging, has shown, this sense of intergenerational interdependence was not confined to the family. In the past, before we had a large number of older Americans, Cole observes, "it was more or less expected that older people carried their weight in the community by helping out. . . whether it was taking care of their grandchildren, teaching kids to read, or being of use in whatever way they could."

An Incurable Disease

In the early 1800s, new ideas about old age and the role of older people in American life began commanding much greater attention. Respect for the aged, the belief that these individuals possessed important skills and experience, and the broader view that the generations needed each other began eroding badly.

A major source of this shift was the Second Great Awakening, a religious and social movement that swept the country during the second quarter of the nineteenth century. Whereas the pulpits had once been a place for affirming the special qualities of older adults, they now were a forum for stressing the importance of youth and progress. Where a cult of age had once existed, notes David Hackett Fischer, one now could find a cult of youth. The old were portrayed as leftover relics from an outdated and regressive world—a past with little to teach the present.

The evangelist Charles Grandison Finney, founder of Oberlin College and one of the leaders of the Great Awakening, railed against the traditions of the old, arguing that they were "the grand sources of most of the fatal errors of the present day." The derogatory term "old fogeys" found its way into popular parlance. By contrast, youth were embraced in this evangelical movement oriented toward self-improvement and progress. Young people could still improve, be redeemed. The old, by contrast, had missed their chance. They had no future in which to improve themselves, and they became symbols of deterioration and sin—as well as symbols of the outdated hierarchy of the previous century.

In the latter part of the nineteenth century, the view of older adults as useless, dependent, and obsolete gained new ground. The new purveyors of antiaging nostrums were not evangelists but an emerging group of professionals—social workers, sociologists, management experts, and, most significantly, physicians—who positioned themselves as the authorities on aging.

Incapable of arresting or treating age-related maladies, these frustrated medicine men belittled the older generation and characterized aging as an incurable, ever-worsening disease. No longer were the elderly seen simply as older versions of younger people. Instead, they were diagnosed as separate creatures requiring a new set of institutions, approaches, and occupations— among them old-age homes and mandatory retirement.

Even in an era when public figures tell us that "we have met the enemy and he is the elderly us," the late-nineteenth-century physicians' characterizations are breathtaking. In the considered opinion of I. L. Nascher, the man who named the medical field of geriatrics: "The old man does not know what is best for him. . . he cannot accommodate himself to new conditions brought about by the progress of civilization." According to the scientific research of Dr. George Beard writing in 1876: "When an old man utters great thoughts, it is not age but youth that speaks through the lips of age."

Probably the most influential and notorious expression of this emergent outlook was a 1905 speech, "The Fixed Period," delivered by one of the nation's best-known medical experts, Dr. William Osler. The fifty-six-year-old Osler delivered the lecture on the occasion of his departure as physician-in-chief of Johns Hopkins University's hospital (personally, he was not about to step aside or to retire, having just been appointed Regius Professor of Medicine at Oxford). In his speech Osler argued that men over forty were a useless drain on society and an impediment to efficiency and progress.

Years earlier he had written that these individuals possessed "a weakened receptivity and an inability to adapt" to new intellectual challenges. Now he was ready to take the case to another level, positing that the period from age twenty-five to age forty constituted the "golden years," during which "there is always a balance in the mental bank and the credit is always good." Older men, by contrast, were useless: "Take the sum of human achievement in action, in science, in art, in literature—subtract the work of the men above forty, and while we should miss great treasures, even priceless treasures, we would practically be where we are today."

As for men over sixty, Osler asked his audience to consider "the incalculable benefit it would be in commercial, political and in professional life if, as a matter of course, men stopped work at this age." Making the connection to the title of his speech, he half-facetiously suggested reconsideration of Anthony Trollope's proposal in *The Fixed Period* that men of sixty should retire for a year to a college for contemplation, before a "peaceful departure" via chloroform. Osler contended that the benefits of this scheme began with honestly acknowledging the personal suffering that befell men in their seventh and eighth decades. He himself could see these calamities coming as he neared that age. Yet not only was it the personal suffering of the aged that we needed to consider, but also—and here it is not hard, on the one hand, to discern echoes of Charles Grandison Finney, and on the other, to hear Lester Thurow and Pete Peterson beginning to clear their throats—we needed to take into consideration "the many evils which they [older adults] perpetuate unconsciously, and with impunity" on the rest of society.

By the early twentieth century, these views had left their mark on private enterprise and public policy. Businessmen used the image of the "superannuated" worker to justify mandatory retirement policies. On the public side, government officials changed rules for distribution of Civil War pensions so that a veteran would be considered "disabled one-half in ability" at age 62, two-thirds disabled at 65, and fully incapacitated by age 70. Independent of actual situation, advancing years were assumed to mean declining capacity.

Given these premises, older people were advised, in the words of another prominent physician, to "lead an absolutely quiet and uneventful life." By the early twentieth century, according to historians Carole Haber and Brian Grattan, maturing men and women were also counseled to avoid the appearance of old age entirely. A raft of articles appeared focusing on how to stay young, sporting titles like "The Quest for Prolonged Youth" and "The Art of Not Growing Old." The aged were counseled to conceal any evidence of "thinning hair, false teeth, arch supporters, hardening arteries, sagging muscles, and failing eyes," all indicators of social uselessness.

At the individual and social levels, old age had been defined as a problem. The Puritans' crown of gold was now a cross to bear, as later life was depicted, in Haber and Grattan's words, as "decay, disillusion, weariness."

There is an irony in the declining status of older adults and the increasing cultural perception of age-related obsolescence that emerged in America in the nineteenth and early twentieth centuries: The real, material condition of older adults actually improved in certain ways during this period. First, industrialization and urbanization, though hardly bringing affluence, nevertheless lifted most working-class families well above the conditions of subsistence farmers in the preindustrial era. In addition, the growth of multigenerational households during the industrial periods generated "family funds"—a pooling of the resources of two or three generations. It also produced continued, pragmatic forms of reciprocal exchange between these generations. For example, older members of the family were often active in helping younger members locate work.

Some middle-class older adults even managed to maintain separate households. These independent arrangements were, in part, a way of dealing with tensions that accompanied multigenerational family living. Although these households had undeniable economic and social advantages, they also entailed substantial sacrifices for members of the younger generation, such as having to quit school, postpone marriage, or give up other opportunities to support aging kin in the household.

As a result of overall economic growth and the emergence of pension plans, some older workers were also able to retire voluntarily during the industrial period. In 1910, one-third of men over sixty-five received Civil War pensions, which originally covered only wounded soldiers but later were expanded substantially. Private pension plans also were on the rise. In 1875, the Canadian Great Trunk railroad system established the first corporate retirement plan in North America, with American Express introducing a plan a year later for workers over age sixty with two decades of experience. By 1910, sixty such plans were in place. Ten years earlier, the Pattern Makers League of North America became the first union to offer a pension plan.

Many other workers faced involuntary departure from the workplace as mandatory retirement was introduced during the latter part of the nineteenth century. To some extent, these policies grew out of the view that older workers were unable to keep up with the pace of industrial change. However, that criticism often cloaked the simple desire to cut costs. As industrial capitalism and scientific management broke the crafts down into interchangeable, unskilled functions with little intrinsic interest, this trend gave rise to a massive labor management problem: turnover. Workers felt little tie either to the work itself or to employers and would constantly change jobs in search of higher wages or out of the simple desire to change. In the words of one historian, William Graebner, the turnover phenomenon constituted "a continuous, unorganized strike."

Henry Ford, for example, faced annual turnover rates of 400 percent. His ingenious response was to create a system of increasing annual wages based on seniority. Because the tasks of semiskilled workers were largely indistinguishable, years of loyal service were used to replicate the career ladder of skilled workers. However, this system led to inefficiencies for manufacturers: Older workers came to be paid higher wages than younger workers for performing very similar jobs. Mandatory retirement provided a way to cap this cost while preserving incentives against turnover, and by the turn of the century a growing number of large U.S. corporations had initiated this policy.

Overall, however, real retirement remained out of reach for most workers through the end of the nineteenth century. Only the most affluent, the most infirm, or the limited number of older adults with guaranteed regular retirement income were in a position to leave work permanently. Most individuals continued to work, essentially dying with their boots on. And those who had left their principal job—either by choice or through mandatory retirement—often turned to self-employment.

Yet tremendous insecurity accompanied this arrangement, note Haber and Grattan. If a worker lost a job, was unable to find some new source of income, and lacked a family to fall back on, there were few alternatives to being institutionalized. After a life of hard work, working-class and even middle-class individuals faced the ignominious prospect of ending up in an almshouse. Few willingly accepted this fate, and relatives made Herculean efforts to keep their elderly kin from having to go to the almshouse, including shoehorning more people into rooms in their house and requiring children to find jobs in the labor market.

Nevertheless, over time, the almshouses came to be dominated by the old (even though, overall, only 2 percent of the elderly population resided in them). These institutions soon came to be public symbols of old age in this country, used by reformers to push for pension policies to support the elderly.

Although sympathetic to the cause of the elderly, these advocates often subscribed to the management experts' and physicians' worst stereotypes of the aged as needy and debilitated. The end result was an unlikely coalition of reformers, labor leaders, and efficiency experts who came together to begin pushing for new measures to deal with those most pathetic of Americans: older adults.

A Life of Their Own

By the early decades of the twentieth century, a new era in the history of older adults in this country was at hand—an era of sweeping changes brought into existence in substantial measure by Social Security.

Throughout the latter part of the nineteenth century and into the early decades of the twentieth, there was modest growth in both retirement rates and in older adults living in independent households. In 1880, for example, 78 percent of men age sixty-five and older were in the labor force. By 1900 that number had dropped to 65 percent, by 1920 to 60 percent, and by 1930 to 58 percent. Similarly, in 1880 only 49 percent of retired men were household heads. By 1900 the percentage had grown to 52 percent; by 1920 to 62. Meanwhile, the proportion of men sixty-five or older who continued working and were household heads remained both high and constant: at 84 percent in both 1880 and 1920.

During this period the elderly were becoming, if not more respected, more sympathetically viewed. Rather than hated signs of the old order, they were portrayed as long-suffering and helpless. As already stated, reformers focused particularly on the almshouse. In the words of Abraham Epstein, a prominent social reformer of the day, "The poorhouse stands as a threatening symbol of the deepest humiliation and degradation before all wage-earners after the prime of life."

An important ally in the push for increased security was the middle class according to Haber and Grattan, even though these individuals harbored less fear of the almshouse than those in the lower rungs of society. However, by the 1920s, the ability of the middle-class old and their children to establish separate households, build up some savings, and maintain a reasonable standard of living had begun to reshape the expectations of family members of all ages. When the depression hit in the 1930s, these and other sources of security were stripped away. The homes that had been so important to the economic survival of the working class were lost, but so too were the private pensions that had supported the retirement of the middle class and the banks that had held their savings. For several segments of society, the depression demonstrated the limitations of the private market to guarantee a decent old age.

The result was a coalition that extended beyond the poor and beyond the older population. The alliance included not only the elderly and their advocates but also younger family members eager to be freed from the sacrifices of multigenerational living and the prospect of having to support older relatives over prolonged periods.

Another contributing factor was high youth unemployment accentuated by the depression. Many in the Roosevelt administration worried about social unrest among the large numbers of young men out of work. To federal policymakers, Social Security looked appealing as a vehicle for inducing retirement and creating more room in the labor market for unemployed youth (the labor unions, seeing a bonanza of new members, eagerly lent their support). At the same time, the business community supported the state pension as a way of advancing the use of retirement to cut costs, in particular through convincing higher-paid older workers to leave the labor force.

This surprising coalition helped to bring about passage of the Social Security Act of 1935 establishing a federal old age pension program, and in 1940 payment of the first monthly Social Security benefits began. At first, coverage applied only to employees in commerce and industry, about 60 percent of the total workforce. The initial age was set at 65, at a time when life expectancy was only 62 and the expectation of payout was modest. Age 65 was already considered the legitimate retirement age, thanks largely to Otto von Bismarck, who had selected that benchmark in establishing the old-age pension plan for the Prussian Army in 1875. Bismarck picked 65, notes Peter Drucker, because he believed it guaranteed that the state would never have to pay a single pension (Bismarck himself was in his 70s at the time, but life expectancy in Germany was only in the mid-30s).

In the 1950s, a steady expansion of benefits began. Social Security coverage was extended to an additional 10 million people in 1950, and benefits were increased by 77 percent. Soon nonprofit and government employees, as well as farm and domestic workers and the self-employed, were added to the rolls. Actuarially reduced, early benefits at age 62 were provided in 1956 for men, and in 1961 for women. Benefits were also provided for disabled workers aged 50 to 64. In 1965 hospital insurance was offered to men 65 and older. Between 1968 and 1973 benefits were increased in every single year—and provisions included for increases due to cost of living—with retrenchment not coming until the late 1970s.

As David Ekerdt of the University of Kansas points out, the period following World War II carried with it "a concurrent expansion of private or job-specific pensions, whose benefits often dovetailed with Social Security provisions." Writing in *The Encyclopedia of Aging*, he notes that in 1949 unions were given the ability to use pensions as an issue in collective bargaining, and came to view these funds as a means both to alleviate unemployment and add to Social Security income. The development of industry pension plans and plans among the self-employed were further simulated by federal tax provisions.

Despite continued growth in private pensions, most individuals (as with today) financed their retirement primarily through the Social Security system. For men and women 65 to 69 in 1991, median Social Security wealth was three times as large as financial assets and employer-provided pensions combined. In 1986, 81 percent of elderly households received over half their income from Social Security, with 40 percent having no income from assets and 74 percent no income from private pensions or annuities. In 1987 Social Security was the only source of income for 14 percent of beneficiaries.

Overall, these changes left the elderly far more prosperous than at any time in the past. Today, the median nonhousing wealth of households with heads aged 60 to 65 is $19,191 in 1917 dollars, whereas it was about $3,000 in 1917—a sixfold increase.

Social Security and the growth in prosperity and pensions in turn produced two major changes in the way older Americans live their lives—and in their economic and social ties to society. The first change was mass retirement. Very few individuals were able to retire in the days of the Puritans, or for that matter throughout the preindustrial period. They were simply too poor living in an agrarian subsistence economy. During the industrial era, retirement became a possibility for the growing number of middle-class Americans, for those eligible for Civil War pensions, and for more prosperous farmers. However, the majority of men and women could not count on the kind of guaranteed income that enabled security in retirement. This insecurity led most to continue working, often through self-employment.

Social Security, building on already existing trends, was crucial in establishing retirement as the norm for older Americans—and it produced a great exodus of individuals leaving the workforce voluntarily. By 1940, the year the first Social Security monthly benefits were paid out, 41.8 percent of men 65 and over were in the labor force; by 1960—the year Sun City was established—that number had dropped to 30.5 percent, and it has continued to decline steadily, spurred in part by benefit increases and the growth in other forms of income. Today the figure is 16.3 percent. At the same time, the participation rate for men 55–64 has dropped from 86.1 percent to 67.6 percent as early retirement has gained in popularity. The pattern for women is different, but the result of low labor force participation is the same, with figures declining for 65-plus women from 9.7 percent in 1950 to 8.2 percent in 1993.

The other major transformation brought about by Social Security and the overall growth in wealth on the part of older Americans was a significant increase in the number of independent households of older Americans. The proportion of men who were retired and household heads grew from 48.9 percent in 1880 to 70 percent in 1940, to 82.9 percent by 1960, to 89.5 percent by 1990. During this same period the rate of nonretired men who remained household heads was consistently high, growing from 83.9 percent in 1880 to 90.8 percent by 1990—reflecting the desire of older adults, when financially able, to remain heading their own, independent households.

The result of these new conditions was that in the years following World War II, older Americans became truly a generation apart. Their status in society, undermined during the nineteenth century first by the clergy, then by the experts, remained marginal. They continued to be a surplus population, cast aside by the supposed imperatives of progress, portrayed as washed up in a society with little apparent use for them. Yet at the same time, they were relieved of much of the economic insecurity that haunted earlier generations of retirees (the widower subsisting on catfood was becoming a less prevalent phenomenon). Meanwhile, their longevity and health were improving significantly, and they were becoming more independent from family ties than ever before in the past.

It was in this new context—and into this cultural vacuum—that a set of corporate interests and leisure entrepreneurs went to work, in the process transforming the nature of later life in America and bringing on the most recent stage in the history of America's aging.

The Making of a Leisure Class

The Roleless Role

On August 3, 1962, *Time* magazine featured a cover story on the rapid aging of America. The article began by rehearsing the long procession of demographic statistics so familiar in magazine cover stories about America's aging today. The centerpiece was a dramatic chart entitled "People Living Longer" showing the nearly sixfold increase in Americans over age 65 between 1900 and 1960. The line indicating increasing numbers of older adults rises so precipitously that by midcentury it appears nearly vertical.

Largely because of the power of modern medicine, *Time* explained, the aged (the article also used the term "oldsters") had become the fastest-growing "minority" group in the United States. People were living longer, with life expectancy at birth increasing during the first half of the twentieth century by 17.6 years for men and 20.3 for women. At the time of the article, 17.4 million Americans were over 65, and this group had increased twice as fast as the rest of the population during the 1950s. Overall, the magazine reported, demographers were estimating that by the year 2000 the number of U.S. citizens past the normal retirement age of 65 was going to double, and that these individuals would come to constitute a full 10 percent of the population. The article noted, by comparison, that this number was equivalent to the total population of Spain and triple that of Australia.

In particular, the cover story underscored, this fast-increasing nation of older adults had both "time and money." At age 65, the average American man in 1962 could expect to live nearly 13 more years. Furthermore, he had "money, or at least a modest income." The 17 million Americans over 65, it was explained, had an aggregate annual income of $32 billion, with the bulk of this money coming from Social Security and private pensions.

In addition to reminding us that the aging society did not start in the 1990s, the *Time* coverage is striking in the way it represented the choices (or lack of them) facing the country nearly four decades ago. As in the case of so many of today's characterizations, the article gave no hint that the massive increase in life expectancy might be a positive development for society. Nor was there discussion about the potential contribution of older adults to families, communities, even the economy, or that efforts to tap this resource were even an option for the society. The overall portrait of older adults was not unsympathetic; it simply described a group of people with time, money, and unprecedented health who were living in a society with no place for them.

The article began in Fair Haven, New Jersey, with a portrait of a recent retiree, "not what anybody would call an old man." His hair was described as gray, but not white, his face as lined, though not wrinkled. As he sat on his son's porch—where his granddaughter was absorbed in play, although there was little contact between them—the man looked down at "strong, freckled" hands and wondered: "I don't know what to do with myself these days." Bewildered, he continued, "I'm supposed to be old—I was 65 last fall—but God knows I don't feel old. The company is right about the retirement age, I suppose; it has to make places for younger men. But what happens to us?" According to *Time*, this retiree/everyman could have been anywhere in the United States in 1962: "His cry and his question are being heard more often and urgently everywhere—in Southern drawl and Northern twang, in city and suburb, cold-water flat and executive suite."

It was a problem catching the country unaware: What was America to do with the vast and growing population of older adults now finding themselves "too old to work and too young to die"? It was truly ironic, the article suggested (anticipating the "failure of success" arguments heard today), that positive developments like advances in medicine should bring about such a cruel dilemma. Also responsible were "progressive" management policies in industry that had standardized 65 as retirement age.

But in a society that valued a man (women were conspicuously absent from the piece) by what he did, these people were being left to live lives in abeyance. To confirm the degree of this decline in status and situation, *Time* sought the views of two experts from the social sciences.

Natalie Cabot, a Boston gerontologist, asked the reader to consider how difficult it must be for retirees to accept the invidious transformation: "Nobody ever suddenly becomes Negro or Jewish, but people do suddenly become retired." The man long attached to identity as a railroad man or an insurance executive, Cabot added, would discover within three weeks of retirement that "he is no longer anything at all." Ernest Watson Burgess of the University of Chicago, author of the 1960 book *Aging in Western Societies*, opined that industrialization ruined the position of older people in America, leaving them with the "roleless role" that was retirement.

To illustrate, the *Time* piece then introduced readers to a further procession of older Americans like the porchsitter from Fair Haven. One, a former factory foreman, explained dejectedly: "I can't think of anything useful I can do any more, and I don't want to sit around doing nothing. So I just sleep for longer spells, hoping it will end." Another man who had migrated to the gray haven of St. Petersburg, Florida, offered his personal prescription for coping with later life in early 1960s America: "What you do is sleep good and late in the morning. That way I eat breakfast for lunch about 11 o'clock, and then I don't have to eat lunch at all. Sure I'm lonely. But it's better to be lonely here in all this sunshine than back in Cincinnati."

The Best Is Yet to Come

The cry being heard "in Southern drawl and Northern twang" of what older adults were going to do with themselves under the emerging new conditions of retirement was already under discussion when *Time* jumped on the issue.

Indeed, since the early 1950s, experts had been arguing about how older adults, and society at large, might contend with the new phenomenon of mass retirement. In 1951, the Corning Corporation convened a group of scholars to help make sense of the relationship between leisure and retirement. One of the participants, Henry Higgins, articulated the prevailing perspective of the gathering, defining retirement as the absence of ideas about what to do with oneself. He went on to propose a national effort, beginning at age fifty, to educate aging individuals into leisure. The session chairman, Lynn White, Jr., the president of Mills College (four decades before Steve Weiner would become that institution's provost), argued that America sat on a new frontier of leisure and consumption. We needed, he urged, a major effort designed "to glamorize leisure as we have not."

While the academics and other experts were busy debating the issue of leisure in later life, those approaching retirement were beginning to be exposed to a "barrage of propaganda" about the wonders of this new life phase. The selling of retirement to Americans had commenced, and the first to exploit this looming market were life insurance companies heavily invested in the pension business. According to historian William Graebner, author of *The History of Retirement*, their new message was a simple one: Retirement need not be a sign of incompetence or maladjustment but rather was "a bounty bestowed by the society and by the pension."

The key, of course, was proper preparation. Addressing the National Industrial Conference Board in 1952, Mutual Life Insurance Company vice president H. G. Kenagy urged preparing employees for retirement beginning at age fifty. He applauded the upsurge in corporate newsletters and magazines for employees as doing "a splendid job of selling the idea. . . that old age can be beautiful, and that the best of life is yet to come." In particular, he advised, the most effective strategy was "constant stories of happily retired people telling what they do, but still more, of course, emphasizing what they did to get ready for the life they are now living."

In fact, insurance companies were the first institutions to create formal retirement preparation programs. Prudential started a special group counseling center aimed at helping employees overcome their resistance to retirement, beginning with the assumption that "many of their fears were not realistic." Soon this approach spread to other industries. Esso Standard saw its efforts as anticommunist in nature, making sure potentially socialistic retirees were aware that industry was "doing something concrete about their uncertain future." They urged employees to see their retirement as "something earned by faithful service, a form of graduation into a new phase of life rather than a 'casting out' process."

By the late 1950s, through their extensive marketing efforts, the insurance companies had succeeded in elevating the idea that retirement might in fact be a new version of the American dream. However, it would be left to a brilliant group of entrepreneurial real estate developers to take this notion and carry it to its logical extreme.

Inventing the Golden Years

Del Webb and his lieutenants were hardly alone in transforming retirement into a lifestyle built around leisure, nor was Sun City singlehandedly responsible for turning older Americans into a leisure class. The conditions for these changes were established long before either the Webb Company or Sun City arrived on the scene. In part, Social Security and the longer-term trend toward prosperity in later life—as well as the century-old rejection of older adults by society—were key. Even in more immediate terms, the insurance companies and others in the financial services industry were the first ones to begin peddling the leisure message.

Nevertheless, Webb's contribution was significant. Webb Company officials didn't just sell pensions or push a leisured ideology; they created whole, self-contained, age-segregated "paradises" ("cities on a hill") built around "an active new way of life." They took the ideal and made it real. In the process, Webb, Breen, and their associates not only fashioned a culture of retirement where none had previously been but even named the new phase of life, inventing "the golden years" as the label for the lifestyle they were selling (along with a lot of long-forgotten labels like "the new leisure set" and "the friendly years"). The Del Webb name, and the term Sun City, soon became synonymous with leisure in later life. Overall, the man was a force of nature, arguably one of the most influential Americans—at least in terms of how we spend our leisure time—of the last half of the twentieth century. An abbreviated account of his rags-to-riches story provides not only a sense of how formidable an entrepreneur he was but also a window on the many ingredients that shaped Sun City and led to its far-reaching impact.

Del Webb was born in 1899, on the eve of a new century, in the pioneer town of Fresno, California. His mother's father was a German farmer who built one of California's first irrigation systems. James Webb, his paternal grandfather, was an English evangelist. The Webb household was both prosperous and deeply religious. However, the young Webb wanted only to play baseball, which was forbidden by a trio of pious aunts. As a boy he would sneak out and play under assumed names, eventually getting to play as much as he wanted when his father's contracting business collapsed, and the fourteen-year-old left home to become a carpenter's apprentice.

Over the next decade he drifted among construction jobs across the West. However, Webb the carpenter was always a means for supporting Webb the baseball player, and he would work only for companies that fielded a semiprofessional team. His single-minded goal was to become a major league pitcher. A picture from the early 1920s shows a clean-cut, confident youth, six feet, four inches tall, dressed in an old-time baseball uniform with "Maxwell Hardware" stenciled across his chest.

Although it is hard to believe that the ferociously determined and magnetic Webb (he was captain of every baseball team he played on) was ever denied anything he wanted so badly, Webb's baseball aspirations ended first with broken ribs, then with typhoid fever. He was stricken with the fever in 1927, the same year the Yankees of Ruth and Gehrig would field what many consider the greatest team in baseball history. As the Yankees tore through the American League, Webb moved to Phoenix "on doctor's orders," convalescing there with his wife Hazel. His weight dropped from 204 to 99 pounds, and he was close to death.

But the desert proved salubrious. Within a year he was back on the job, this time working for a small Phoenix contractor building a grocery store. After the contractor absconded with the payroll, the grocer, in a panic, asked Webb to take over the construction job. He did—setting up the Del E. Webb Construction Company on Ninth Street in Phoenix—with total assets consisting of one cement mixer, ten wheelbarrows, twenty shovels, and ten picks (all inherited from the deadbeat former employer).

After Webb finished the store, he was rewarded with a contract to build a chain of groceries. By the mid-1930s, amazingly, the Webb Company had mushroomed into one of the biggest contractors in Arizona, a $3-million-a-year business. In 1937, ten years after moving to the state, he was selected to construct the new annex to the Arizona state capitol building. By World War II, Webb's company was operating in twelve states, constructing the majority of military bases and air stations in Arizona and Southern California. A number of these contracts called for Webb to build entire cities.

The most dubious came in March 1942. A month earlier FDR had signed the order moving Japanese and Japanese Americans from designated "military areas" to internment camps. Webb was retained to build the so-called Theater of Operations at Parker, Arizona, a large Japanese relocation camp. He threw 5,000 employees into building the internment camp around the clock. After finishing he signed another contract to expand the camp to hold 25,000 more Japanese Americans who were being rounded up. For Webb none of this posed an ethical problem; a job was a job.

In the midst of so much business expansion, Webb again began experiencing health problems. The army physicians who examined him during the war said he was suffering from the "flu." But the symptoms persisted, and Webb decided to see another doctor. In the course of the visit he casually mentioned his habit of drinking "10 to 20 bourbons a day." On the stunned doctor's orders, Webb agreed to quit. "Not another drop of whiskey has passed my lips since that day," he recalled. "All that time I spent drinking, I could now spend working." The result was a business empire that made him one of the biggest builders and wealthiest men in the country.

Throughout, government contracts provided the basis for Webb's empire. After the war, a new round of defense contracts enabled Webb to expand further, including the commission to build Howard Hughes's new airfield and factory, the beginning of a long business relationship (and friendship) between the two men. He later co-built a $62-million Minuteman missile silo complex in Montana, and a nearly $500-million housing development covering 15,000 acres southeast of Houston to house the employees of NASA.

Years earlier, in 1945, Webb had gotten back into baseball, for "public relations" reasons. He and two partners purchased the Yankees for $2.8 million. During the twenty years the developer owned the team, the Yankees won an unprecedented ten world championships, raising the owner's national profile and making yet more money for him. But baseball for Webb was more than the realization of a childhood fantasy. He used to boast that he applied all that he learned playing baseball to his business dealings, but in reality it was the other way around. As one associate recalled: "He brought business principles to major league baseball. Before that, baseball was a game, and most of the people involved in it were not business people. He organized it." Webb knew how much every fan spent on hot dogs, popcorn, programs, and souvenirs. He rationalized every aspect of the game (with the exception of what happened on the field, which he left to his excellent manager, Casey Stengel.) By the time Webb was finished with baseball, he had organized the major leagues into a business.

In all his business dealings, Webb was notorious for his lust for standardization. The builder's offices were operated according to something called "The Blue Book." The manual specified every detail of protocol and appearance, down to the type of desk calendar pads and the kind of lettering on each door. (One employee who drove a tan car when Webb wanted the entire company in black sedans left the office at the end of one day to find that his car had been removed from the parking lot during the day and repainted black.)

Another chapter in Webb's postwar empire building was the development of Las Vegas. Bugsy Siegel's dream, the Flamingo Hotel, was built by Webb. ("Don't worry, we only kill each other," Siegel told the apprehensive Webb when first discussing the construction of the Flamingo—which was called "Del Webb's Flamingo.") Later, Webb would go on to build the Sahara-Nevada Hotel and coax Howard Hughes—with prodding by a Nevada gaming commission eager to attract reputable business types and clean up Las Vegas—to join him in developing the city.

When one adds in Webb's prominent role in launching the first motels (Hi-way Houses), the long list of construction projects he completed (including Madison Square Garden), his role in shaping both Las Vegas and the DiMaggio-Mantle Yankees (Yogi Berra called him the "ideal owner"), the scope of the man's impact begins to become clear.

Perhaps more than anything, Webb was—as his company touts in its official history—"an expert at building something in the middle of nothing." He was someone who could transform the barren desert into a vision of paradise—or at least a source of profits. Over and over again, Webb would metamorphose it: into missile silos, into army bases, into internment camps, into company towns, into gambling casinos, into resort facilities—and ultimately, into a new vision of retirement in America, a vision that turned this much maligned stage of life into a seeming second spring.

A New Way of Life for the Old

Given Webb's stature, it was no surprise that when *Time* did its 1962 cover story on the aging of America, Webb was selected for the cover (Tom Breen had by then receded behind his boss's shadow). Under the banner "The Retirement City: A New Way of Life for the Old," Webb's massive head and resolute expression were set against a backdrop of shuffleboard courts and palm fronds, the new Webbian symbols of active retirement living.

In stunning contrast to the older lives of rejection, inactivity, and confusion recounted in the first part of the article, the *Time* cover story upheld a new and compelling alternative: abandoning society to join age-segregated retirement enclaves located in the middle of the desert and built around the unabashed pursuit of leisure. Under headings like "Healthy and Busy" and "Pioneer Spirit," Sun City was described as a place for those older adults who had "enough energy and gumption. . . to pull up stakes, sell the house, dispose of the furniture," a preferred alternative for that "growing army of active oldsters willing and able to cut out and start a new life." Against the backdrop of alienation and uselessness, Sun City—with its shuffleboard courts, golf course, and activity center—was described as a "dramatically successful solution" to America's aging problem.

In contrast to the earlier cast of pitiable elderly, readers were introduced to Sun City residents like Dr. Chester L. Meade, "a tanned, lithe" man who gave up his dental practice in Mason City, Iowa, to move to Sun City with wife Mabel. The couple articulated the Webb Company's formula for successful aging: activity plus friendliness plus age segregation. "People say, 'But don't you miss Mason City?'" Mabel recounted. "Those dear friends, yes, but not Mason City. We're not lonely here at all, and the people are so friendly." Dr. Meade explained, "Back there, you can play golf only a few months of the year. The rest of the time you go to the Elks Club and play two-bit rummy." As for missing contact with the younger generation, Mabel explained that the Meades harbored no antipathy for the young ones, "But as you get older, you don't care about having a lot of them around. The fact that you can have your own yard and flowers without worrying about children traipsing through is appealing."

Another original Sun Citian featured was former Sonotone Corporation president Dean Babbitt, who unlike many of the working-class and middle-class residents of the community moved to Sun City from a large estate in New Hampshire. He described himself and his neighbors as pioneers on the frontier of age: "People here have pulled up stakes and started over. Whether you're living on Social Security or a bunch of money, it makes no difference." Babbitt emphasized the equality of life among residents of Sun City, where all the status and achievement anxieties of midlife were set aside—and where society's adulation of youth was irrelevant.

The article concluded that for the "oldsters" of Sun City, being apart from the rest of society offered a kind of liberation: They no longer needed to fear being "shouldered aside" by the younger generation, while they were free to enjoy the camaraderie of their agemates. Overall, Sun City offered them a better life, especially compared with what society was willing to make available outside the walls of the enclave.

Over the coming years the utopian message of the *Time* article was reproduced over and over again in a wave of early 1960s idealizations of Sun City. With titles like "Where Life Begins at 65" (*Reader's Digest*) and "For the Retired a World All Their Own" (*Life*), these articles hammered away at the message that the leisured life—that "year-round vacation," to quote one of the Webb Company's press releases—was the highest aspiration for older Americans.

Making Sense of Sun City

As Sun City approaches its fortieth anniversary and we mark Webb's centennial year, it is an appropriate time to reexamine what this archetype of the most recent phase in America's experience with aging has to teach us—both about the role entrepreneurs and institutional inventions can play in social change and about the nearly half-century-long career of leisure as the reigning ideal for later life. This reexamination reveals a mixed legacy containing both inspiring and distressing aspects.

A Major Step Forward

From the perspective of 1999, Sun City's offerings of activity and leisure seem commonplace. Perhaps more than anything else, however, this fact is testimony to the degree to which Webb's formula succeeded over time. In 1964, a vehicle for making retirement something active and enjoyable was nothing short of revolutionary.

In 1964, *The New Yorker* sent then-neophyte writer Calvin Trillin off to the desert to check out the social experiment generating so much attention. On the second morning of Trillin's Sun City visit, he turned on his motel television to watch the Phoenix morning news. The top story was about a retired pump mechanic who had lost his mind and wounded a police officer while holding six others at bay on his front yard. When the man was finally led out of the house by a local police captain, he provided a simple explanation for his behavior: "You can't be retired and live." Trillin observed that as he spent time at Sun City, he found the comment a pithy, if especially harsh, summary of the outlook of many older adults in a society "that has managed to extend their life span but not their working years."

What Trillin found at Sun City was a refuge from a society that had no place for the deranged pump mechanic or for a great many people in his stage of life. At one point Trillin asked Louis Inwood, a Sun City resident, about the theory among gerontologists that older adults didn't want to live in age-segregated communities apart from the rest of society. "As a theory, it's fine," Inwood reacted. "But in practice nobody is going to do any listening to them." Inwood had been Delaware Valley Man of the Year when he retired at 65, a civil servant who got a unanimous vote of thanks from Philadelphia's city council: "And despite that kind of record, I couldn't get a job if I tried," he told Trillin, angrily. "I'm an outcast because I'm 67 years old. I think the whole damn bunch of us are outcasts, who have found a way of living without impinging on anybody or bothering anybody."

In this context, is it any surprise that 100,000 people showed up to Sun City's opening? Webb and Breen found a gulf in American society you could drive whole age-segregated cities through. There were so few compelling options for older Americans in mainstream society at the time that people were willing to flock to places like Sun City where they could start all over again—in the process becoming, in Dean Babbitt's characterization, pioneers on the frontier of a new kind of aging. It was a place where they could forget the curse of age. Indeed, Frances FitzGerald comments that people moved to

Sun City not to be old—but to be young. Surrounded only by agemates, they could forget that they were no longer in the "prime of life." (One great story about Sun City's early years is that a speculator purchased the land across the street from the retirement community, threatening to build a cemetery there until Webb paid him twice his purchase price for it.)

Webb not only created "a paradise town" for a group of older Americans to commence this new experience in aging, but he played a significant role in filling the broader cultural void as well. Along with the pension sellers, Webb and the other retirement community developers who followed his lead put forth a positive vision of later life and retirement that countered "the absence of ideas" and the long history of negative characterizations that had existed. In the Webb Company's jingles and full-page ads, aging was depicted not as an incurable disease but rather as a reward and a privilege ("Lucky enough to be 50?" one Sun City ad asked). Later life was recast in the company's marketing efforts as a special phase of life, something to look forward to.

The motives of company officials were far from utopian. Breen was the first to admit that the company was in this for a buck. However, along with the insurance companies so heavily involved in marketing a leisured later life, they contributed greatly to improving the image of older Americans and elevating the notion that it was possible to attain happiness in retirement. They gave us "the golden years"—and in the process provided respite from the overwhelmingly negative outlook toward age that had reigned essentially unchallenged for nearly a century and a half.

The Henry Ford of Retirement

Another of Webb's contributions was simply to show the kind of impact an entrepreneur armed with an idea could have, both in terms of those individuals directly served and in relation to the broader culture. In important ways, he might be considered the Henry Ford of retirement living, in the sense that he made this kind of existence accessible to the average American. Webb figured out how to keep per-unit cost low, drawing on his feel for standardization, his long experience building for the military, and the fact that land in the desert was dirt (sand?) cheap. And Webb was an alchemist of sorts, one who knew how "to build something from nothing."

The initial houses at Sun City were priced from $8,750 (the "Kentworth") to $11,600 for three bedrooms with two baths. A house directly on the golf course cost an additional $1,450. Not a bad bargain even in the early 1960s.

Half the buyers paid for their homes in cash. They were in a position to capitalize on the post–World War II real estate boom (government assistance after the war had enabled returning veterans to own their homes), buy a bigger house in Arizona, and have money left over to boot.

But Webb went beyond affordability. He found a way to combine affordability and luxury, which fed the overall Sun City message that retirement could be a kind of aristocratic existence. The central vehicle for conveying this sense was golf. Webb was the man who put golf into retirement. As the journalist Mike Steere observed in a recent *Worth* article about Webb's achievement: "The most conspicuous, defining amenity," at Sun City, "was and is golf," adding, "golf courses make industrial-scale tract housing look more like paradise, and also like a terrific deal. No way, especially back in 1960, could a regular Joe on a pension expect a golf-course retirement—until Del Webb provided it."

Part of Webb's genius—perhaps inherited from his irrigation-building maternal grandfather—was to translate revolutionary ideas into projects on a vast scale. Although Sun City started small, the plan from the beginning was for it to get much bigger—as it did. And the growth was not confined to the original site, although after the initial Sun City went through a series of phases, Webb launched Sun City West, then Sun City Grand, until more than 100,000 people (and still growing) were living in the communities on the outskirts of Phoenix. Soon, Sun Cities were sprouting up elsewhere in the state, in Southern and Northern California, Florida, Texas, Nevada, South Carolina, even Illinois. Webb knew how to go to scale, and his organization had the resources to do it. Here, too, he was like Ford; as Steere commented in *Worth*: "The company did what others did, but bigger, faster, at better value."

The other part of Webb's entrepreneurial gift might be traced to Jimmy Webb, his evangelist paternal grandfather (the one who used to grouch about the waste of being old with nothing to do). Webb not only could turn an idea into practice but also could proselytize about it. As Jim Dietrick, the company's advertising manager explained in the early days of Sun City, "We've always sold a way of life. The homes are secondary."

However, the marketing side of the company's work was far more than glitz. Officials did their homework. The company from the outset was devoted to research. Even at the most basic level, Breen spent years reading, visiting, and talking to people before he would marshal the evidence to convince Webb to invest in the Sun City idea. Over time, the company developed an increasingly sophisticated research machine—constantly surveying Sun City residents about their needs and preferences and conducting focus groups and other studies of older Americans outside the walls of their own communities. And the company was willing to make adjustments when research suggested they were warranted.

Webb also made the most of public policy. He built his business developing whole towns for the military, state capitals, missile bases, airfields, even internment camps. In the case of Sun City, the developer was helped by the government in many other ways, both direct and indirect: Purchasers of Sun City homes were buoyed not only by government pensions but also by FHA loans. Furthermore, age-segregated housing was specifically protected under fair housing legislation. At almost every turn, it seems, Webb benefited from—and manipulated—public policies. A lifetime Democrat, Webb was nevertheless close with politicians as diverse in outlook as LBJ, Barry Goldwater, and Ronald Reagan. He had their ear and was not reluctant to use his access when needed to advance the prospects of his developments.

In the end, Webb's breakthrough did not redound only to his company's benefit. The Sun City experience produced thousands of reproductions and variations, not only spawning an entire retirement community field but also providing impetus that led to massive public efforts in age-segregated public senior citizen housing. Furthermore, the Webb Company's pioneering efforts spawned a whole set of subsidiary businesses.

This burgeoning industry is on display in contemporary magazines like *Where to Retire.* Its summer 1998 issue features a quiz, "Are You Cut Out for Relocation? Take Our Quiz to Find Out" (echoes of the "gumption" referred to in the 1962 *Time* piece). The magazine is filled with glossy spreads for "Ocean Ridge Plantation: The Best in Country Club Living," "Port Ludlow: The Unparalleled Life Experience," and "Wyboo Plantation: We've Got a Handle on Your Lifestyle." All these ads are filled with vigorous, stylish, affluent-seeming older adults tromping through meadows, playing golf and tennis, and rediscovering love. And if romance is not enough, there is a feature article on "10 Tax Friendly Retirement Towns: Small Tax Burdens Make These Places Especially Attractive."

Finding the Package

Just as Bill Berkeley and Elderhostel found the "package" that produced customers in droves, the Sun City formula combined the right ingredients to satisfy customers and enable expansion. Already mentioned was the second plank in Tom Breen's original plan: affordability—as well as the Webb Company's ability to dress a low-cost, accessible product in a sense of luxury through the provision of golf and the use of golf courses.

It's worth noting that golf was not employed simply because of its status appeal. This choice was part of a whole variety of amenities that balanced activity with a sensitivity to the potential physical limits of men and women who would be growing older. Golf was a low-impact sport that could involve either walking or carting about the course. Sun City was also designed to be flat and amenable to easy bicycle riding.

There was also an effort to create an egalitarian feel at Sun City. Especially in the early days, the community drew individuals ranging from Dean Babbitt to plumbers and bricklayers. Webb himself had been a carpenter and was interested in having working people be able to live in the community. Its egalitarian climate seemed to appeal particularly to individuals tired of all the jostling for position and status associated with midlife, as well as the sudden decline in status in mainstream society that accompanied retirement.

Two other ways through which Webb made a genuine contribution were to emphasize both activity and sociability. Sun City was a vigorous community. A generation after the initial Sun City was built, gerontologists are telling us that active engagement and strong social networks are the cornerstone of sustained health and well-being in later life. The internal studies the Webb Company was conducting in the early 1960s led to the same conclusions—and the company was well ahead of its time in putting these insights into practice.

Furthermore, to its credit, the Webb Company also put great stock in the self-organizing capacities of older adults. Rather than orchestrate the many clubs and activities available at Sun City, the company let the residents do it themselves.

One of the most significant activities over time has been volunteerism. Unfortunately, most of this activity occurs within the Sun City grounds, helping the immediate community but doing little to build bridges to the outside world. For example, hundreds of residents serve on the all-volunteer "posse," a law enforcement group whose members wear uniforms and police the grounds. In fact, Congress even declared Sun City the "Volunteerism Capital of the World"—in a testimony more to the power of lobbying than clear-headedness. That said, some aspects of this service are impressive and extend beyond the walls of these towns. For example, Sun City volunteers today contribute a fair amount of volunteer service each year to the Westside Food Bank near Phoenix. Habitat for Humanity projects are also increasingly popular among members living in the retirement communities.

By latching on to a compelling idea, transforming it into an affordable, reproducible, and high-quality institution, and marketing it in a sophisticated, well-researched fashion, Webb and his associates were able to make a fortune and change the face of aging in this country. Yet for all their entrepreneurial verve and admirable achievements, over time the Sun City approach has revealed numerous disturbing signs that simultaneously call into question a culture of retirement built around age segregation and leisurely recreation.

Insularity and Prejudice

When Calvin Trillin visited Sun City in 1964, he noticed that all the residents were white, a characteristic nearly all those he interviewed were quick to mention and to mention approvingly. At the end of his visit, he decided to ask Thomas Breen about this aspect of Sun City.

Breen's immediate response was that Sun City salesmen were instructed to show no discrimination whatsoever and to assure "Negro" customers that they could buy any house they wanted to buy. However, Breen went on to explain that "when it comes to a sale, the sales manager handles it, and he explains to the people what they're getting into, because, let's face it, a Negro would be miserable in Sun City." Trillin then asked Breen whether there were any blacks living in any of the Sun Cities. Apparently, one woman had purchased a home in Sun City, California, but "we told the people near her they could transfer lots, although as it happened, the people on one side said it made no difference to them. But actually we were just one step short of a revolution out there." When people get older, Breen added, they get set in their ways. Besides, "what would happen if she should want to have a swimming party and invited all her colored friends from Los Angeles out there a couple of nights; it would amount to having the swimming pool taken over by colored people a couple of times a week." The woman decided not to move in.

Ten years later another reporter (from *Life*) visiting Sun City was struck by a similar situation, observing the tendency for Sun City residents to think of their town as an "oasis," not just from a society that didn't have a place for older adults—but from anything different from them. "The town has no hippies, no smog, no race problems (since, in fact, it has no Negroes), no riots, no bombings, no LSD and no relief rolls. It is the rare inhabitant who is not ('by God') against them all."

The racism expressed by Tom Breen and the whiteness of all the Sun Cities reflect a broader tendency in retirement communities, and this factor is disturbing even adjusted for the prevalence of racial segregation in housing throughout the country in the early 1960s. Breen's comments were hardly an isolated incident. University of Southern California (USC) researcher Maurice Hamovitch found widespread racism and anti-Semitism in California retirement communities a decade later. Salesmen at one of the communities he studied were quick to let prospective buyers know that the two things they didn't have to worry about were "colored people and mosquitoes." Fifteen years later Francis FitzGerald found anti-Semitism widespread in the Florida Sun City she profiled in her book *Cities on a Hill*.

However, the homogeneity and ethnic suspicion that have long dogged the retirement community movement are dwarfed today by the issue of insensitivity toward younger generations and their needs. This trend has become a major problem in many places these age-segregated enclaves have appeared.

Generational Tensions

When Calvin Trillin visited Sun City in the early years, he found the place so inhospitable to children that he was forced to wonder whether the young people who visited weren't more eager to leave than their grandparents were to see them go. As one person told him, "I raised my kids, but I don't feel like raising anybody else's." One young employee with the local air conditioning repair company was initially permitted to move onto the Sun City grounds in order to provide quicker maintenance service. However, when the Peoria School District bus rolled up to his curb on the first day of school, the outrage was so enormous he was forced to leave Sun City. By the second year of the community, the residents were already voting in a bloc to defeat local school measures.

The pattern continues today, fueling the view that older adults are "public enemy number one" of education. A recent example is especially distressing. After defeating three consecutive local school bond issues—which resulted in the elimination of music, sports, and other enrichment programs, tremendous shortages in materials, a halving of school librarians and nurses, and an

exodus of underpaid teachers—the residents of Sun City West elected themselves to a majority position on the school board and attempted to pass measures that would "deannex" the entire Sun City development from the
district. As a result the schools—which are 70 percent Hispanic—would lose
a full third of their tax base. The argument by the Sun City West leaders was
that they were being unfairly taxed in relation to other local retirement communities, which had already removed themselves from the school district.
This justification is vivid illustration of how withdrawal and disengagement
can snowball.

It also shows how the seeds of generational conflict can be sown by residential segregation. It is a short step from selling freedom from having to
care about other people's children to the kind of voting patterns evidenced in
Sun City. As one school board member—the target of a recall vote by the Sun
City residents—argues: "The point is to supply them with a lifestyle where you
can recreate [as in recreation] for the rest of your life," she states. She then
added: "they leave whatever sense of community they had where they came
from." The student editor of the local high school paper, Alicia Alonzo, con-
curs: "It's not like hating old people, but you feel this type of resentment because everybody pays taxes and they're trying to squirm out of it."

A less far-reaching but, in some ways, even more disturbing story occurred in Youngtown—that true pioneer retirement community—in 1997.
(In addition to being the first age-segregated retirement enclave, Youngtown
became the first field chapter of AARP in 1963.) Youngtown sought to expel
a couple for harboring their grandchildren. Forget all the lines about having
to care about other people's children—this was a case of punishing residents
for caring for their own kin. In fact, Youngtown officials boasted in the
process to *The Arizona Republic* of expelling 300 young families during the
first half of the 1990s.

According to *The New York Times*: "Fresh-faced and direct, 16-year-old
Chaz Cope would seem to be the ideal poster boy for this Phoenix suburb of
sunshine and orange trees. Instead, this retirement community sees him as
human contraband. While Youngtown allows dogs, the City Council has
voted unanimously to fine Chaz's grandparents $100 a day for illegally hous-
ing a child." According to Lynn Rae Naab, Chaz's grandmother, "All we
wanted was permission for him to stay until he finished high school, only 16
months," to provide asylum from abuse by a stepfather elsewhere in the state.
When the Naabs applied for a variance on the age ban, in addition to charging them $300 for filing the application, Youngtown officials posted a sign

on the lawn of their bungalow to notify neighbors that the couple was housing a child.

In places like Arizona, these cases are not simply anecdotal, idiosyncratic examples—like Thurow's case from Michigan. Half of Arizona's 530,000 residents 55 and older live in age-segregated retirement communities—nearly 100,000 in the various Sun Cities. The battle lines are already drawn. According to Floyd Tharp, acting president of the Sun City Taxpayers' Association, "What we are concerned about is protecting the lifestyle of the old folks," and he voices the complaint that education is already too high a share of the state budget.

Worsening Sprawl

There are environmental as well as human issues associated with the growth in retirement communities. The success of Sun City–like communities with their active lifestyle is contributing to significant sprawl in the Southwest and other parts of the country. The transformation of desert into housing communities is just part of the problem. The impact is made much worse by golf courses. Developers can charge a minimum of 10 percent more for a lot in a golf course retirement community than in a standard development. And a lot on a fairway goes for as much as 200 percent more (so much for the $1,450 extra for a fairway house in the original Sun City).

As The New York Times reports in a recent article on Phoenix: "If all the fairways and greens in this hot, cactus-studded metropolis—165 golf courses, in all—were placed in a straight line, the swath of grass and sand traps would stretch hundreds of miles across the Sonoran Desert." In other words, they would create a carpet of artificially induced green stretching a good part of the way between Phoenix and Tucson. Given that an average of six new courses a year are being built in the Phoenix area—many of them to accommodate the continuing influx of retirees—the day may not be too distant when the courses of Phoenix and Tucson eventually meet.

The environmental consequences of this movement are, to say the least, troublesome. The amount of water, alone, required to feed the golfing frenzy is staggering in an area where it rains only a few months a year and temperatures can exceed 120 degrees.

The Limits of "Activity"

Activity has its virtues, but a life built around activity for activity's sake can be vapid, self-indulgent, and ultimately boring.

Most visitors to Sun City are struck by the frantic "busyness" of its residents—rushing about from one activity to the next as if to block out the emptiness of their lives. Sociologist David Ekerdt calls this phenomenon "the busy ethic," a way for retirees imbued with the work ethic yet without any real role in life to maintain a sense of continuity with their previous lives. According to Ekerdt, "Marketers, with the golf club as their chief prop, have been instrumental in fostering the busy image," adding that in general "one cannot talk to retirees for very long without hearing the rhetoric of busyness." Indeed, a motto of Sun City is "The town too busy to retire."

At the close of his visit to the retirement community twenty-five years ago, Calvin Trillin challenged Breen on the already-evident obsession of Sun Citeans with activity, independent of content: "I asked Breen if he had considered the possibility that he had created a community dedicated to self-indulgence on an unprecedented scale, a place in which the distinction in value among various kinds of activities had all but disappeared." To this Breen replied: "Well, there *is* a feeling that as long as they keep active they'll be all right, and they're not too selective, sometimes, about how they keep active. They believe that if they keep active—keep that ever-loving blood circulating, keep those organs functioning—they'll keep alive."

Scientific research supports the instinct of those original Sun Citeans. With individuals spending thirty years or longer in retirement, however, the hollowness of a life dedicated to keeping the blood flowing is hard to overlook. This point was driven home to me recently in interviews with current residents of Sun City West.

One person I talked to was Bob Moore, a seventy-something man who spends half the year in Arizona and the other half in Seattle. His partner is Katie Hickel. Both are widowed.

Bob and Katie are caring, responsible people. Bob's children have become teachers and environmentalists. His wife, who passed away several years ago, was a teacher. Katie learned about Sun City West while taking an Elderhostel course (on "How to Play") offered across the street from the retirement community. She spends some time volunteering with Habitat for Humanity as part of a group of twenty retired women who build houses for the poor.

When asked about life in Sun City West, both Bob and Katie immediately commented on how full their days are. She begins early with exercise class. Then there is line dancing, followed by plenty of socializing. Katie tells me she has met people from all fifty states at Sun City West, "wonderful people—there is a real sense of community here."

Bob adds that Sun City West—even though far more upscale than the original incarnation—remains an egalitarian place: "Nobody down here has anything to prove anymore. Whatever we have and have not done, it's over. In our forties, everybody was wondering how they're doing compared to everybody else. Now my goal is to shoot my age in golf," he jokes, noting that he's come within one stroke. Bob adds that he feels blessed just to be alive and active at this stage. "I'm so busy, I don't know what to do!"

I asked him if this was the happiest time of his life. As soon as the words left my mouth, I worried about having committed a faux pas—inadvertently asking Bob to compare his time with Katie and the years with his wife. But Bob didn't take my question the wrong way. Nevertheless, his answer surprised me.

"Is this the happiest time?" he thought. "You know, I raised six kids and worked full-time. When you just quit all that and are not giving back, something's missing. We're not producing anything now, and there is something about making a contribution that I do miss very much." After more thought, Bob continued: "My wife was a teacher, and I've had a teaching credential all my life [Bob worked for a defense contractor and was an officer in the Army reserves]. I would like to teach reading, English, science. In the younger grades. But some of the teachers resent people coming in. And the biggest problem with volunteering, at this stage of life, is that you don't want to give up everything. You want some moments to give and some moments to be selfish!"

Bob's answer reminded me of Steve Weiner's comments. It also made a point about continuity and change in the period since Sun City was founded. There was precious little room for a Bob Moore or a Steve Weiner to "be retired and live" in 1960, to quote Calvin Trillin's deranged pump mechanic. A place like Sun City was, in many respects, welcome relief for those "outcasts" whose sole offense was reaching their fifties, sixties, or seventies. Now, however, both types can easily conduct pleasantly leisured lives within places like Sun City, or outside them, in Seattle or Oakland or a multitude of other towns across the country. Indeed, they can lead lives that many people still in the working world might envy for their abundant free time and relief from work-related stress.

The hard part is *not* to lead pleasantly leisured lives. Both Bob and Steve have struggled to assemble lives that move beyond leisure to involve a sense of contribution to others as well. Steve has faced peer pressure not to do so—the suggestion that his ongoing need to do something worthwhile is akin to being a workaholic. Both men describe the frustration of being shut out by nonprofit groups or schools unprepared to take advantage of their desire to help or to make good use of their talents. Both continue to stay active and busy—to keep the blood flowing—but both also articulate a desire for a greater fulfillment in their days.

The End of an Era

Frances FitzGerald argues that Sun City is a prism on the broader culture of retirement as leisure that has evolved over the past half century. She is undoubtedly correct. Since Sun City came into existence, leisure has become the defining ideal of retirement. A survey of men who began receiving Social Security benefits in 1951 revealed that a mere 3 percent retired because they preferred leisure over work. By 1963, in Sun City's infancy, the figure had grown to 17 percent. By 1982, nearly half the new Social Security recipients retired in order to pursue leisured lives. The career of Sun City reflects this trend and provides a useful window on it.

However, Sun City (and the retirement community movement it helped promulgate) has been as much *catalyst* as *prism*. The emergence of mass retirement presented many options for the society. The ascendancy of leisure had a great deal to do with the marketing and institution-building talents of not only the insurance companies but also a set of savvy developers and other leisure entrepreneurs who defined the issue and our response to it. And the savviest of them all was the Del Webb Company and its formidable leader. Webb filled the cultural vacuum of retirement in the early 1960s by peddling propaganda about a new active way of life and by providing an accessible vehicle for average Americans to live daily lives organized around leisure. He showed the kind of impact an entrepreneur armed with a good idea can wield.

Indeed, Webb provided an antidote in that context to the kind of structural lag Matilda White Riley describes—where the images and institutions of society lag behind the interests and capacities of the changing older population. Webb's creation was—to borrow the term of Cornell University sociologist Phyllis Moen—a form of "structural lead." His invention got ahead of society, providing a glimpse of what retirement could be like and helping to make that vision real.

Over time his approach has proved to be a magnet for approximately 5 to 10 percent of the older population who relocate each year to Sun City–esque settings. However, the influence of Webb's way of life resonates far beyond those who move to retirement enclaves. As one scholar notes, "The impact of the retirement village phenomenon on America's elderly. . . did not depend upon the number of individuals housed" but rather on the new image and vision of retirement—as a lifestyle focused on leisure that was marketed broadly. Sun City and its residents were both institutional and individual role models whose influence was widely felt.

The resonance of the retirement community movement has by no means been confined to retirees and the lifestyles they choose to lead. It can be argued that the perceived self-indulgence of places like Sun City has contributed mightily to the backlash by younger generations against older Americans—deemed by some as "greedy geezers" concerned only about their own needs and enjoyment.

But the most disturbing impact radiating from the Sun City idea is the rapid increase in gated communities for Americans of all ages, one of the fastest-growing housing trends in the country. More than 3 million American households have decided to wall themselves off from the perceived problems of the larger society, moving to communities featuring guard gates, imposing fences, and twenty-four-hour-a-day patrols by armed security forces in military-like uniforms.

According to Edward Blakely, dean of the School of Regional Planning at USC, gated communities were rare "until the advent of the master-planned retirement developments" of the 1960s and 1970s. Sun City and Leisure World "were the first places where average Americans could wall themselves off. Gates soon spread to resorts and country club developments, and then to middle-class suburban subdivisions." In his 1997 book *Fortress America*, Blakely chronicles the damage this phenomenon has done to our broader sense of community by contributing to the rise of disengagement in the society and widening social gaps between haves and have-nots.

The gated community phenomenon is a reminder of the kind of impact a relatively small number of older Americans can have on American life. Imagine if a new movement inspired 5 to 10 percent of the retired population to reenagage with the same intensity that 5 to 10 percent have disengaged through Sun City–like arrangements. This movement might produce positive reverberations echoing throughout our civic life.

·

When initiated in the early 1960s, Sun City and the retirement community movement engendered many advances—especially given the wasteland that was life for older Americans in the country at that point. Forty years later, there is strong reason to question whether the leisure ideal (and its close companions of disengagement and age segregation) has not outlived its usefulness.

As we consider moving beyond this questionable ideal, it is worth remembering that the equation of leisure and retirement is a recent phenomenon, the product of particular circumstances that came together in the post–World War II period. It is also worth remembering that this stage in our history of later life is not only recent but invented, invented by real people like Tom Breen and his boss and invented primarily for the purpose of profit.

Today, all signs indicate that the old conditions that helped support the leisure ideal are coming apart. The Steve Weiners of the world are not likely to be content with thirty years of shuffleboard and a tract house in the sunshine—or the dressed-up versions of this diet that many are still offering. As Dave Schreiner, vice president of the Del Webb Corporation told *Time* magazine in 1997—thirty-five years after its original cover story on Sun City—the new generation of older Americans will be looking for "more than endless weekends." According to Schreiner, "Five years ago, we were in the last quarter of a market that was reward-oriented. . . . Now we're finding a different audience that is perhaps still working. They may want to learn, volunteer or try an experience that may not be related to recreation."

Just as Dean Babbitt and his neighbors were pioneers on the threshold of a new kind of aging in the early days of Sun City, so too are Steve Weiner and an ever-growing number of Americans approaching the third age. Although they won't be averse to taking it easy—at least easier than in their middle years—they will also insist on contributing. And they will require new arrangements in order to redefine retirement in a way that can take us past "the golden years."

The next chapter describes just such a pioneering arrangement, one that was born at nearly the same time as Sun City was launched and that has existed in quiet obscurity ever since. In many ways it is the mirror opposite of Sun City, providing opportunities for individuals over age sixty not to escape the annoyance of "other people's children" but to develop what are essentially second careers focused on transforming the lives of these young people—and in the process becoming surrogate family to them.

If Sun City was the *emblematic* institution of the outgoing era of later life in America, then this little-known initiative might well be characterized as *embryonic* of what we will need to devise in the next stage. It points the way toward a new era of aging defined more by the desire to leave a legacy than to lead lives consumed by leisure.

PART TWO

ALEX HARRIS

Aggie Bennett (right) and Louise Casey (left), both now
eighty, served together for well over a decade as Foster Grandparents on
the pediatrics ward of Maine Medical Center in Portland. For that entire
period, they showed up virtually every day, week in and week out, to work
one-on-one with children in dire shape. For both Aggie and Louise, their
service as Foster Grandparents has been a second career. Aggie was a waitress for many years and part of the time was a single mother raising two
children alone. Louise worked in a sawmill with her husband, a minister simultaneously starting a church in a small Maine town. When he died, the con-
gregation asked Louise—by then in her fifties—to take his place. She studied

to become a licensed minister and served the church for a decade before retiring—to the Foster Grandparent Program. Born and bred in Maine, Aggie and
Louise continue to live near Portland, each in senior citizen housing on the
outskirts of the city.

·

Aggie: I came for one week but stayed for sixteen years. I saw that there
was a need for you. And it was something actually that we needed. Older people don't want to sit around the house all day. I'm sure I don't. We get more
out of being with the young people. They keep you young.

Louise: I've been here going on ten years. I'll be seventy-seven in a couple
of weeks.

Aggie: Ever since Louise came in I've had nobody but Louise as my partner.
In fact the kids refer to us as cousins. We see each other every day—unless
one of us is sick or takin' a vacation. . . .

Louise: Not only that, I think we serve quite a purpose because these children come from all over Maine and the northern border, sometimes four
hours to get here, and these children with cancer—there's a lot of cancer—
these children have to stay several weeks for chemo and radiation. Their
parents have to go home. They have siblings to take care of. And the children
get to know us. We're the red coats [the Foster Grandparent uniform in the
hospital]. The white coats, the staff, have the needles, you know. The kids
kind of shy away from them. But they know that we comfort them and play
with them. And they get real close to us, and we just love them, and the parents appreciate it so much. Send us notes.

Aggie: That little girl that just came up—just had an I.V. put in—I've had her
since she was six days old, first time we saw her. She's fifteen [years old] now.
I was saying today she sometimes seems to be mine. Sometimes we have to
remember—don't we, Louise—that the children go home sooner or later. But
they do come back to see us.

Louise: And some of the children cry when they have to go home. One little girl who broke her leg said last week, "You know, I've gotta come back to get my cast off, and I'm awful glad because I'd never see you otherwise." So you get real close to the children. And there's a lot of abused children today. I can't get over some abused children coming along, just wanting to be loved. . . .

Aggie: I only came because of one individual, Jeannie [the former supervisor]. She called me up and said, "I heard you might be a candidate for a Foster Grandmother." I said I can't be a Foster Grandmother, I don't have any grandchildren. They said we can find you some! So she came up to see me and I said to myself, now how'm I gonna get rid of this woman, you know, but you don't get rid of her very easy. My daughter had called her. My husband had died, been gone a year, and my daughter didn't like the way I was living. After my husband died I didn't want to go out, to see people. Anyway, I said to Jeannie I'll go up and spend one week, but I won't promise you any more than that. That one week was sixteen years.

It wasn't a hard decision—you just see the need. You can't be here an hour that you don't see those children need you, and you know you need something besides just sitting home. [Besides] I don't like to rust away, I want to wear away!

Louise: I had retired, about three years, and I was doing crocheting, things like that, makin' satin coat hangers. And I got so stiff I didn't even want to get out of the car to walk to the grocery store. I saw in the paper that there was Foster Grammies, and it said, "See Jeannie," so I thought I'll take a ride up to Parnell [where the program office was located] to see Jeannie. She said, "We have an opening in Yarmouth with handicapped children this summer. Would you like to work with handicapped?" I said I'd love it, and later I moved here to the hospital.

It's like a family, the Foster Grandparents. We meet once a month and we kind of have a fellowship together, and speakers and trips, all kinds of things going. It's really like a family when we get together.

Everybody will say, how can you take it when you lose a child, and I think Aggie and I feel the same way—heartbroken. . . . But if we can do something when they're here to make that little child happy, to smile, it's worth it all. We lose them, and it is heartbreaking.

Aggie: I don't think I'd been here a year—when Sue Forth was head of the unit—and she asked me, "How strong a person are you?" I said "Well, I've always prided myself that I was strong." She says, "We got a baby that is dying, and we promised that mother that her baby would not die in a crib. Do you think you could hold her?" Well, they put me in a room here, they kept checking on me, and that baby didn't die in no crib . . . that baby died in my arms. And I was always so grateful for that. I didn't feel fear . . . I just felt good. You know how it is, Louise, when you just sit with them, and your heart's aching, but you don't let them know it, that's all.

Louise: They let me go in and sit with Tanya after she died. They said would you feel better, because I loved her so. And they said would you feel better just going in and sitting for a while. And I said yes I would. And Cheryl, I was there when Cheryl died, almost in my arms. This is a family. When anything happens, and we can get there to the funeral, we're there.

Aggie: You know something, though, it does make you a stronger person. It does. It's hard, but I don't think I could be anywhere else. This is home.

CHAPTER 3

The Quiet Revolution

Today we are wasting resources of incalculable value: the accumulated knowledge, the mature wisdom, the seasoned experience, the skilled capacities, the productivity of a great and growing number of our people—our senior citizens.

.

Senator John F. Kennedy, 1956

Just as Bernie Nash and Marv Taves finished packing up the van, lightning appeared overhead and the thunderstorm predicted all day for Washington, D.C., began unloading heavy rain on the city. Already soaked from carrying twenty-two boxes of applications in the July humidity, Nash and Taves climbed into the van and headed out from HEW (Department of Health, Education, and Welfare) headquarters to Sargent Shriver's office across the city. Their appointment with Shriver was for 4:30, but they pulled up to headquarters for the War on Poverty just a few minutes after 4:00. The rain was still coming down steadily.

Parked in a loading zone, they started hauling the cardboard boxes up the stairs to Shriver's outer office, hurrying in vain to keep the boxes from getting drenched. After a dozen trips up and down the stairs, it was hard to tell whether the beads of water running down Bernie Nash's forehead were sweat or rain. Both men were wringing wet and breathing heavily. But they were, characteristically, on time, seated outside the office of the director of the OEO (Office of Economic Opportunity) a good ten minutes before their meeting was to start—the boxes neatly piled in the corner, the cardboard already beginning to curl from the moisture.

Nash and Taves were meeting with Shriver to decide which agencies across the country would be selected to participate in the new Foster Grandparent Program, a War on Poverty effort that would be launched by Lyndon Johnson in just a few weeks and that was designed to pair older adults living in poverty, one-on-one, with needy children. The effort leading up to this point had been frenetic and pressure-packed, but the environment in Shriver's office that day made their experiences seem relaxed.

Bernie Nash, a former Navy fighter pilot from Minnesota with a crew cut and military bearing, was stunned by the harried environment. "All hell was breaking loose," he recalls. "I'd been in war rooms that were less hectic." Young men in suits were racing between the offices, occasionally emerging from Shriver's suite, closing the door carefully as they exited.

Amid all the anxiety, Nash and Taves sat, and waited, for hours. At seven o'clock they were still sitting uncomfortably in their damp clothes. Nash approached the secretary to suggest that perhaps they could reschedule the meeting for another time more convenient for Mr. Shriver. That would be impossible, she explained, leave now and they could be assured of not getting another appointment.

Finally at 7:25, Shriver himself came out to fetch them. Once inside the office it became clear that, in fact, a crisis was in progress. The Watts riots had broken out in Los Angeles, and Mayor Sam Yorty—in London at the time—was blaming the violence on Shriver. If only the OEO had put more money into Los Angeles, Yorty was contending, the situation could have been averted. As Nash and Taves methodically made the presentation they'd been planning for days, the phones continued to ring insistently. At one point President Johnson was on one line to Shriver while Yorty was screaming into the OEO director's other phone. Bernie remembers being amazed at how Shriver could navigate this mayhem without ever losing his concentration in the meeting. Each time he'd hang up the phone, he managed to resume the conversation at precisely the place where they'd left off. Mostly, he wanted to know why they hadn't shown up with thirty-five applications, as originally instructed.

Shriver told the men he would have to think about next steps. They'd hear from him later that week. Each day they didn't hear, Nash and Taves, back at their tiny quarters in HEW's Administration on Aging, grew more worried. What if the boxes of applications and mimeographs, already beginning to mildew by the time they left Shriver's office, had been hauled off by garbagemen, mistaken for trash?

An Untapped Resource

The notion of older Americans contributing in substantial ways to their communities, as we have seen, is not an unprecedented idea. Indeed, these kinds of contributions were an essential and expected part of American life in the days of the Puritans. However, most conscious efforts to enable them, through creating new roles designed for that purpose, date only to the 1960s—to a period when a small renaissance of creativity in this area briefly flourished.

The first part of the 1960s involved a much larger rediscovery of the older population in several spheres. As Del Webb and his lieutenants were doing their part to transform later life into a lifestyle focused on leisure and aimed at lining their corporate pockets, Washington, D.C., was focusing greater attention on the economic security and health of older Americans.

At the time, despite steady expansion of Social Security, nearly a third of the older population continued to live below the poverty line, and most had no health coverage. The benefits of Social Security were real, but they still hadn't reached five and a half million older adults mired in poverty. In 1961, JFK had hosted the first White House Conference on Aging, and a year later he established the President's Council on Aging to address the problems of older Americans. The following year, Kennedy's HEW secretary Anthony Celebrezze stated, "Fear of illness and lack of sufficient money are uppermost in the long list of worries that plague most of the nearly 18 million older Americans," and he announced the administration would commit more federal resources to the task. However, the watershed year in American aging policy would be 1965.

In the midst of federal government activism not seen for thirty years, 1965 produced a wave of major policies enacted to help transform the circumstances of older Americans. Most important, Medicare was launched as an amendment to the Social Security Act. On July 30, LBJ flew to Independence, Missouri, to sign the new health insurance program for older Americans into law in the presence of the elderly Harry S. Truman, who twenty years earlier had unsuccessfully attempted to enact government health insurance.

Alongside Medicare, the Older Americans Act was also passed in 1965. This legislation created the U.S. Administration on Aging within the Department of Health, Education, and Welfare, now led by John Gardner. The

Administration on Aging was set up to stimulate the development of community programs aimed at meeting the needs of the elderly and to be an advocate for older Americans within the federal bureaucracy. Over time, the Older Americans Act was largely responsible for the creation of state and local agencies focused on aging and for the tremendous expansion of senior centers around the country—now numbering more than 10,000. The Older Americans Act also provided for activities such as nutrition programs for older adults, with many of the programs administered through senior centers.

During this period Social Security benefits were expanded dramatically in their coverage and amount. In 1967, for example, a 13 percent increase in benefits raised 800,000 people over age sixty-five above the poverty line. From the early 1960s to the present, these changes contributed to transforming older adults from the poorest segment of the population to the least poor (with rates now below 12 percent.)

Taken together, these measures aimed at meeting the tangible needs of older Americans were nothing short of revolutionary, and they further fulfilled the promise initiated with the creation of Social Security in 1935. However, the 1960s also witnessed a much smaller revolution, one that has been largely overlooked ever since. This little revolution produced a set of social experiments displaying another side to America's aging, creating opportunities for older women and men to make a contribution to their community while receiving certain benefits in the process.

Adding Life to Years

At the White House Conference on Aging in 1961, President John F. Kennedy challenged the delegates. Now that we had added "years to life," it was time to think about how we might add "life to years." In spring 1963, Kennedy delivered his most important speech on aging, decrying the loneliness and isolation afflicting older Americans, "heightened by the wall of inertia" standing between a great many seniors and their surrounding communities. And Kennedy did more than issue this rhetoric; he proposed a concrete remedy: the establishment of a new National Service Corps (NSC) "to provide opportunities for service for those aged persons who can assume active roles in community volunteer efforts."

Kennedy's proposal was a radical departure. At that point only one in ten older Americans was involved in any formal or informal volunteer activity. Furthermore, the presence of older adults in the kind of intensive and challenging assignments being proposed—full-time service with support for living expenses and a minimum one-year commitment to fighting urban and rural poverty—was virtually nonexistent.

Besides, historically, service efforts of this sort meant mobilizing young people. Although Kennedy had every intention of including youth in this attempt to formulate a domestic equivalent of the Peace Corps, the potential contributions of older and younger Americans would be given equal weight in the new NSC. According to Attorney General Robert Kennedy, who chaired the task force to develop the program, the NSC was a call to service to "college students and retired persons," a challenge to youth but equally "to millions of older and retired people whose reservoir of skill and experience remains untapped." Testifying before Senator Harrison Williams's special committee to investigate the feasibility of the NSC, the attorney general delivered a remarkable appeal for the prominent place of older Americans in serving the community:

> Millions of Americans who have years of productivity and service to offer are dormant. Retired teachers, craftsmen, tradesmen really don't want to go to the seashore to fade away. They want to help. So many of these people have come forward that I am convinced they can accomplish something unique in this country, something undone by all the Federal, State, county, and private agencies, something still to be done.

Over the ensuing period of testimony, RFK's perspective was endorsed and amplified by a procession of government officials and private citizens. HEW secretary Celebrezze described seniors as a "vast manpower and womanpower resource," arguing that older adults would bring wisdom, skills, and maturity to the corps. Echoing Kennedy's list of occupations, Celebrezze offered as evidence the composition of the retiree population in 1963, which numbered among its ranks 126,000 schoolteachers, 36,000 lawyers, 3,000 dietitians and nutritionists, 18,000 college faculty members, 12,000 social and recreation workers, 11,000 librarians, 32,000 physicians, and 43,000 professional nurses.

The program had enthusiastic backing from the president, Robert Kennedy, and others in the administration; outside support from a wide range of social service and civic organizations (even Malcolm Forbes testified on behalf of the legislation); and leadership from Harrison Williams, who would go on to promote similar efforts in the Senate throughout the 1960s. Nevertheless, the National Service Corps was defeated in Congress, where reactionary lawmakers portrayed it as a back door to racial integration in the South.

With the demise of the NSC (and a set of unsuccessful variations on it proposed periodically over the next few years) went a more encompassing vision of a national effort to mobilize older Americans on behalf of communities, one that remains unfulfilled today—that is "something still to be done," to echo Robert Kennedy's challenge.

They Suffer in Silence. . .

The death of JFK's National Service Corps was followed by the birth, through the Economic Opportunity Act of 1964, of VISTA (Volunteers in Service to America). Gone, however, from the reincarnated effort was emphasis on the contribution of older Americans. In general, the participation of this group was a low priority for the newly created Office of Economic Opportunity (OEO). OEO's focus was on youth, and its philosophy was that programs involving the younger population were the key to breaking the poverty cycle. A social investment in youth, it was hoped, would pay a higher dividend over the long term.

Furthermore, these oldsters seemed particularly hard to involve. OEO director Sargent Shriver was reluctant to integrate older adults into the agency's efforts. He told a Senate committee, "The majority of persons over 65 will not be effectively reached" by programs involving them in community service, instead recommending bolstered income transfers and enhanced social services. His deputy Robert McCan stated, "It's harder to reach the old," who he doubted would come forward to enlist. "Unlike young people in poverty," he explained, "they suffer in silence."

However, the fact remained that a vast proportion of the older population was poor at precisely the time America was supposedly fighting an all-out battle against poverty. Many in Congress felt OEO could do more to help, and once again Robert Kennedy—this time joined in the Senate by his brother Edward and George Smathers of Florida—was in the forefront. The three senators brought increasing pressure on OEO to find a way to involve and assist low-income older Americans. Smathers declared, "There is a clear need for much more widespread understanding that the War on Poverty is directed at all age groups, not only at youth," and he held hearings on the subject. The bottom line was becoming clear: The OEO would do more to help older Americans or the OEO would face additional difficulty in getting its budget passed by the Senate.

Shriver wasn't the least bit unsympathetic to the elderly poor—as stated earlier, he just felt the best approach was to give them more money. However, Lyndon Johnson was adamantly opposed to any more "doles." In fact, Lester Thurow, then a junior staff member of the Council of Economic Advisors, was dispatched to review the Economic Report of the President to flag anything that might be construed as putting more cash directly in the hands of poor people. In this context, a programmatic "back door" would need to be devised: By creating community service roles for older adults, proponents simultaneously created an excuse to put more money in their pockets—while sidestepping political opposition.

Facing considerable time pressure for developing this effort, OEO contacted the Office on Aging (soon upgraded to the Administration on Aging) within HEW offering $20,000 in demonstration funds for a concept paper building on some rough ideas being discussed by the OEO planning group. In fact, the contours of what would become the Foster Grandparent Program had already been largely developed by Sandy Kravitz, head of the OEO unit in charge of demonstration projects. This paper fleshing out the program would need to be completed almost immediately.

In the spring of 1965, Bernie Nash was lecturing in social work at the University of Missouri in Columbia. He was fresh out of graduate school at the University of Minnesota, where his thesis had focused on the issue of time use in the context of children's institutions. While researching his thesis, Nash became acutely aware of how little time staff in these places had for connecting with and nurturing children. As he would later write, "Children in group settings are often denied the intimate adult-child interaction which is essential to personality growth and development." After graduate school, however, Bernie ended up working at the opposite end of the age spectrum, taking a job with Minnesota's state aging office.

As he was nearing the end of his first year of teaching, Nash received a surprise phone call from Professor Marvin Taves, a rural sociologist and aging expert Bernie knew from his graduate student days. But Taves wasn't calling to recruit Bernie for his department. In fact, he wasn't even calling from Minnesota. The professor had temporarily relocated in Washington, D.C., where he explained, he'd been urgently summoned to help develop a new War on

Poverty initiative focused on engaging older adults in the community. Most important, he was in over his head and needed help. This project was due almost immediately. Did Bernie already have plans for the summer?

Like most junior faculty eking out a meager salary, Bernie was all too happy for the moonlighting opportunity. The next day he was headed to Washington to join Taves in the insanely rushed effort to get something in place by the end of the summer—the time the White House wanted to announce these new efforts. Altogether, Bernie Nash wrote six concept papers, but one in particular met with Shriver's strong approval.

The OEO chief had recently traveled to Cincinnati to look at issues of poverty. During a visit to a large public hospital, he was walking down a corridor when he was suddenly overwhelmed by noise coming from one of the wards: "It was the size of a small gymnasium—there must have been a minimum of 100 cribs in there, each one with a little baby. It was bedlam. The children were crying. Maybe there were three practical nurses in there rushing from one crib to another. . . . It was a sad and shocking experience. I have never forgotten it." Shriver talked with the nurses, who told him there simply were not enough human beings to care for these children, to hold them or to nurture them. The hospital certainly couldn't afford to pay for people to provide this kind of support.

Before he had time even to recover from the experience, Shriver found himself at "an old people's home," the next stop on his tour of poverty in Cincinnati. "I saw these old people sitting around, looking at space," he recalled, "most of them sedentary, bored, hopeless, and empty." When Shriver began talking to them, he came to the conclusion that he was witnessing a parallel problem to the one at the hospital: "It was clear that they were suffering from a lack of human contact." They were complaining about their ailments—albeit more quietly than the children. Why wouldn't they, Shriver thought, they had nothing but time to think about their aches and pains.

As Shriver left this second stop, he realized that these two problems might be solved—or at least alleviated—simultaneously:

I was riding around, and I said *by God,* here you have all these older people who complain they have nothing to do, and here these nurses are telling me they need people desperately to just hold these children. I said, *for God's sake,* why don't we just take those old people out of this one building—which was in easy walking distance of the place where the children were—and put them to work doing just what those nurses said that the babies needed.

He thought that paying "a tiny amount of money" for the service would make sense too—by helping to ease the economic situation of the older adults with "money they had earned."

When I interviewed him about this little-known corner of the War on Poverty, Shriver showed me an ashtray he gave all the OEO employees when he left his job as director. Stenciled around the edges were the more familiar efforts like Head Start and VISTA. But there was the Foster Grandparent program as well, which Shriver highlighted proudly: "It worked! And it worked for two reasons. First of all, it's human—it's about human relationships. Second, it's simple. It was one of those simple ideas that, I think, are frequently the best ideas."

Creating Foster Grandparents

Despite these virtues, the idea for what was to become the Foster Grandparent Program initially met with considerable resistance from the very children's organizations who were supposed to be lucky beneficiaries of it. Shriver, through Sandy Kravitz, informed Nash and Taves that there were to be thirty-five Foster Grandparent sites by July 4—a little over a month after Nash arrived in Washington. So the two men went to HEW Children's Bureau officials requesting their recommendation on the 100 most forward-thinking institutions working with children. These groups were then invited to Washington to attend a meeting on either June 8 or June 21.

The June 8 meeting was a disaster. The children's groups tore into the proposed project. The idea was ridiculous, they told the organizers. Some suggested that the older adults would bring diseases into their agencies and spread it among the children (after all, if age was an "incurable disease," might it not also be infectious?). Others contended that the seniors would molest the children. Besides, how would these people get to and from the institutions, given that most didn't drive? The agencies were furious about their time being wasted by such a silly proposition and stormed out without a single group submitting an application to participate. In short, they wouldn't take the government's money to do the Foster Grandparent Program.

Their response was yet further illustration of why so many older adults in the early 1960s viewed Del Webb as a savior—someone who could deliver them from a society where they had absolutely no place. Despite some highly visible supporters of the notion that older adults weren't a useless drain on society—such as the Kennedy brothers, Senators George Smathers and

Harrison Williams, and HEW secretary John Gardner—these voices were still rare in the 1960s. Indeed, as Gardner sized up the situation in a 1967 speech: "Today there is a cruel and ironic contradiction in the fate of our older citizens. Never before have older people been able to look forward to so many years of vitality. But never before have they been so firmly shouldered out of every significant role in life—in the family, in the world of work, and in the community."

Nobody had to tell Taves and Nash. They were crushed by the response to their creation. Not only that, they faced the prospect of fifty more organizations arriving in less than two weeks and of the disastrous reception repeating itself. Even worse, it was now less than four weeks from Shriver's July 4 deadline. In an absolute panic, they threw themselves into redesigning the program, working eighteen-hour days—sometimes remaining in the office throughout the night.

The operation consisted of Taves, Nash, and Barbara Pitwell, a young single secretary who often was asked to work long and late hours. In the midst of the marathon effort, at three o'clock one morning, Pitwell's father made a surprise visit—worried about her hours and convinced "hanky-panky" was occurring. Instead he found his daughter at the typewriter with the two earnest Minnesotans, Taves and Nash, engrossed in rewriting the request for proposals.

In the end, the men emerged with an improved version of the program, including provisions for medical exams for all the older adults to ensure they didn't carry communicable diseases, allowances for volunteers' transportation, advisory committees to screen applicants, and other measures designed to address the earlier criticisms in practical or symbolic ways. However, the core elements of the Foster Grandparent Program—engaging low-income older adults to work one-on-one with disabled or disadvantaged youth, twenty hours per week, for a minimum wage, in the context of large children's institutions—remained intact.

The June 21 meeting arrived, and much to Nash's and Taves's relief, the organizations evinced mild receptivity. A total of thirty-seven expressed some interest in applying, although the response was hardly enthusiastic. However, July 4 was closing in fast. By July 1 only four applications had come in, and Nash and Taves successfully pleaded for a two-week extension from OEO on the condition that Nash fly around the country to help potential sites complete their applications. In most cases, he ended up writing the entire proposal for the projects—they liked the idea of funding but cared little about undertaking the Foster Grandparent Program. At the end of the two weeks, twenty-two applications had been submitted, and Nash and Taves headed off with them, in the rain, in their van, to see Shriver.

A month later—with Shriver's approval of twenty-one new Foster Grandparent Programs complete (one group dropped out at the eleventh hour)— Bernie Nash was back in Columbia, Missouri, preparing to teach the fall semester. On Sunday, August 29, as he was sitting in his easy chair thumbing through the *Kansas City Star*, a headline jumped out at him. Lyndon Johnson, meeting with the press at the LBJ ranch, had the previous day announced $41 million in funding (soon to be cut in half) for a new set of programs involving older adults in service. "The aged poor have maturity and experience to offer," Johnson pronounced. "They are eager to help themselves and others. We are going to use this rich untapped human resource to help others less fortunate. In turn, it will enable these elderly people to find the dignity and usefulness they seek."

The first of the four new service programs involving low-income elders was Nash's invention, Foster Grandparents, which set out to match 1,000 "needy" older citizens (with incomes below $1,500 per year) with 2,500 children living in orphanages and other institutions in twenty-one locations around the country. The older women and men would serve as "substitute parents," spending four hours a day, five days a week, feeding, cuddling, rocking, and exercising disabled children. In return they would receive stipends of $1.25 an hour.

The other programs created under the new directive were Home Health Aides, which recruited low-income seniors to provide in-home unskilled nursing tasks and personal contact to frail and needy individuals; the Medicare Alert program, which engaged senior citizens around the country in the process of informing the elderly poor about new benefits available through Medicare; and Project Green Thumb, sponsored by the National Farmers Union and initiated under the federal government's Operation Mainstream program. Green Thumb began as a pilot program putting older rural residents to work on projects in Arkansas, New Jersey, Oregon, and Minnesota; it was enthusiastically supported by Lady Bird Johnson, whose interest in highway beautification influenced the early shape of the program.

As Nash was scanning the article, one item in particular caught his eye: Foster Grandparents would be individuals *age 60 and up*. He was stunned. The last big battle between the Administration on Aging and Shriver was over the eligibility age for Foster Grandparents. Shriver and his associates,

reconciled to the fact that this was not going to be a program involving
youth as volunteers, was still angling for as low an eligibility age as possible.
He pushed for 45, while the Administration on Aging staff—true to their
mission—was pressing for 65 (the eligibility for Social Security and Medicare). In fact, in the boxes of applications that Nash and Taves lugged to the
OEO office, all described a program for Americans 65 and above. Finally a
compromise was reached at age 55—and Taves and Nash had to go through
every page of every application (including mimeographed copies), crossing
out 65 and inserting 55.

However, when LBJ stood up to announce the new programmatic initiative (which would be funded by OEO but run by the Administration on Aging), he spontaneously changed the eligibility age to 60. Johnson, it turns
out, was at the ranch to celebrate his fifty-seventh birthday the day before,
August 27. And there was no way—despite all his exalting of the maturity,
experience, dignity, and usefulness of the "untapped resource" of older Americans—that he was going to include himself in that codgerly lot. Furthermore, he was sensitive about not being a grandparent yet himself—and
loathe to do anything to draw extra attention to this fact.

To this day, the Foster Grandparent Program—which now involves over
25,000 older Americans serving 100,000 children one-on-one each year—
turns away thousands of individuals annually because they are not yet 60.
This fact is a reminder of not only the idiosyncratic nature of public policy
but also of how whimsical—indeed, almost accidental—the creation of this
landmark program was. (And it highlights tellingly the contrast with
Thomas Breen's years of painstaking research and planning before launching
Sun City.)

The issue of age eligibility further illustrates the great ambivalence about
age and aging that prevailed in 1965—from Johnson's empty rhetoric to the
reaction of the "progressive" children's organizations. Indeed, once funded,
many of the children's institutions quickly abandoned the Foster Grandparent model that Nash and Taves had labored so hard to design. Soon the institutions had the older volunteers changing bedpans, and Nash was back on
a plane threatening to rescind the money.

But quickly, within two years, the program had won over skeptics. One
reason was some early research—from the University of Utah Medical
School, North Texas State University, and the Merrill Palmer Institute in
Detroit—that showed strong mutual benefits emerging from the program.
As noted in one study from 1966: "A viable role for the aged has been

demonstrated, aged persons have been lifted out of poverty, the majority of children involved in the program have benefited, and institutions have become oriented to a new service role."

Demand was also strong. When the program was launched, there were 20 applicants for each available opening, and by 1968 the number of Foster Grandparents had leaped from 800 to 4,000—with another 8,000 applicants on the waiting list. (It is remarkable how poor the Foster Grandparents were, with the average income in 1968 being $900 a year.) The number of projects grew from 21 to 68, with most based in children's institutions, such as hospitals, orphanages, and centers for the developmentally disabled. Throughout this initial spurt, Bernie Nash played an active role in the program—for a period as director, then as deputy commissioner of aging in the Administration on Aging. Later, he would serve briefly as the head of AARP.

Throughout the early years, Nash continued to champion the program—arguing that it was valuable in and of itself and a harbinger of great future opportunities. In a 1968 issue of *Public Welfare*, the journal of the American Public Welfare Association, Nash wrote that this country was on the verge of a longevity revolution: "The increasing numbers of persons enjoying longevity today and the decreasing age of retirement from the labor market have presented society with a potential issue of major proportions. . . . One solution is the utilization of older persons in service roles such as demonstrated in the Foster Grandparent Program."

The value of the program, he continued, lay not only in highlighting an untapped resource and one important way this resource could be mobilized to help meet society's needs, but also in illustrating the importance of human relationships in social policy. "The conscious involvement of two persons in a relationship of concern does much to relieve the relatively impersonal climate" that prevailed in so many public institutions, especially those for children. Expressing a heretical view in the midst of the increasingly technocratic field, Nash concluded his article by asking, "Isn't this what public welfare and social service are all about?"

Everyday Heroes

Patsy LaViolette

Patsy LaViolette was the first Foster Grandparent I met. I visited her in Portland, Maine, in the late 1980s, two weeks after encountering Nick Spaneas and the Work Connection mentors. She shared a number of traits with Nick. She was a survivor. A tough French Canadian woman born in northern Maine. And like Nick she was using her education in life—having raised three children alone after her husband died—to help teenage mothers navigate their way through lonely waters. "What I have in common with the teen mothers," she told me when we first met, at a Dunkin Donuts on a freezing Portland morning, "is that I was widowed very young." Her youngest daughter was ten months old at the time. "I brought up my three children alone," working as a cashier, bookkeeper, nurse's aide, and beautician.

Why would somebody who survived all that want to spend so much time in retirement "raising" other people's children (to recall a perennial comment of Sun City residents)? According to Patsy, it wasn't very complicated. She was looking for something to fill her time, "I am not ready to retire yet, but I don't want to work full time." The Foster Grandparent Program was perfect, involving twenty hours a week and a stipend of about $200 a month. (In the 1970s, the Foster Grandparent stipend was decoupled from the minimum wage and exempted from taxation. In the process, the program moved from being an "employment" initiative to a "service" program.)

But the stipend was only one piece of Patsy's decision to serve. Best of all, she was out of the house and working with people. She was a "people person." And she would visit one of her young mothers each day, Monday through Thursday, spending five hours with them each time. Then she would take Fridays off and enjoy a three-day weekend.

Several of the teenagers became surrogate daughters to Patsy. One, Cindy Burke, was, like Patsy, from a working-class Catholic family. She lived in Portland public housing with her two young children, ages one and three. Between these two births, Cindy lost a son to Sudden Infant Death Syndrome. She dropped out of high school after her first child was born and was subsisting on AFDC (Aid to Families with Dependent Children). Cindy's relationship with her family was strained, at best. After learning about her second pregnancy, her grandfather told her she was "breeding like a rabbit" and disowned her. Her ex-husband was long gone (Cindy heard he was living in another state), and her most recent boyfriend had just committed suicide. Her closest girlfriend had recently relocated from Portland to Indiana.

"I see my mom when she drops off Steven [Cindy's brother] on Mondays, so we don't have that much chance to even talk or sit down. So that Wednesday when Patsy comes over we just talk about everything," Cindy explained. "There are some things I don't even dare talk to my mother about." Then, she added a comment reminiscent of Eddie Dillon's words to describe Nick Spaneas: "I guess her husband died. It's like she's been through it, and she knows what I am going through." Eddie told me that what Nick had seen made him a wiser man. Cindy was fumbling to register the same point.

I asked her to say more, and she started talking about her boyfriend's recent suicide: "The day that it happened, she [Patsy] was right over and she gave me a great big hug and asked me. . . if I was going to be all right. I really didn't think we were that close until that happened and she was right there. I called my dad and he really didn't want to talk about it. . . . So I. . . hung up on him. But with Patsy you can talk about it and she's not going to shut you out."

When Patsy first met Cindy, the teenager was "offensive to a certain extent, most of the girls are." So Patsy just played with Michelle, Cindy's daughter. ("She's very attention-grabbing.") She read her books, played games with the little girl. The next week when Patsy showed up, Michelle was excited, ready to play. But Patsy told the little girl, "Now is your mother's turn. This time Cindy is number one." At first they mostly talked about Michelle and how special she is. Over time, Patsy turned her attention to Cindy and to bolstering her confidence.

"I tell her not to down herself so much," Patsy explains. "She feels so inferior. She's a pretty girl, to me. She's got an awful lot going for her. She downs herself, says, 'I have two children.' I say, 'You had a bad marriage, it didn't work. That's not your fault.' It's just little things to make her feel good, to love herself." But after I talk to Patsy for some time, it is evident that these pep talks were more than pep talks. She had grown to appreciate the young girl and to genuinely value their time together: "I really enjoy being with her. In fact, I wouldn't mind if my son brought home a girl like her to me. She's a very good mother. It shows in the children."

Given so much good feeling, I asked Patsy if she felt as if Cindy had become another daughter. Patsy hesitated, then said the relationship was distinct: "In fact, she's a true friend. My relationship with her is different than a mother/daughter relationship. I'm too domineering with my own children, but I do not dominate her."

John Curtis

Patsy and the other Foster Grandmothers working with teenage mothers in Portland were a no-nonsense group of (mostly) grandmothers, who—like their male counterparts in the Work Connection—were very loving yet utterly unsentimental. One of Patsy LaViolette's few male colleagues in the program was John Curtis.

John Curtis looked like a folksinger from the 1950s, or perhaps a balding, northern New England version of Colonel Sanders—thin face, hair brushed back on the sides and a little long on his collar, and a thick snow-white Vandyke. (He once told me, at the age of seventy-three, he wished he had more hair—so that he could grow a ponytail.) His voice was raspy from sixty years of smoking but retained its Maine accent. We used to meet for coffee at the bakery-café that Martha Elkus—the former Portland Foster Grandparent director—opened in an old firehouse. The entire front door of the engine house was composed of glass panels, and the building was flooded with light on the cold February morning I last saw him. John died a year later, a week before I was scheduled to visit him again.

At the time, John Curtis was in his fifteenth year in the Foster Grandparent Program. Over the previous several years we'd gotten to know each other as I kept returning to ask him questions about his life and his work with kids. In the process, I also met his wife Jean, who was so involved in helping John with his service that she was declared an "Honorary Foster Grandparent" by the program. When I was in town they would invite me over to their small apartment in a low-rise senior housing complex, feed me dinners of roast chicken, mashed potatoes, and Jello, and treat me like a long-lost relative.

I loved visiting them and found spending time in their apartment both comforting and strongly reminiscent of my own grandmother's place. Although tiny, John and Jean's apartment had two windows, one facing a small forest, the other overlooking a pond. The living room was taken up with a small sofa and a pair of matched, reclining easy chairs—and an abundance of photographs of their children and grandchildren. The last time I visited, a copy of the latest James Michener novel sat on the coffee table next to a large-print edition of *The Shipping News* by Annie Proulx and William Bennett's *Book of Virtues*. The TV set was on in the background, with Peter Jennings covering that day's highlights from the O. J. Simpson trial.

As soon as I arrived, Jean greeted me warmly, then quickly went over to turn off the television. In her early seventies, she remained an attractive woman, with bright blue eyes and stylish hair. She would be a real—as opposed to an honorary—Foster Grandparent were it not for inane federal regulations that prohibited two members of the same family from being involved in the program. Yet as her honorary status bespeaks, over John's many years in the program she had also done her part. Most commonly, John brought over his young charges for Jean to cook them grilled cheese sandwiches at lunchtime, not only assuring that they had one decent meal that day but also adding to the children's overall feeling of being cared for. (One youngster, however, had protested recently when Jean substituted real cheddar cheese for the usual Velveeta.)

In the process, the children were exposed to a stable and loving household. Jean and John had been married fifty-two years at the time of his death. They met at a Quaker meeting in 1936, although neither was Quaker. John attended periodically, and Jean had accompanied her aunt. They married in 1944 when John returned from the war. That last time I was at their house, John sat me down in his easy chair and showed me pictures from his Navy days during World War II. Jean rolled her eyes in feigned protest, but I didn't mind. John was never overbearing, and I enjoyed hearing about the experiences of this humble, funny, intelligent, and enormously good-hearted man I'd come to respect so much.

While in the Navy, John was a radar man on a transport ship, the *Dickman*, that was in the midst of considerable action. It was a horrible experience. He was serving in North Africa when two nearby ships were torpedoed, spilling hundreds of men into the water. His ship was ordered to leave the area immediately, and John describes vividly what it was like to watch helplessly as the *Dickman* plowed through screaming sailors in the water—many of whom were not only drowned by the ship's wake but even pulled through its engines.

The greatest threat to his life came not aboard a ship in the war but in the late 1970s, when he nearly died. In his fifties, John was forced to quit his job as a manager for W. T. Grant's in Lowell, Massachusetts, due to a heart attack. He decided to go home to Portland to live out what seemed to be very little remaining time.

One day when we were walking around the lighthouse in Portland with one of the boys he was mentoring through the Foster Grandparent Program, he told me the story of this turning point in his life:

Eleven years ago I had open-heart surgery with four bypasses. I was miserable before that. I'd had a heart attack in Lowell, in the middle of the street. I went into Boston, the best hospital. They tried something new, cardiac catheterization they called it. And it took five hours when they did it to me. Then they told me there was nothing more they could do for me. I said, "No surgery?" They said no. I had to quit work. I was an operations manager for the W. T. Grant Company. It was one of those twenty-four-hour jobs, all the time something to do. I moved back to Portland to die. I figured, hey. . . my folks were gone, but my son was here, and all of Jean's family was here. And we got into HUD housing, where they take 30 percent of my income, and that takes care of the rent and the lights and the heat. And it's a beautiful spot. So we moved there.

But I got sicker and sicker. Finally, my doctor up here sent me to some cardiologists that said they thought things could be done. So I said, "Let's do 'em!" because I was going to bed nights hoping I wouldn't wake up in the morning. There was pain, but I think mainly it was that everything had come to a screeching halt.

The bypass surgery was effective, and while John was home recovering he read about Foster Grandparents in the Portland paper: "I couldn't do any lifting and nobody was gonna hire me, and I looked into it and, bang, they said, 'How would you like to work with some drug kids?' I could see leather jackets and chains and whips. I said, 'I don't know. . . .'" But he agreed to give it a trial run, and the Foster Grandparent Program assigned him to a drug rehabilitation center for teenagers called Day One. "And they said, 'Yeah, you are just what we want.' I said, 'How do you know that? I am not sure I want to be here!' But it turned out really good. So I stayed there for five years."

John was revered at Day One, where he mostly taught classes to help young people make the transition back into mainstream society. At the same time, he worked one-on-one with a series of young people. John, like Nick and Patsy, had been through a lot himself. When he was two, "my father decided he didn't want the family life and he took off—so I have a pretty good idea of how that can be." The family was poor. His Uncle Harry stepped in to be a substitute father, and although he did a good job keeping food on the table, "I didn't see him often enough."

But John didn't like to talk about the hard times he'd been through, and instead he started telling me about one of his most moving experiences as a mentor to a young girl recovering from drug and alcohol addiction:

One girl, Julie, who had gone through the whole program and was about to be out on her own, asked me if I would be her "grandfather." I knew her history. She had a terrible childhood. She'd been molested, been raped by her father's friends. Her mother would prepare her by getting her feeling good on beer. This was when she was about fourteen. I mean, it was terrible stuff. But she went through the program, stayed the entire year and came out. That's when I met her. I used to teach a class there on how to open a bank account, how to job interview, and all that. So I said "Sure." We went out to the mall, she had to get a job lined up, and I walked her through the mall. She had no idea what she wanted to do, but all the stores were looking for help. I said, "You decide which one you'd rather do." Well, we walked for about an hour and I said, "Let's have a cup of coffee while you are thinking." We went into McDonald's and I said, "How would it be working here?" She said, "Okay".

So she filled out the form, turned it in, and we left. And just after we were leaving the manager, who was a woman, comes running out after her, and says, "Are you Julie? You want to come in and talk to me?" They hired her on a part-time basis, working around her hours. She had to transport quite a ways. Then she decided that she would go to U. of M. [University of Maine] on a part-time basis. She wanted to get into the counseling field. I would pick her up nights after work. She would come over to our house and she'd have dinner with us, bring her studies with her. But all she wanted to do was take a nap! Although she lived with her aunt, she was just like our daughter, or our granddaughter. And she went to school and she stayed sober. In fact, I stopped being her "grand-father" through the program then, because she was doing so good. We just became friends.

Then one day she called up and says, "I've met a young man." And I says, "Oh good," but I was hoping it was somebody that didn't have problems. And he didn't. He was straight as an arrow, had a good job. She said, "I wonder if we could come over? I want you to okay him." So she came over with him, and then they got engaged. Had a wedding in September of that year. They still come over once in a while, and we visit them. Then in her Christmas card this year she says, "I'm pregnant." They had been married three years; but they waited till she was going to graduate from college to have a baby. They bought this little house and fixed it up nice. I am telling you, the most successful story that I can think of is hers. We were the *second or third people* she called after the baby was born!

Another time, I was on my way to shopping when this big guy across the street hollered, *"Hey John."* I looked. He said, "Grampa." Who the hell is that, I thought? And he was tall and he came over and hugged me. I was thinking holy. . . I am worried about my wallet! Then he gave me his name, and he was from Day One. But he had grown so. He is the same boy that had been in this class I was teaching, "Living in the World," and he had really cleaned himself up, gotten a job. He looked at me and said, "Well, aren't you going to say anything?" I said, "Congratulations, you look great." Not all of them turn out that way!

Another boy, Josh, that I am mentoring now, made me laugh the other day. He says, "You know, John, you shouldn't be afraid to die." And he says, "You know what happens when you die?" I said, "Well, what do you think happens?" And he touched me on the chest and he said, "You, you. . . what's inside of this body goes up there." And he pointed up. "There you stay forever and you are happy. They bury you. But that really isn't you." And I thought that was great, and I agreed with him. Pretty important questions at this stage of the game.

In light of these stories, I asked John about what he was getting out of this work and his second life—after the reprieve from heart problems the bypass operation gave him. "I really feel that the last thirteen years have been the best years of my life, as far as rewards go," he responded, "and as far as realizing you are doing some good, or at least you are trying." Then he added:

I feel this way: I feel I owe my community. I have to pay back, be thankful for my life, and maybe this is one way of doing that. The other thing is, my own grandchildren are a hundred miles away from me, and I can't see them as much. And I would hope that somebody where they live had interest in them too. They are not in the predicaments of the kids I see, but I think they also need somebody, with a little experience, who really cares. And it just helps me to know that I am needed somewhere. Now I could stay home, but I'd probably die. I honestly don't know if I'd have made the thirteen years just hanging around the house, doing nothing, reading the paper.

That is how I first got on the program. I was reading *The Press Herald* one morning and it was about kids being abused. I went back and read it again and read it to Jean, and I said, "Why in hell doesn't somebody do something?" Then I thought, I'm somebody. And that is when I called the program. There is another thing too: I am working with people my own age [the Foster Grandparents] who share, pretty much, the same feelings. I really feel that most of them, if not all of them, really care about what they are doing. And honestly, the stipend helps too. Because my stipend takes care of my car. Otherwise I wouldn't be able to have that car probably. I also love coming home evenings and having dinner with my wife. It is more like I am coming home from work, and that fills a void somehow or other.

Then, realizing how out of step all this must sound, given the prevailing expectations for retirement as a time of kicking back, John suddenly seemed embarrassed: "I must sound weird. I guess I *am* weird!"

Aggie Bennett and Louise Casey

I had little difficulty locating Aggie Bennett and Louise Casey on any of my many visits to see them on the pediatrics ward of Maine Medical Center in Portland. Ask anybody on the ward and not only would the person know exactly where Aggie and Louise were, but simply asking for them conferred special status on the visitor. Any friend of Aggie's and Louise's was a friend of the ward.

On my last visit to see them, there was no need to ask directions. Aggie was positioned at the nurses' station, arms on her hips, showing off a pair of thick, round, tortoise-shell glasses of the type George Burns started wearing in his nineties. "See, Marc," she yelled, turning the "r" into a Maine "ahh," "I wore my glasses so that I could look intelligent for your book." Louise was beside her, smiling shyly, while Aggie turned to one of the nurses. "When I put these glasses on and I'm playing cards, the other ladies start laughing so hard, I always win the hand!"

The children who come to the pediatrics ward at Maine Medical Center sometimes confuse Aggie Bennett and Louise Casey. It is an understandable mistake. In addition to being exactly the same age, Aggie and Louise both stand four feet, eleven inches, speak with the indelible accents of women born and bred in small Maine towns, share an equal antipathy for how they look in slacks, and carry the same stocky frame ("built like a grammy," says Louise). The children call them cousins, a label they have long since given up protesting.

Yet upon meeting the two women, one is also struck by obvious differences. Aggie is devilish, bawdy, and theatrical. She dresses up as a tiger in the July 4 parade at the medical center (which she also marshals) and loves being the center of attention. She drives a car with a vanity license plate (VFW832—she heads up the ladies auxiliary of the local VFW) and a fur-covered steering wheel. When we go out to eat at the local clamhouse, Cap'n Newick's, she brings her own plate and silverware, shunning the plastic and paper versions offered by the restaurant. Louise, by contrast, is demure, deeply spiritual, and eager to avoid the limelight. She is a retired minister in the Church of the Nazarene, and it takes Aggie to bring out her wild side—or the kids on the pediatrics ward,who once tied her up with scotch tape as a gag.

Their supervisor and friend, Linda Angel, tells a story to explain the difference between the two women she has worked closely with for many years. When the hospital was recently rearranging its parking system, Aggie refused to relinquish her parking permit until she could be guaranteed a good spot in the new arrangement. "Louise would never do something like that," Linda chuckles. "Instead, she'd pray for a good spot."

For well more than a decade—thirteen years for Louise, twenty for Aggie—the two women have showed up essentially every day, for half a day, as Foster Grandparents on the ward, partners in helping to bring "a human touch" to thousands of young people ranging from infants to teenagers. Some of the children are in the hospital for relatively minor problems, such as broken legs, others to recover from serious illness. A substantial number come back periodically over numerous years. For them Aggie and Louise are a source of continuity and comfort.

Many—the ones on whom Aggie and Louise focus—are in dire shape. Some will never leave the hospital, while others are in and out before succumbing to fatal illnesses, birth defects, and other tragic conditions. Because Maine Medical Center is the best hospital in the state and located in its southeastern corner, many parents are separated from children who are so sick that they must come to Maine Medical for extended stays. It is not uncommon for these parents to live five or six hours away, near the Canadian border. Usually they are poor in a state that is desperately poor. And with other children to take care of, these parents are compelled to return home after a few days. The result is almost unthinkable: Imagine being eight years old, stricken with cancer, and alone in a hospital ward in a city many hours away from your parents.

This is where Aggie and Louise come in. They become like family for these children. This work might seem overly sentimental. After all, what do the women actually do? They hold babies, play games with children, help feed young people during mealtime. However, to dismiss what Aggie and Louise do by focusing on these surface activities would be to miss the great significance of their contributions at many levels. The real work the two women do lies in the close connections they forge with the young people, offering not only the chance to have fun but also the opportunity to temporarily forget their plight.

And the work is, in many ways, quite fun. Both women possess a gift of being able to bridge the generations. They are as good with babies as with teenagers, and children gravitate to them. Watching Aggie or Louise on the ward at Maine Medical is to see two "old" women transformed—youthful, lighthearted, and playful. And their own joy is infectious, as one exchange between the two of them conveys:

Aggie: Now, the teenagers are great too. We got a teen unit down on the end. The other day I come in and one of them put his arms around me. I knew he was up to something. He put a sign on my back, "Kick Me Now!" I went down that hall and I got after him. Oh they're buggers. They got squirt guns, and they'll squirt you coming around the corner. But it's nice. Here we are old enough to be their grandparents and they are trying to play with us.

Louise: I think I told you how they took the tape and went around me and around me. And I thought it was loose, you know. When I went to get out I had to call the nurse to help me. And then I went to the ladies room and the two of them stood outside the door, "Oh, you can't come out, Granny." It's fun. You get laughing with them.

The fun is intensified by the constant presence of death. At their age, Aggie and Louise have learned to live life "one day at a time." This approach is not surprising, since, together, the two of them have outlived four husbands and one child. However, the primary sense of urgency comes from the situation of the children. Many are living under death sentences, and the two women have watched hundreds die prematurely over the years.

As Louise recalls, the closeness she develops with the children is both enormously fulfilling and a source of great pain:

It can be heartbreaking. One girl, Cheryl, was sixteen, with cystic fibrosis. And children with cystic fibrosis do not live too long. She was so, so talented. She made Christmas cards you would think you bought them. She was always doing paintings of the playroom. She was just marvelous, such a sweet girl. And her cystic fibrosis grew worse, and it was near Christmas time. They called me in, the day she passed away, and wanted me to say a prayer with her while she was dying. And I went in there, with the family. And Cheryl told me, "I am making you a teddy bear out of a jar, with a head and the glasses and a floppy hat. I am going to fill it with Hershey kisses for you, Granny. And if I should die before Christmas—I hope I don't, I hope I live through Christmas so we can have a time together with the family. But if I don't, I told my mama to finish that for you and give it to you for Christmas." She died two days before Christmas. Her mother came to me afterwards with the jar with that little hat. "Cheryl wanted you to have this and wanted me to finish it." I thought, what a beautiful thing. I have it at home by the bed. And the parents still write me. Christmas time, I always get a card from them.

Cheryl's death reminded Louise of another boy, a small child who had been abused and whose mother was in jail. He would smile when Louise held him. "To me, that was worth the world." At the child's funeral, the police brought the mother in. "He was so precious, and she used to get so upset with him, even though he was so sick. She would scream, 'Why don't you eat your supper?' But I would hold him and he would smile at me. I felt he might not have had too much love at home. But I loved him."

Overall, the losses have taken their toll, along with driving to the hospital in the Maine weather. "I am seventy-seven, and I think, oh, can I do another winter?" she confessed to me several years ago.

Despite so much outward bravado and obvious courage, Aggie agreed that losing so many children has been very difficult:

I remember one little girl I had, Susan. The first time I met her she was thirteen, and they discovered that she only had a third of a heart. How she ever lived all these years with a third of a heart, I could never understand. She was somebody that you just wanted to reach out to. Her mom and dad used to come with her, but she'd say, "I can't talk to them, Aggie, like I can you. I know I am going to die, and I can't talk about that to my mother and father, especially my father."

I asked the hospital, "What am I supposed to say to that child? She's only thirteen." They told me, "The best thing to do is just let her talk to you. Just let her pour it out." So I used to. Well, she finally died, four years later. And then, she just knew that she was dying. She said to me, "Dr. McCall told me that I couldn't live." She says, "You know, Aggie, this is it." I said, "Don't even think that." She said, "Well, I do. But, you know, I am tired, and I am ready." She wasn't crying. And that was the last conversation we had.

Her father called me at about a quarter to three in the morning, and he said, "Aggie, Susan just died. Can you come?" So I stayed with the family until they removed her body from the hospital, seven or eight hours later. Then I went to Oakfield for the funeral. I said to my girlfriend, "I got to go." And she said, "You are not going alone, Aggie, because I know how much that child meant to you. I'll go with you." Off we went. We went right to the house and then to the church. And later the parents sent me her obituary sealed in plastic, and it said, "Susan is survived by her parents, and by a Foster Grandparent, Aggie Bennett." That I wouldn't part with for anything.

Friends often ask Aggie and Louise how they can stand losing so many children. Aggie admits, "I think you really have to have a feeling for it. Because it isn't everybody I know that could do it, could face it."

I could understand directly what she was saying. It is scary, at first, even to spend time on the ward. So many of the children are "baldheads," having lost their hair from cancer treatments. Others have massive scars from brain surgery and other disfiguring procedures. But after their many years at Maine Medical, Aggie and Louise aren't fazed by much. Louise does wish she didn't take her feelings for the children so much to heart, but she still finds an upside. "If you can get a smile, even when they are real sick, just get a little smile, that's terrific." She admits, "You are heartbroken when you lose them, of course, but you feel that you did something to make them a little happier while they were here."

Louise's feelings are anchored in her religious beliefs and conviction that the young people are headed to a better place. She wasn't born into a religious family, but someone took her to church when she was a teenager and she loved it: "I was fourteen, and I realized I wanted to do something with this." But it was the depression, and college was out of the question. However, at nineteen she married Wilbur Casey, a licensed minister of the Church of the Nazarene. They were married for thirty-five years.

At first they worked together in the S. D. Moran Paper Mill in Wyndham, Maine, while Wilbur was opening a church in the town. He worked downstairs on the rollers, putting on glue and paper, while Louise was upstairs in the sorting room with a group of other women. Their salary was tied to production, and the pressure was intense. But every day Wilbur would come upstairs during his fifteen-minute break: "He'd come in smiling, waving his hands, and the girls thought he was wonderful." He too had been denied a college education by the depression but was licensed (as opposed to ordained) as a preacher in the Church of the Nazarene. He built the Wyndham church up over the next four years, so successfully that the Church of the Nazarene enlisted him to create new churches in hamlets throughout Maine. In the ensuing years, they moved to Bath, Cuddy's Harbor, Rockland, and a variety of other small towns.

In the late 1960s, Wilbur—who was considerably older than Louise—had a massive cerebral hemorrhage. The doctors said he would not live, but in six weeks he was out of the hospital and a year later was back to preaching. He was more tired than usual, and Louise began assuming more responsibilities at the church. But Wilbur continued to drive, preach, and be active in the community. His doctor called him "the miracle man." In fact, he preached right up until the day he died.

Louise remembers his passing, the turning point in her life, with a sense of peace and closure:

> It was on a Sunday. The day before, you won't believe this, he said to me, "I hope we don't have any calls on the telephone. And I hope no people come to visit." He said, "I just want you and me together to talk over our lives." We were like bread and butter. He would preach and I would play the piano. We just worked together. He said, "I worry about you if something happens to me." I said, "Oh, I'll go into the hospital and pass out trays of food or something." And I said, "Don't talk about it, because I'll cry." So we didn't, and we had such a wonderful day. We talked about our love for each other.

The next day was Sunday. We were living in Rockland. The church had bought him a new suit. I had a rose corsage. He preached in the morning and then again at night. Then we had a "Sing-spiration," with singing groups from all the churches in the area. It was in the auditorium, and to get into the auditorium you had to go upstairs. He came running up, taking off his topcoat, saying, "Wait for me, honey." And the church was packed. We had to sit in chairs right in the very back. And I said to him, "There's a window open behind. We better change." So we moved a seat. And I no more sat down when the usher tapped me on the shoulder and said, "Your husband!" And I looked. He was leaning on the man that was sitting next to him. He'd gone. He had a heart attack coming up the stairs, I guess. Hurrying.

And the preachers, they all carried him because the hospital was right around the corner. And they carried him out down to the hospital. It was only a matter of, maybe, three minutes. I held him in my arms, going down, in the back of the beach wagon. When we got to the hospital they began to pound on him. I knew it was bad. They worked on him for forty-five minutes. But they couldn't bring him to. All I can say is that he said he didn't want to rust out. He'd rather die preaching, and he did.

When her husband died, Louise was fifty-four years old, didn't know how to drive, and had spent the past thirty-five years serving as a minister's wife. She assumed she would have to leave the church, where they lived. However, the church board came to Louise and asked her if she would consider taking over for her husband. She was stunned. She couldn't, she reacted, she didn't have any training or education. But the church leaders countered that they wanted to pay for her to get licensed. And that they would pay her a good salary, if she only accepted.

So at the time most people were beginning to retire, Louise embarked on a second career as a clergywoman. "On the first Sunday I got up there, I was shaking all over," she remembers. "There were babies to dedicate and people that wanted to join the church. I was just shaking. And I had to do everything. In those days you didn't have assistants." Louise prayed a lot, got through the early jitters, and served the Wyndham church for a decade. Then, feeling she couldn't continue the pace, she elected to retire.

Retirement turned out to be a big disappointment, very sedentary, living in senior housing, occupying her days crocheting and making satin coat hangers as gifts for people in nursing homes. Soon she was climbing the

walls. Indeed, Louise joined the Foster Grandparent Program out of desper-
ation. "I thought it would be so wonderful to retire. Don't mention it to me
now," she remarked to Aggie during one of my visits. "Retirement is for the
birds, isn't it?" (To this question Aggie responded, "It's not for me. My
daughter, Lord love her, she means well, but she is always saying to me,
'When you going to give it up? You know, Mother, you should *take trips.*'" To
this Aggie tells her daughter, "I take a trip every day—five miles to Maine
Medical!")

It was Aggie's daughter Vonnie who orchestrated her mother's involvement in the program, convinced Aggie was on the verge of unraveling as a
result of retirement. It is hard to imagine the peripatetic Aggie, who'd
worked her whole life, grinding to a halt.

Like Louise, Aggie married young, as a teenager, and by nineteen was the
mother of a boy and a girl. Her first husband was killed in an industrial accident that year, leaving Aggie a single mother in the heart of the depression,
in impoverished East Machias, Maine. She came from a French Canadian
family—her father (who shortened his name from Lundeaux to Lund) was
Catholic, and her mother a "rolling-terror Baptist."

Both parents were illiterate (Aggie's middle initial, "U," is for the mis-
spelled Eunice). Aggie raised her brothers and sisters while her parents
worked to keep the family afloat. The lifestyle made it much easier for her to
become a single parent, as she was already accustomed to commanding an
army of children. However, having children so young is Aggie's great regret;
it cut short her dream of being a nurse.

Needing to support her children, Aggie left East Machias in the late 1930s
for Portland, where she first took secretarial work in a dentist's office. Looking for something less isolating, she switched to waitressing during the day
and working as a cocktail waitress at night—while her younger sister moved
in to care for Aggie's children. Over the years she married twice more, both
to men named James. The first James, whom Aggie called "P," died of a heart
attack in the middle of the night in Aggie's arms. They were married
twenty-five years. The second James—"Jim"—was a chiropractor, who also
was killed by a heart attack just short of their tenth wedding anniversary.
Aggie jokes that no other man would dare marry her, after three dead husbands: "No way, they are scared of me now!"

Despite the jokes, Jim's death was a terrific blow. As tough as Aggie is,
and as resilient, she essentially became a recluse after he died. Her daughter
was so worried about this change that she went searching for some means of

getting her mother back into the world—contacting the Foster Grandparent
Program, which recruited Aggie as if she were a new MBA coming out of
Stanford. Someone from the program even visited her at her home, convinc-
ing Aggie to give Foster Grandparents a try for one week. That one week,
Aggie is quick to remark, turned out to be nearly twenty years. (The length
of her tenure—and Louise's—reflects the difference between being a Foster
Grandparent and showing up at the local soup kitchen for an hour or two
every month. Theirs are true second acts, new careers in service.)

Why do they do it? As Aggie and Louise both make plain, it's not the $9
a day they receive in stipend money—although they say the stipend makes
life much easier. The main reason is the children, the sense of doing something that is important. "It's so rewarding," states Louise, while Aggie adds,
"It's a great feeling to know that you are wanted by everyone." They are also
good at it and have gotten better over time. In Aggie's words, "You learn
your children," a comment that refers both to specific children and to the
general capacity to understand the needs of young people.

Another part of their commitment relates to alternatives. Aggie was sick
in 1995 with a two-and-a-half-pound tumor ("in my belly—I didn't stand
still long enough to even know I had it!"). At home, convalescing in her senior housing development, she decided to contact some of her neighbors for
a little social life.

> I was so lonesome, being away from the hospital. So I called them up, got
> six of them to play cards. It was the biggest mistake I ever made! I
> thought we was havin' a little card game or something, and out come the
> pill boxes, and they start comparing how many pills they took in the run
> of the day. And I said, my God. So I sat there. And after they had all made
> their comparisons, I said, "Well, I think I will go home, feeling a little
> tired." And I never went back.

On the pediatrics ward, the women are part of a multigenerational community with connections radiating in all directions. The recurring metaphor,
which one hears from all involved, is that it is "like a family." Of course,
among the most important of these relationships is the sisterly bond between
Aggie and Louise. As Aggie describes it: "Louise and I get along famously. I
can really say to Louise what I can't ever say to anybody else."

Another important source of community is their supervisor from the Foster Grandparent Program, Linda Angel. A tall, elegant, dark-haired woman

in her late thirties and the mother of an eight-year-old, Linda receives as much support from Aggie and Louise as she gives the two older women: "You come here and you've got people who will support you when you need them," she reflects. "I know, I lost my mother two years ago, and I don't know how I would have gotten through it without Aggie and Louise and a couple of the other Grandparents. I have a wonderful family, but you need so much help to get through something like that. I can't imagine what it would have been like without them."

Aggie and Louise also feel appreciated by the nurses and doctors on the ward, where they are thoroughly integrated into the ongoing life of the unit. When staff members go out each month to have fun together, Aggie and Louise are an essential part of the group. "It makes you feel so good to know you are part of a team, not just a 'volunteer,'" says Aggie.

They are also part of a community of Foster Grandparents. For example, Louise rides to the monthly Foster Grandparent training sessions with three other Grandparents from Yarmouth—Minnie, Molly, and Ethel. Afterward they go out to dinner. "We look forward to that," Louise explains. "We have such a good time. And if one of us doesn't feel good, we look out for each other. Minnie calls me up, 'How's your knee?' 'Getting old!' I tell her. Everybody's concerned about each other."

"It's my life. It really is." says Aggie, "It's a family here. You know you come here and you've got people who will support you when you need them."

Reflecting on the Foster Grandparent Program

I n 1968, Bernie Nash wrote that the Foster Grandparent Program posed a basic question: "Can a new and useful role be found for older citizens?"

A generation later, after tens of thousands of them have been involved in the program, the answer is an unequivocal yes. As the accounts from Aggie and Louise, John Curtis, and Patsy LaViolette reveal, there is much in the accomplishments of this little-known legacy of the War on Poverty to give inspiration.

However, three and a half decades after the Foster Grandparent Program was launched by Lyndon Johnson, it is hard not also to be struck by how marginal this common-sense effort remains—especially in comparison to far more influential institutions from the same era like Sun City. Both sides of the Foster Grandparent story—the accomplishments and the marginality—contain important insights for us today as we try to create again "new and useful" roles for a coming wave of older Americans.

It Can Be Done

The Foster Grandparent Program, at the most basic level, reveals that it is possible to create a national initiative recruiting older Americans to provide assistance to the younger generation. The program broke new ground at a time when the broader views of older adults were especially retrograde, and it managed to become established despite considerable early resistance from its supposed beneficiaries, human resource–strapped children's institutions.

Today there are 25,000 individuals putting in twenty hours a week through the Foster Grandparent Program, and another 14,000 in the Senior Companion Program—a spinoff of Foster Grandparents identical in every respect except that the recipients of service are frail seniors struggling to maintain independent living. Altogether, there are 500 projects nationwide between the two programs, with federal funding nearing $110 million. Although participation is hardly massive in comparison to the vast numbers of older adults, these projects nevertheless involve a total of nearly 40,000 high-intensity volunteers. These efforts constitute, along with the Retired and Senior Volunteer Program (RSVP) program administered by the National Senior Service Corps, the country's largest infrastructure for enabling older Americans to contribute to their communities. And the numbers are not insignificant: For example, Foster Grandparents serve more children one-on-one than even the Big Brother/Big Sister program (over 100,000).

Making a Real Difference

Most important, these projects show not only that a national initiative across all the states is possible, but also that these efforts can make a genuine difference beyond simply keeping the "old folks" busy. They are vivid illustrations that older persons—rather than being "superfluous people dangling at the end of the lifespan," to paraphrase one observer—have much of importance to contribute to society.

The Foster Grandparent Program was far ahead of its time in emphasizing the importance of one-on-one relationships on behalf of disadvantaged youth. Thirty-five years later there is virtual consensus that these bonds are of essential importance in the development of young people. For example, the largest study of adolescent health ever done, the $25 million National Longitudinal Study of Adolescent Health surveying 90,000 young people, recently found that caring relationships with adults are the most important factor protecting young people from all sorts of social and psychological hazards. As the study's principal investigator, a professor of medicine at the University of Minnesota states, what matters most for children is "that there is a sense of caring and connectedness that comes through from at least one person," either related or unrelated, "that really protects kids from all sorts of negative outcomes."

Over the past three decades, thirty-one studies have been conducted directly on the program, with most concentrating on benefits to the older volunteers. A seven-year study of the Detroit-area Foster Grandparents program by the Merrill Palmer Institute and Wayne State University Institute of Gerontology found, for example, that "forming intense, personal bonds with their individual foster grandchildren was easy and natural for most of the elders in the project, and that the children also soon 'adopted' them as grandparents." The study further states that "foster grandparenting had a very positive impact on the children's development in both intellectual and social areas."

Other studies examining various aspects of the program echo this endorsement. Research on a state-funded teenage parenting project in New Jersey placing Foster Grandparents in homes where child abuse or neglect was suspected found that the seniors "often became 'special friends' to members of the family; they provided on-going support, acted as role models to parents of the children," and produced significant improvements in the family environment and interactions and in the life satisfaction and morale of the elders.

More recently, a 1998 study by Westat of Foster Grandparents serving in Head Start centers—a wonderful pairing of two War on Poverty creations—found that "the majority of Foster Grandparents engage in a wide variety of activities and interactions that are associated with positive developmental outcomes for children."

These studies reflect that the older women and (occasional) men serving as Foster Grandparents don't simply bring warm bodies to the task—just more people to be plugged into environments short on people. They are very good at relationship work. Much of this comes down to the issue of *time*. Having enough time to pay attention—to notice the small things, for example—seems to pay off in numerous and subtle ways. Bernie Nash noticed the time factor in the early days of the program, arguing that "children in the process of growing need time to experience life and test their reactions to it," time that many of the adult staff at schools, in Head Start centers, and on pediatric wards simply don't have. "Time is a special possession of the older person," Nash argued from his observations of Foster Grandparents in the mid-1960s. "It may well be the major gift of age if properly channeled."

A related gift is perspective, the long view that comes from having wrested some lessons from life. Patsy LaViolette admits that she is a much better mentor to Cindy than she was a parent to her own children, a view echoed by another older mentor, who describes his work with teenagers as "a golden opportunity to do some of the things you would have liked to do better as a parent." This is possible because "you have become more humble, more gentle, you listen to the children, what they have to say." He adds, "When my children were coming along, many times I couldn't take time to listen to them, to hear the things they wanted to say to me."

Overall, this is work that goes beyond mere sentimental value, the heartwarming notion of old people hugging kids—although there is increasing evidence that hugging itself is extremely important. For examples, studies by scientists at Duke University School of Medicine are showing that for infants separated from their mothers, providing human contact can stimulate hormone and brain development. And as one expert quoted in a recent *New York Times* article explains, "The cornerstone of early childhood education involves touching."

However, there are functions provided by the Foster Grandparents whose importance cannot be captured by these studies, that can only be described as essentially human. Aggie holding a baby who is dying and whose parents are five hours away is probably the most vivid example. Obviously, this act—like so many things that she and Louise do for the children at Maine Medical Center—won't show up on the bottom line of any evaluation. They won't save the life of the child, or even prolong it dramatically. These functions are simply the things that distinguish a caring and civilized society—yet are all too often absent in our technology-driven and cost-conscious world.

There are other benefits as well emerging from the work of Foster Grandparents. One is to help humanize the settings where they serve. The pediatrics ward at Maine Medical is a kinder, gentler, more personal place for their presence. The Westat study finds the same thing about Head Start centers where Foster Grandparents are involved, reporting that these volunteers are "a calming influence on the classroom environment" and provide "continuity for children when teaching staff are absent or leave." The continuity point is worth emphasizing: Because Foster Grandparents show up four or five days a week and tend to sign on for numerous years at a time, they provide the kind of continuity often missing even with staff. Interns and residents come and go, teachers come and go, Head Start staff come and go—yet Foster Grandparents quite frequently remain a lone steady presence in the institution.

The value of one-on-one bonds and of the ability of older adults to provide them is reflected in a raft of studies of the Senior Companion program as well. Since 1975, thirty-five studies have been conducted of the Senior Companion program consistently indicating that this effort is addressing a real community need and doing so effectively.

Every Dollar Spent Twice

The Foster Grandparent program, like the Senior Companion Program, demonstrates powerfully that this work is based on mutual benefit—that it is a win-win situation. Sure, there is reason to believe that people who depart for age-segregated enclaves in the desert are happy, but working with children seems to bring with it not only happiness but a sense of meaning and purpose hard to find on the shuffleboard court. Hence, the Foster Grandparent motto: "Every dollar spent twice," once on the children, and again on the older volunteers themselves. (Often this is literally the case, since many of the volunteers use their stipends to buy school supplies, presents, books, meals, and other items for the children.)

In fact, the engine driving the program seems less utopianism than a straightforward desire for structure, purpose, community, growth, and meaning—not surprising given the salt-of-the-earth quality of the volunteers themselves. And studies examining the benefits for Foster Grandparents and Senior Companions support the broader research finding that productive engagement and strong social networks are extremely important in maintaining physical and mental health in later life.

One of the most important of these broader studies, by Stanford University psychologist Laura Carstensen, focuses on the notion of socio-emotional selectivity. Rather than running around from one activity to another, trying to keep busy, the successful agers in Carstensen's research manage to winnow their lives down to the most important elements—in particular, to close relationships, often shedding those that lack special meaning.

Research specifically on benefits to older adults participating in the Foster Grandparent Program runs the gamut from meaning to mental function. A ten-year, ongoing study by two professors at the University of California at Irvine began by assigning 175 older adults to either a control group or to a Foster Grandparent Program. The findings showed that the Foster Grandparents had more complex brain activity, better memory, and better sleep patterns than before they became involved in the program and demonstrated gains compared with the control group.

A three-year Foster Grandparent study released in 1983 included fourteen projects and 471 respondents and set out to determine the impact on participants as compared with seniors on the waiting list to become Foster Grandparents. The study found that participants' mental health and social resources improved over the three years, whereas these characteristics of individuals on the waiting list declined. Among the study's findings was that 71 percent of the Foster Grandparents reported they "almost never" felt lonely, compared with 45 percent of the waiting-list group. Overall, 83 percent of participants reported being "more satisfied" with their life, compared with 52 percent of those waiting to become Foster Grandparents.

So the broader link between engagement and well-being in later life that is a central part of the MacArthur Foundation's Successful Aging project as well as of numerous other studies is supported as well by research on these conscious vehicles aimed at enabling older adults to serve their communities. And the range of benefits extends beyond improved brain function and declines in disability.

Another clear benefit of efforts engaging older adults whose income places them below the poverty line is financial. For some individuals living on extremely limited incomes, the tiny Foster Grandparent or Senior Companion stipend is used for food, medicine, and other essentials. For others, it permits small indulgences, like going out to dinner once or twice a month. For others still, it provides additional resources to enhance the service experience, such as for purchase of learning materials or even for mundanities like the grilled cheese sandwiches that Jean Curtis makes for the children her husband John is mentoring. One of the biggest benefits, as John Curtis himself describes, is in being able to keep a car. For John, the Foster Grandparent stipend covers car insurance, maintenance, and gas. He uses his car extensively in his work as a Foster Grandparent but also has it available for personal tasks like market shopping. In this way the stipend simultaneously makes a major contribution to continued independent living for John and his wife.

Older adults interviewed repeatedly expressed gratitude for having "something to get up for in the morning," a structure in their lives and the chance to be engaged. They also love being part of a community, as John Curtis and Aggie and Louise attest in their comments in the previous section, in particular a community of other older adults who care. The MacArthur studies come to a similar conclusion, as does other research, about the importance of such communities for older adults.

The Most Value—From the Least Valued

Because the roots of the Foster Grandparent and Senior Companion programs in this country are in the War on Poverty, these efforts exclusively involve low-income older Americans, the segment of the population most likely to be overlooked and undervalued by virtue of age, income, education levels (and often gender). All participants in these programs are older and poor, the vast majority are women, and just over half are members of minority groups.

In some ways this development is ironic. We did not begin with those retired doctors, lawyers, accountants, teachers, and other professionals reeled off by proponents of Robert Kennedy's National Service Corps. We did not begin with the group of older adults with the most obviously well-respected skills. Rather, we started with the group most program developers thought had little to contribute—a result largely of the "back door" origins of the Foster Grandparent Program, which was designed in large measure to be an income support mechanism for down-and-out senior citizens. Few expected much, in terms of contribution, from the older volunteers. To nearly everyone's great surprise (Bernie Nash, Marvin Taves, Sandy Kravitz, and a few others excepted), these low-income older adults filled a great gap in the lives and places being served.

Furthermore, over time it has become clear that many of these individuals possess special advantages. Shriver himself made this point, arguing from his Peace Corps years that "human nature and human experience is better, often, than advanced degrees. Anybody who goes to any place in the Third World gets to see that for themselves."

An Enabling Role for Policy

The Foster Grandparent Program is the product of federal government innovation and was developed during a great era of imagination and experimentation, so much maligned today, that led to the War on Poverty. One would think that a program based on creating that most delicate of things, an intimate human relationship, would be inimical to promulgation by the federal government. However, the history of Foster Grandparents shows that there can be an important enabling role for public policy in the creation and sustaining of these efforts. These programs have established themselves as part of the annual federal budget and as a result remain a reliable annual presence in communities across the country. They have also managed to leverage a considerable amount of private and other public, such as state and local, funding (totaling $50 million a year for Foster Grandparents and Senior Companions).

Beyond direct financial support, one of the most important roles policy plays in this program is through making the stipend (now equivalent to about $9 a day—approximately the same amount most locales pay for jury duty) tax-free, protected from minimum wage laws, and free from affecting any other benefits or entitlements. The stipend is ingenious. Because it is not taxed or tied to the minimum wage, it doesn't feel like a wage, yet it plays an important role: making it possible for individuals of modest means to make a major commitment to service, covering many of their out-of-pocket costs, and keeping them from having to take jobs where their skills would likely be used in ways of far less benefit for the community. The stipend seems to be large enough to induce many to join the program but not so large that people "do it for the money."

One of the most important lessons emerging from the Foster Grandparent Program for us today and in the future is the possibility of blending income support and significant service to the community without transforming these efforts into "make work." At a juncture when early retirement (both voluntary and involuntary) remains a reality and the eligibility age for Social Security is scheduled to be pushed back, the question of what society will do with the large number of Americans between their midfifties and midsixties, most of whom are healthy, skilled, and vital yet out of the labor market and not yet eligible for entitlements, will soon loom very large. These "gap people" have an enormous amount to offer, but any scheme to make use of their talent will need to incorporate some form of income support.

A related issue within the context of policy is sustainability. Foster Grandparents (and Senior Companions) have managed to sustain themselves across seven different administrations both Democratic and Republican, picking up an amusing collection of supporters along the way. What other effort can claim Sargent Shriver and Nancy Reagan among its champions—in fact, not only among its champions but among the ranks of individuals (I've identified at least five) who claim to have created the program. In *To Love a Child*, her 1982 book about the Foster Grandparent Program, the former first lady declares: "The Foster Grandparent Program is my baby, and my involvement during the past fifteen years has been like watching my child grow up." She even convinced Frank Sinatra, in what must count as one of the most bizarre moments in the history of American social policy, to croon about the Foster Grandparent Program as part of its twentieth-anniversary festivities. The Chairman belted out "The Right Chemistry," a song penned by one of the Foster Grandparent directors, in a 1985 gala sponsored by a major New York bank.

A Legacy of Limits

For all these many virtues, it is hard not to come away from the story of the Foster Grandparent Program without a profound sense of limits. The fact is, three and a half decades after its creation, the program has had little overall impact on how America ages—even when combined with the equally admirable efforts of the Senior Companion Program. The program's numbers are large compared with participation in most other opportunities, but in any given community the scale is minuscule. In Philadelphia, for example, a city of 2 million people, there are fewer than 200 Foster Grandparents. Few even know the program exists. Furthermore, there is no sense of critical mass either in a particular city or in the specific sites where most volunteers do their service—as these individuals are generally scattered about, one or two at a given school or Head Start center.

At the same time, the strengths of the Foster Grandparent Program's history are closely linked to certain weaknesses. While demonstrating the significant contribution of low-income older adults, the program is at once restricted to these low-income individuals. Those living above the poverty line are, for all intents and purposes, excluded. The program's restriction to one-on-one work with children means other kinds of important work are out-of-bounds. Older adults who have much to offer—for example, acting as advocates on behalf of schools, getting parents involved, or assisting in program development—are restricted by current regulations from undertaking these activities. Nor is there room for someone unwilling or unable to serve twenty hours a week. This issue becomes increasingly problematic as individuals in the program get older and become unable to keep up the same schedule (many program directors finesse this restriction by surreptitiously creating job-sharing arrangements among two or more Foster Grand-parents).

In all these (and other) ways, the program is profoundly inflexible. It could never accommodate a Steve Weiner, for example, and is generally ill-suited to capture the imagination of a new generation of retirees. And despite the occasional John Curtis, the program continues to struggle in finding men; 90 percent of current Foster Grandparents are women. Yet so many boys need one-on-one connections to an adult male.

It is worth noting that another strength of the Foster Grandparent Program also qualifies as a weakness. The long-standing government support of the program has helped expand this effort nearly thirty times over its initial size as a pilot project of 800. However, this growth has been insufficient; even without advertising or appealing to men or younger retirees or the vast segment of the older population living above the poverty line, the program maintains a waiting list of aspiring volunteers equivalent to a quarter of the number of participating Foster Grandparents.

Ultimately, there have been few steadfast champions of this work, despite much lip service the program receives for its sentimental appeal. The Nancy Reagan case is telling. When Shriver learned Nancy Reagan had become a champion of the program, he immediately contacted her to express his appreciation. I asked him whether it was well-received, given all of Ronald Reagan's bashing of the War on Poverty. He laughed: "I wrote her a letter and thanked her very much for supporting this program—which I, like her, thought was just wonderful. A) I never got an answer, and B) she stopped supporting the program!" Whether the Shriver letter had anything to do with it is unclear, but Nancy Reagan dumped Foster Grandparents for her "Just Say No" campaign shortly thereafter.

The Last Great Wave

In considering the history of the Foster Grandparent Program, one is hard-pressed not also to feel the loss of what might have been. During the five-year stretch from 1963 to 1968, there was a reevaluation of the role of older Americans being pressed by a set of key leaders within Congress and the federal government that is stunning even today and that was far ahead of the country at the time. To review the mid-1960s record of the Senate Aging Committee, or to read the speeches of individuals like HEW secretary John W. Gardner, is to glimpse a period when the federal government was on the verge of becoming an entrepreneurial actor in reinventing retirement. Sadly, the end result of this rich period of creativity and many proposed initiatives is but a few categorical projects like Foster Grandparents and Senior Companions, each of genuine value but none comparable in scale or scope to what was on the table thirty years ago.

What Might Have Been

Throughout the mid-1960s, while most people's attention was on the "big" policy innovations related to health care and economic security for older adults, dozens of proposals were put forward for a massive new institution aimed at expanding the contribution of older Americans to the country. The story begins with JFK's support for more vital roles for retirees beginning with his time in the Senate. Later, as president, he spearheaded legislation leading to the first White House Conference on Aging and calling for "immediate action. . . to permit the country to take advantage of the experience and skills of the older persons in our population." Robert Kennedy's National Service Corps proposal was one of the most significant attempts to realize this appeal, although by no means the only one.

The great champion of this issue during the period was Senator Harrison Williams, Democrat of New Jersey, who succeeded George Smathers of Florida as chair of the Aging Committee. Throughout the mid-1960s, Williams promulgated one bill after another aimed at vastly increasing opportunities for older Americans to become vitally involved through serving their communities. In 1966, for example, he sponsored two separate bills, one to create a National Community Senior Service Corps and another to establish a Talented American Senior Corps. One after another these efforts were

put forward, knocked down for lack of broader support (or for reasons of bu-
reaucratic territoriality), and reintroduced in altered form, before ultimately
being defeated.

In 1967, Williams wrote that older Americans must not be thought of
"solely as a 'problem group,'" even though the problems of poverty and ill-
health were a reality for many in this population. Despite these challenges,
"the older citizens of this nation are rich in talent and energies and wisdom,"
Williams continued, urging that "many new ways must be found to free such
resources for public good." Just as high school graduation is commonly
thought of as the start of a career, "so should we recognize that retirement
can become the beginning of a rich and rewarding stage in life's development."

The years 1967 and 1968 would turn out to be a watershed period. Frustrated with the slow pace of progress to date, Williams was becoming increasingly urgent in his appeal for a massive national effort involving
millions of older Americans in contributing to society. Although he was
moved by what he saw coming out of pilots like Foster Grandparents, he saw
them not as answers in and of themselves but as suggestions of what might
exist.

The Senate committee made this perspective plain in its annual report,
arguing that we'd had enough pilot projects. The time had come to move to
something that might really matter on a national scale. "The soundness of
the concept of community service by older Americans—either as paid participants or as volunteers—has been amply demonstrated in many promising
pilot programs," the report stated. We should take heart in this confirmation,
however: "The Committee renews its recommendation that advantage be
taken of the lessons learned within recent years, and that a *comprehensive national program*—using all available resources at Federal, State, and local levels—be considered by the Congress and enacted into law *at the earliest
possible date*."

In 1967, Williams proposed a bill that would pay individuals age sixty and
older a sum up to $1,500 a year (enabling all individuals to remain within the
Social Security maximum at the time) to do intensive service in the community. The goals were twofold: to inspire local organizations to create "entirely
new service programs enlisting the services of older Americans" and to support already existing efforts of this type. The stipend was not restricted to
low-income individuals but instead was designed to offset the out-of-pocket
cost of making such a substantial commitment to service.

Directors of local programs of this sort, the Senate committee explained, have discovered "that their very worthy activities often face a fundamental difficulty—the participants find that it costs them money to give service. Bus fare, for example, can be a burden to a person who lives on a tight budget," adding that clothing requirements can also entail significant out-of-pocket expenses.

There was need as well for program funds, the Committee urged, to help administer efforts that wouldn't be free: "Private organizations often find, too, that the directors of such programs begin on a part-time basis but often find themselves working around the clock. Even a small infusion of funds would help keep such programs going and growing but usually there is no help to be found." (In other words, without such support, even compelling projects like The Work Connection might go under.)

The committee listed some of the activities that older adults might be involved in, including serving as classroom assistants (with particular focus on helping potential school dropouts), teachers of illiterate adults, companions to the homebound elderly, and organizers and workers in community improvement projects.

Testifying on behalf of the legislation, HEW secretary John Gardner argued that the older population was the country's greatest untapped source of not only talent and experience but also time. According to Gardner, we needed a new "helping corps" to release these possibilities and tap this time: "To the typical man retiring at 65, retirement means at least 25,000 hours of 'extra time' for the balance of his life expectancy. Male retirees alone now number well over 5 million. The total time freed by this amounts to over 100 billion hours."

Of course, Gardner added, we can't expect that all retired men and women would build community service into their later years. Like everybody else, older Americans have a wide range of interests, and we should respect the need for options: "Some will want to work until the day they drop; others will want to pitch horseshoes; others will want to watch someone else pitch horseshoes." And although we surely need to create a society in which older people have choices, "in designing such a society, we shall have to work harder on some choices than on others." It was already easy for older adults in society to be alone or to disengage or "to find a park bench to sit on." What was difficult, Gardner made clear, was to find ongoing opportunities to contribute and to find meaning in the process.

The death knell for a major new institution aimed at mobilizing the time, talent, and experience of older Americans came not from enemies of the concept but from those who were sympathetic. Secretary of Labor Willard Wirtz testified that "there is a crying need in people's lives for continuing 'social opportunity' and for the need to be useful as well as to be secure." Furthermore, Wirtz argued that our "continuing inattention" to this issue as a society contributes to "encouragement of the idea of 'retirement' as being a good thing," adding that we will look back on this position as "one of the real marks of our present immaturity as stewards of life's experience."

However, Wirtz and Department of Labor (DOL) officials opposed the creation of a major new service initiative. The focus, they argued, should be on employment programs, and they proposed as a compromise the dividing up of "service" programs to HEW (including Foster Grandparents) and "employment" programs to DOL. The compromise was adopted, and the dream of something more ambitious passed. As a result the pilot programs essentially became larger pilots over time but remained categorical and limited.

A First Rough Draft

The Foster Grandparent Program can hardly claim the impact of a Sun City, and indeed it pales compared with much of what Robert Kennedy, Harrison Williams, John Gardner, and others were proposing at the time it was created. Nevertheless, this project is of real significance to us today as we think about moving forward. It illustrates that a national effort engaging the older population to help communities and the younger generation is possible, that this kind of involvement can result in powerful mutual benefit, and that public policy has a key role to play in realizing these possibilities.

In reflecting on the significance of Sun City in her masterpiece on community in America, *Cities on a Hill*, Frances FitzGerald observes that in her visit to the pioneering retirement community, she felt she was witnessing "a first rough draft" of the kinds of new institutions that will be demanded by a graying America. Her characterization might apply equally well to the Foster Grandparent Program. As Sargent Shriver stated, the program's beauty is in its simplicity, modeled essentially on the grandparent-grandchild relationship. It remains viable today and points the way to more encompassing developments in an area of great and growing significance.

As a result of the Foster Grandparent Program, and its offspring Senior Companion Program, the notion of reengaging older Americans in important ways is not simply an untested, enticing ideal today. We have "usable" models, not only in the long-past practices of the Puritans but also in the ongoing efforts of individuals like Aggie and Louise and John Curtis. It is in this context that new types of social entrepreneurs—"Del Webbs" of the civic sector—are building the next generation of opportunities for reinventing retirement in America.

PART THREE

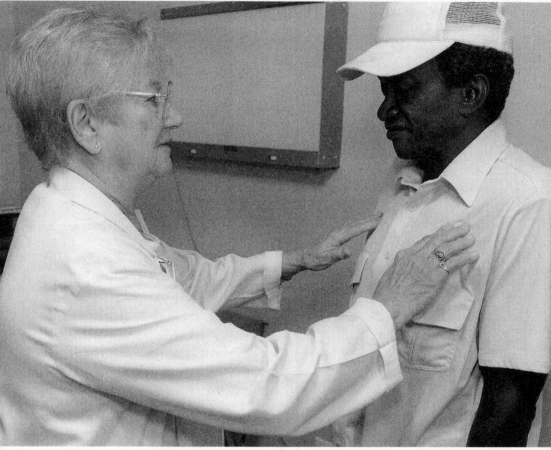

THOMAS ROMA

Dorothea Glass, M.D., is a twice-retired physician in her mid-seventies serving at the Volunteers in Medicine Clinic in Stuart, Florida. Born in New York, she comes from a family of women physicians (both her mother and aunt became obstetricians in post–World War I Manhattan). The mother of four children, she decided instead to specialize in physical and rehabilitation medicine and become a physiatrist. After a distinguished career as a department chair at Temple University Medical School, medical director at Moss Rehabilitation Center, and head of service at Albert Einstein Hospital, all in Philadelphia, she "retired" to Florida where she promptly became a professor at University of Miami Medical School and assumed new professional responsibilities. The centerpiece of her second retirement is volunteering to provide free care to working-poor patients in Stuart, a small town just north of Palm Beach. Her husband of over fifty years, Bob Glass, died a week after this interview from complications related to his diabetes.

·

I first retired in 1982 in my early sixties. I had very bad arthritis and was holding down three jobs. It had just gotten to the point where I couldn't do it all. So I retired and we came down here. But I didn't retire completely. I had both of my hips replaced. And then a friend of mine at the Veterans Administration in Washington said, "Come to the Miami VA because we want to start a residency training program in physical medicine and rehabilitation there." And I love teaching, love being with young people, so I said okay.

For four years I commuted to Miami every day. Then I became president of the American Congress of Rehabilitation Medicine, which took about four hours a day of my time. So I worked at the VA and was on the faculty at University of Miami for close to ten years. Then my husband and I both decided to retire a second time.

But I missed medicine. It is the most interesting thing I've ever done. I love the hospital and the interaction between people there. And I love physical medicine and rehabilitation because it involves such teamwork. It is truly holistic medicine. You know your patients. You follow them almost for the rest of their lives, especially if they are seriously impaired.

When I retired that second time, I joined the Treasure Coast Council for Planned Parenthood, and the League of Women Voters, the AAUW, all those things. We have a little boat we go out on, and I love my garden. I am lucky enough to be close to my daughters and I see my grandchildren. It is really a very pleasant life—but there was something missing. Then this great doctor at Martin Memorial [the main hospital in Stuart], Fred Carter, came up with the idea for the clinic and got the legislature to pass an act that more or less protects us from malpractice issues. He just did fantastic work, and it has been wonderful volunteering there.

I see patients who fall into my specialty. And we don't have a neurologist, so I do gross neurological evaluations. I also do a lot of—for lack of a better word—psychotherapy, because many of my patients are pain patients. As we get older, we all have aches and pains. But these are people, many of them, who simply have not been able to cope with life. And life is tough, especially for people with such marginal incomes. They are just overwhelmed. And the pain oftentimes becomes an explanation for it all.

In any case, I do not think that you can separate the body and the mind. The mind changes what happens in our blood, in our nerves, in our muscles. There is no way of dividing them. You cannot treat a patient if you treat only the physical part, at least not treat them well.

I had some wonderful mentors, and they helped me to understand that. They also taught me that you practiced the best medicine you could, regardless of a person's ability to pay. You treated everyone as though it was yourself or your child. And they taught me that when a disaster occurs to somebody—a terrible accident—you can't just treat the fact that a spine got cut. There are ripples. There's a person and then there's a family and then there's a community. You have got to take all of those into account. We physiatrists don't know as much as a neurologist about neurology, or as much as the urologists about what they do, but we know enough about all of these things to put them together and be an advocate for the patient.

At the clinic I get a lot of the patients that nobody else knows what to do with. A lot of them come in with lung disease, or heart disease, or terrible wounds that won't heal, diabetes out of control. But mostly they are people who have used up all their resources, emotional and financial. Some of them are living in cars.

First of all, I try to tell them that someone really cares to listen to them. Because they have worn out their families, worn out their friends. You need to make them know "you are still an important person to listen to." One woman I am treating, we know that her disability is hysterical because the symptoms are so bizarre. But she believes in her symptoms, and we are treating them. And she is getting better! We are giving her physical therapy exercises to do. We're giving her psychological support, really a kind of mentoring. And her symptoms are starting to disappear. She is a nice person—I love her. She is just a person who has been hit too hard. And what is any person's breaking point? It's how strong you are—and some people are stronger than others.

At the clinic, there are also a lot of people who are lost between the cracks. And because we are all in there together—the volunteers, Diane [the clinic director], the nurses who run the clinic and who are very skilled—we make fewer cracks. Or we rescue some of these people from the cracks.

We have the luxury of practicing medicine the way we think it should be practiced—and without having to worry about the money side. I believe it is very high-quality medicine. When I was working for money I was so over-committed. I don't think that I could do as good a job then as I can do now. What's more, everyone at the clinic is here because they want to be here, and they aren't harried. They are people who loved what they did and like it even more without all the pressures they had.

There are other things we get out of it as well. It's intellectually stimulating. Every patient is a puzzle. They are coming to you because they have problems that they haven't been able to solve otherwise. It keeps you on your toes. I read my journals because I need to know what's going on. I'm going to prevent Alzheimer's in myself by doing all this reading [laughs]. And I just love the interaction, between not only the patient and the doctor but among all of us treating patients.

And I guess I was brought up to believe that it is important that you contribute. Maybe contribute is too arrogant a word. You participate in what makes the world good. So many of us contribute to what makes the world bad. And, you know, once we are at this stage, there is a joy in seeing what you know not only being used but being used to help others.

And, as I was saying, we are also a family for each other. Diane has been wonderful to me. She comes down to see my husband in the hospital. She has allowed me to consult with her. She is going to help us set up when we go back home. I am sure she would do that for anyone. I think the other people in the clinic would do it for me too.

I know that I can't change everything as one person, but I can do what I can do. And hopefully that little thing will make a difference to somebody, besides me. Because it does make me feel good. And I think the thing about the clinic is you get a lot of encouragement and accolades for something that you just love to do. It's no sacrifice, it's a benefit. I would be devastated if it was taken away from me.

CHAPTER 4

Reinventing Retirement

The best way to predict the future is to create it.

.

Peter Drucker

Volunteers in Medicine

When Jack McConnell was a child, his father, a Methodist minister working in Tennessee and West Virginia, eschewed owning a car for fear that he could not "support Mr. Ford" and ensure that all seven McConnell children had the opportunity to go to college. So he did a considerable amount of walking as he carried out his ministerial duties. He was also fortunate to receive many rides from friends and neighbors, and this early experience instilled in the younger McConnell—who went on first to become a pediatrician and later a corporate executive at McNeil Laboratories and Johnson and Johnson—a lifetime habit of giving a lift to others.

This habit ended up playing a pivotal role in altering McConnell's retirement plans. Having done well financially, well enough to retire to a large house in one of Hilton Head's poshest gated communities (he played a role in the development of the MRI, Tylenol tablets, and the Tyne test for TB), McConnell was planning on a leisured third age with his wife—many rounds of golf, a steady diet of upscale dining, and long hours reading on their deck overlooking the water. However, this lifestyle didn't work any better for the energetic McConnell than it had for Steve Weiner: "I soon realized my fulfillment would not occur on the golf course," he recalls in "Circle of Caring," his essay about creating the first Volunteers in Medicine clinic in Hilton Head, South Carolina. "If anything, it diminished me more than I would have liked."

This desire for a more fulfilling retirement was becoming clear at the same time that McConnell was realizing the real town of Hilton Head was not quite the one advertised in all the Chamber of Commerce brochures aimed at luring affluent retirees to the resort community: The PR conveniently neglected to mention that alongside all the upscale snowbirds like the sixty-four-year-old McConnell, were a great many native islanders and others employed as maids, gardeners, and servants living at or near the poverty line—nearly one-third of the island's population.

In many cases, the haves and have-nots were divided literally by the walls of gated communities. On the inside, McConnell and his peers lived in palatial houses distributed around golf courses and waterways, while on the outside working people scraped by in unheated shacks without running water or sewers. The contrast became a galvanizing force for Dr. McConnell. Referring to his regular trip from the gated community to town, he commented in 1993: "It's a short drive, but a hell of a long journey. . . . Sitting cheek by jowl, you couldn't ignore the squalor."

McConnell was in the habit of driving out the back gate of the community and of giving rides to workers walking home along the side of the road. These encounters taught him something further: that these men and women—most of them earning the minimum wage—rarely had any health coverage. Meanwhile, he was spending his days on the golf course with scores of retired physicians and dentists who, it seemed to him, were restless, bored, and lacking real purpose in their lives.

The idea of bringing these two groups together, of devising a new route to providing inexpensive health care to the working poor while creating new roles for retired medical professionals, became an obsession for him (in much the way that a similar, common-sense insight drove Peter DiCicco to forge The Work Connection). As he began testing out the notion with his friends and contacts around town, McConnell became increasingly convinced that a free clinic staffed by retired physicians, dentists, and nurses was not only a good idea in theory but even a viable proposition.

Along the way, McConnell did encounter some resistance from local physicians convinced that an operation of this sort might end up competing with them. (For what? McConnell asked. Nonpaying patients they weren't treating anyway?) However, he also acquired a pair of key allies in the CEO of the local hospital and its director of emergency medicine. They were concerned about the mounting costs of nonpaying patients in their ER, individuals who required urgent care after untreated conditions became medical disasters. These were costs they were required, by law, to bear, and they felt a clinic like the one McConnell was proposing might save them money and help avert some of these personal crises by providing individuals with care earlier in the process.

Once the clinic idea began taking shape, there was essentially no stopping McConnell. Courtly on the exterior but relentlessly hard-driving underneath, he commented in 1995 that once he got rolling he "never looked back," even if the process wasn't always a smooth one. According to McConnell: "I kept moving forward. I just didn't know how many bumps we were going to hit in the road." But he tirelessly built local support for the clinic, by then named Volunteers in Medicine.

McConnell also managed to secure a planning grant from the Robert Wood Johnson Foundation (using corporate connections from his job at Johnson and Johnson), then a $300,000 grant from the health care philanthropy for three years of operating support. He next turned to state politics, cultivating the support of the governor of South Carolina, then locating a physician in the state legislature, Dr. Billy Houck, who helped shepherd through legislation establishing a special volunteer medical license for out-of-state physicians practicing in free clinics—despite strong resistance from the South Carolina Board of Medical Licenses. (According to McConnell, the board even solicited a letter from Dr. Sidney Wolfe, director of Ralph Nader's health watchdog group, charging "There is a renegade doctor loose in South Carolina trying to create a two-level heath-care system with a good one for those who can pay and a poor one for those who cannot." However, McConnell was able to convince the board that there was already a two-level system in practice: individuals who received care and those who had access to none.)

Next McConnell tackled the other formidable obstacle: malpractice insurance. He negotiated a deal with Joint Underwriters Association, the largest malpractice insurer in South Carolina, which for a total of $5,000 a year agreed to provide unlimited coverage for all involved in the clinic—professional and lay volunteers. McConnell then set out to build a 7,000-square-foot Volunteers in Medicine facility on land the city agreed to rent the clinic for $1 a year (McConnell jokes that in a fit of reckless abandon he paid off the entire lease on the clinic's groundbreaking, a total of $30.50). In the development phase, he raised a half million dollars to build the facility, which opened in June 1994. Next he convinced dozens of businesses and individual donors to provide support for a full range of state-of-the-art equipment for the clinic.

By 1997, a little over five years after initially conceiving of the notion, McConnell was overseeing an operation involving 44 retired physicians, 64 nurses, 3 dentists, and 128 lay volunteers who treated 6,000 patients a year— an average of about 50 a day on those days the clinic was open. The annual budget of just under a half million dollars covered upkeep of the facility and salaries of 5 full-time and 2 part-time paid staff, including among the full-time staff a medical director, nursing director, development director, and office manager.

As Jack McConnell envisioned, patients of Volunteers in Medicine are overwhelmingly working-poor men and women who neither qualify for Medicaid nor are covered by private health insurance. For them, the clinic is a place of last resort. And based on the overall cost of $35 per patient visit to the clinic, Volunteers in Medicine saves the local hospital between $350,000 and $500,000 annually. In fact, Steven Caywood, president of Hilton Head Hospital, estimates that it costs his emergency room twenty times as much as Volunteers in Medicine to treat the same cases.

On a social level, Volunteers in Medicine is regarded by many in Hilton Head as one of the town's few bridges between the large numbers of wealthy retirees who have relocated there and the far less affluent, and often younger, local population. According to Thomas Barnwell, an African American community leader and third-generation Hilton Header, the clinic is "the glue" of this community, one that connects individuals from dramatically different circumstances and "bind[s] them together. . . like nothing before."

The clinic's reputation spread beyond Hilton Head quickly. By 1995, Jack McConnell had received 492 requests from towns around the country interested in setting up variations on the Volunteers in Medicine clinic. In response to this outpouring of interest, McConnell passed on the operational reins at the clinic in October of that year to devote all of his time to helping other communities adapt Volunteers in Medicine to their particular circumstances.

Healing Hands

"Now Is Later"

I first read about Jack McConnell and the Hilton Head Volunteers in Medicine Clinic in a newspaper article on Christmas Day 1993—before

McConnell had even built his new home for the project. For the next several years I followed the clinic's evolution from afar. Then, four years later, as I was preparing to write this book, I decided to call McConnell and arrange to see the Volunteers in Medicine operation firsthand.

To a large degree, my interest came from a desire to counterbalance all the mentoring projects I was writing about. I was filled with respect for The Work Connection and Foster Grandparents and for the relationship skills and compassion of outwardly "ordinary" individuals like Nick Spaneas (the former bus driver and barber) and Aggie Bennett (who'd worked as a waitress). I was convinced they were involved in work of immense—although all too often undervalued—importance. Yet there was another group of retirees—also overlooked—who possessed an array of sophisticated professional skills just as desperately needed by society.

In thinking about Volunteers in Medicine and this other end of the skills spectrum, I was reminded as well of the testimony that former HEW secretary Anthony Celebrezze offered to Congress thirty-five years before (in 1963) as a rationale for Robert Kennedy's National Service Corps. It was the speech in which Celebrezze described the older population as a "vast manpower and womanpower resource" and ticked off the skills residing in the early 1960s retiree population: 126,000 teachers, 36,000 lawyers, 18,000 retired professors, 43,000 retired nurses, and 32,000 physicians. The numbers for all these groups have grown dramatically since that time. Today, for example, there are approximately 140,000 retired physicians, with many thousands more leaving active doctoring each year.

My hope was to include the story of Volunteers in Medicine alongside those of Foster Grandparents and The Work Connection to remind people of both the rich range of experience in the retiree population and the need for a variety of vehicles in attempting to tap that talent. Besides, what better example than medical professionals to highlight how we are wasting prized skills in the older population at a juncture when the nation faces an acute health care shortage?

As I flew into Hilton Head in February 1998, however, I was feeling trepidation. I had already written glowingly of Volunteers in Medicine in several articles, focusing on the idea behind the institution. What if the reality fell short of the ideal, not an uncommon experience in the world of social programs?

In fact, what I encountered at the clinic was, in many ways, more impressive than I had imagined. Located on a quiet, shady side street just off the main thoroughfare in Hilton Head, it felt like an oasis—professional yet peaceful. The clinic facility itself was spacious, immaculate, welcoming, even accompanied by abundant parking. All the obstacles for perspective patients, psychological or logistical, seemed to have been thought through and eliminated.

Inside, a sizable portrait of a lithe, tanned, doctorly McConnell hung behind the reception desk, just above the clinic's mission statement: "May we have eyes to see those rendered invisible and excluded, open arms and hearts to reach out and include them, healing hands to touch their lives with love, and in the process, heal ourselves."

Those hands seemed especially apparent in an alcove just to the left of the front door: the children's reading room. The walls are brightly painted with big colorful fish. There are plenty of toys and many books, which the children are encouraged to take home with them. The message is clear: Volunteers in Medicine treats the whole person, the whole family, the whole community.

As I walked past the waiting area into the clinic itself, I was struck by something else. The doctors, nurses, receptionists, and others moving so purposefully through the corridors were only *slightly* older than those at the average clinic or doctor's office. There it is not uncommon to see many people in their fifties and sixties. Here there are many people in their sixties and seventies, along with some younger individuals and a few older ones. The difference is subtle. Yet it is still quite moving to see so many people who might otherwise be prematurely put out to pasture—or at least out to the pasture in Hilton Head called the golf course—so thoroughly engaged in doing important things.

This work is not limited to professionals either. Key to the operation, for they set the clinic's atmosphere, is a group of older volunteers—none with medical backgrounds—who meet all individuals who come through the door, warmly welcoming them and asking them how they can be helped. This climate is a striking contrast to the impersonal experience one typically expects in going to the doctor, much less to a free clinic.

The person who greeted me is Jeanette Mayer, age sixty-five. Jeanette's husband Norman, seventy-five, was an executive with the Travelers Insurance Company. Originally from Connecticut, the couple now spends six months of the year in Hilton Head and the other six in New Hampshire. She worked as a buyer for a department store. When they are in Hilton Head, both volunteer at the clinic. Jeanette spends two days a week greeting patients and helping them negotiate their way to medical care, while Norm spends three or more days every week as a "screener." Because the clinic is restricted to individuals who neither qualify for Medicaid or Medicare nor have any private insurance, Norm is part of a group of volunteers who determine eligibility. This role is important for two reasons: Volunteers in Medicine wants to concentrate its efforts on those who do not qualify for other care, who have fallen through the cracks. The institution also wants to avoid any perception of being in competition with local practicing doctors, of stealing away potentially paying patients. (In practice, however, it is very rare for patients to be turned away.)

Jeanette told me that upon retiring and moving there, the Mayers discovered that two or three decades of leisure would simply not do for them: It "wasn't enough, wasn't fulfilling," explained Jeanette. "When you retire you can only sit around so long—you can only play so much tennis." She didn't sit around. "This," she said, referring to the clinic, "is probably the most rewarding thing I've ever done."

To make her point, she told me about a woman who had visited the clinic in late December with three sick children and as she left was looking frantically for the cashier. "The woman asked me, 'Where do I pay?'" Jeanette said. Tears rolled down the woman's face as Jeanette explained that the clinic was absolutely free. "The woman said, 'I thought this was going to cost me fifty dollars that I don't have.'" For Jeanette, that brief encounter was "the best Christmas present of the year."

Jeanette and Norm both talked about the sense of community at the clinic, the egalitarian atmosphere among the doctors, nurses, and lay volunteers. "Ten years ago I wouldn't have dreamt of answering the phones for a day," Norm chuckles, "but somebody has to do it! No job is too menial, none of us is too fancy to do it." By the time you retire, he added, you've already proven yourself, one way or the other. There is an acceptance of limitations and some liberation from the burdens of ego. Many other men I interviewed at the clinic, physicians and lay volunteers alike, articulated a similar perspective.

The Mayers also spoke movingly about the rewards of being part of a community of people giving something back and about how this work had left them more compassionate. Jeanette explained, "I think I can speak for both of us when I say we have a much greater appreciation of the large number of people living right on the edge, who never got a chance. This is a very different perspective than sitting on a United Way allocation committee."

"We just get a lot more than we are giving," Norm adds. "It's a shame—

there are so many retired people with so much to give, who don't need the income, who are healthy. But there are not the opportunities to get involved." At the same time, there aren't the opportunities for so many of their patients to get adequate health care: "If it wasn't for this clinic, where would they go?"

One of the stars of Volunteers in Medicine is Art Friedman, a retired general practitioner from Youngstown, Ohio. In his early eighties, Friedman works at the clinic every day, from opening until closing, which he has done since his wife of fifty-three years passed away three years previously: "When I lost her, I was lost. . . . I'm still depressed." On the surface there is no evidence of Friedman's depression, only his commitment. The other doctors describe him as the "backbone" of the clinic. In part, this status is due to the shortage of general practitioners at Volunteers in Medicine. Hilton Head is the kind of place that attracts more retired surgeons than family doctors. And in our interview Friedman expresses his delight at all these fancy specialists from elite hospitals and universities coming to him each day for advice about treating common ailments.

When I ask Art Friedman about his extensive commitment to Volunteers in Medicine, he complains in mock frustration, "Yeah, this clinic has *wrecked* my golf game!" But the work does keep his mind sharp. "I'm reading more now than when I was a medical student," he says, referring to all the continuing medical education and other study required to remain current. But one line of his in particular resonates. When asked where the clinic fits into his life, Art tells me, "This clinic *is* my life."

Harry Nelson and Oliver Crawford are two of the other doctors I interviewed at Volunteers in Medicine. Nelson, a recently retired vascular surgeon, was on the clinical faculty of the University of Pennsylvania; Crawford, who is African American, was a pediatrician at Northwestern University's hospital in Chicago. Both are in their early sixties and look younger. They defy in appearance and demeanor every stereotype of the "senior citizen." They could be mistaken for the typical middle-aged doctors one might encounter at the local teaching hospital.

Nelson learned about the clinic from his real estate agent, who used it as a selling point. The doctor should buy a house in Hilton Head—as opposed to the other resort communities Nelson was considering—the agent explained, so he could keep his hand in medicine. An obviously kind and deeply religious man, Nelson always reserved an hour each day in his surgical practice just for talking with patients and their families about the stress they were under. In this way, Volunteers in Medicine, with the "circle of caring" it tries to create, is a perfect fit for him—and he for it.

The great luxury of the clinic is time, both doctors underscore, specifically time for relationships with patients. Dr. Crawford observes that although he wears a watch now because his wife gave it to him as a present, there is no "watching the clock in the clinic"—a consuming preoccupation in his previous practice. Nelson shudders: "The pace that I lived by in practice was so horrendous. I had so little time to spend with people, with patients. And when I retired and came to Hilton Head, I was tired." Now there is not only time but flexibility as well. If they need time off, they can take it. They simply notify the clinic administrator in advance. And they can volunteer the number of hours that enables them to achieve some balance in their lives.

"As you get older, you often realize how valuable time is," Dr. Crawford notes. "There are so many things that I'd like to do that I never took the time to do before. When you're thirty or forty, or even fifty, you think, 'I'll do that later.' Well, *now is later!*"

One of the things Crawford is doing with his newly abundant *and* precious time, in addition to the clinic, is working as a mentor for local youth, along with twenty other African American professionals in Hilton Head. They are focused on exposing eighth graders to higher education, with a particular emphasis on historically black colleges. This includes organizing trips and college fairs, along with providing one-on-one attention.

As the two men were leaving the room, Dr. Nelson pointed out that there are other, tangible side benefits to being a part of something like Volunteers in Medicine. Recently, while waiting in a long line at the local DMV, it came to the attention of the clerk that he was a doctor at the clinic, and he was immediately reassigned to the front of the line. But there was another perk as well: The surgeon met his wife at the clinic, where she was serving as director of volunteers.

Fred Carter's Dream

After my time at the Hilton Head clinic, I was left with the desire to explore another of the free clinics inspired by Volunteers in Medicine. I was concerned by the prospect that the original clinic was possible only because of the charisma of Jack McConnell and the unusual talent pool in a place like Hilton Head. So I decided to visit the Volunteers in Medicine Clinic in Stuart, Florida, led by Diane Montella, the first medical director of the

Hilton Head clinic. Stuart is on Florida's "Treasure Coast," forty-five minutes north of West Palm Beach, itself a prime retirement destination.

The driving force behind both the Stuart clinic and a Florida state law licensing retired volunteer doctors is Fred Carter, an internist who practiced in Stuart for twenty-six years. By all accounts a much-beloved and wonderful doctor, Carter was already volunteering for the county health department when he heard from "Doc" Myers—a state representative and physician—about the clinic idea. It sounded like a dream come true. As the *Palm Beach Post* put it in 1996, "If he had his way, Dr. Fred Carter would spend an hour examining each patient, asking lots of questions, and charging nothing."

One of Carter's great achievements—and arguably an important improvement over the Hilton Head model—was to avoid setting the clinic up as an independent, free-floating entity dependent on continuous community fundraising. Carter convinced the local hospital, Martin Memorial, to make a major ongoing commitment to the clinic from the outset, building it into the hospital's operating budget. The hospital's volunteer services director functions as administrative director for the clinic, and Martin Memorial pays approximately $450,000 a year to cover the clinic's expenses. In addition, it provides a myriad of supportive services free to the Stuart Volunteers in Medicine, including laboratory work and testing. The hospital also extends legal protection to the clinic and helps line up private physicians in the community who will see referrals from the clinic for free.

In addition, the Martin Memorial auxiliary provided $200,000 toward a new facility for Volunteers in Medicine, a 4,800-square-foot building near the hospital. The attractive single-story building, while not as vast as the Hilton Head clinic, contains eight examining rooms, two counseling rooms, a library, a pharmacy, an ophthalmology clinic, and a dental clinic. In addition to primary care, many subspecialties are offered. And all services are completely free ("Free but not cheap!" one of the doctors exclaims, emphasizing the quality of care delivered). At present, the clinic operates at 64 percent of the cost of private doctor visits, on a per-visit basis, and hopes to bring that number down to 50 percent.

For Martin Memorial Hospital, Volunteers in Medicine is both good economics and good public relations. It is good economics because the program helps to prevent poor patients from developing acute conditions that then end up in the Martin Memorial emergency room. It's good PR because the hospital—a nonprofit—is striving to project an image of continued commitment to the community.

Overall, the clinic sees about 700–1,000 patients a month during its primary season (when snowbird physicians are in Florida), with 35–40 retired volunteer doctors and a slightly smaller number of retired nurses. That number drops dramatically during the summer when the retirees head back north, and the paid staff—six in all (Montella, a nurse manager, an office manager, a lab technician, a secretary, and a patient services representative)—struggle to provide for the ongoing patients, taking no new cases except the absolutely urgent ones.

Many of the best features of the Hilton Head clinic are evident in Stuart, including the volunteer greeters. Diane Montella, a compassionate young physician instrumental in shaping the culture of the Hilton Head Volunteers in Medicine, has managed to cultivate a similar environment of dignity and respect for indigent patients in Stuart. The majority of these men and women are working-poor—although, unlike the Hilton Head facility, the clinic treats no children under five. Florida provides medical coverage for these children, and the clinic is careful to avoid taking any insured patients from local doctors.

Montella explained to me that patients come to the clinic because they are not "feeling well," and that she and the volunteers see to it that they leave having been "cared for." That includes first-class medical care but also a lot of emotional support, pats on the back, even hugs (her comments recall the part of the Hilton Head credo about "healing hands"). The result is reciprocal exchange of caring. Not only do the physicians care for the patients, but the patients care about the physicians. When one of the doctors is absent, the patients often send cards expressing their concern. Indeed, the older physicians frequently find themselves on both sides of the medical relationship—sometimes as doctors, sometimes as patients or the spouses of patients. When I visited the clinic, Fred Carter was out for two and a half months with a hip injury.

I met many inspiring volunteers in Stuart, among them Noah Barish, a ninety-two-year-old pediatrician who recently completed his bar mitzvah. One of my favorites was Dr. Norman Gehringer, who graduated from medical school in 1939. In the course of his practice in Pontiac, Michigan, as a family doctor, Gehringer delivered an estimated 5,000 babies. During World War II, he delivered thirty a month—including eleven in one remarkable day. "I could never say no," Gehringer confesses. Now the grandfatherly physician, with a gentle disposition and pencil-thin mustache, is a mainstay at the Stuart clinic. (In fact, when Gehringer was hospitalized recently, the other doctors visited him daily, teasing him about shirking his duties at Volunteers in Medicine.)

It was in Stuart that I met Thea Glass, a walking embodiment of the Hippocratic oath. Having spent most of her professional life being a role model for women in medicine, Dr. Glass continues to model the possible, providing a vision of retirement as a time of beautifully balanced continued contribution and meaning.

Thea Glass came by her love of medicine naturally. Her mother emigrated from Russia to New York just after the turn of the century, at age ten. Although she didn't speak a word of English at the time, the young woman proved to be a brilliant student and was accepted to Cornell Medical School (where Thea's aunt also followed in her footsteps). On the recommendation of her high school principal, Thea's mother's education at Cornell was sponsored by the founder of the Upjohn pharmaceutical company.

After she became a successful obstetrician in Manhattan (as well as a friend and colleague of Margaret Sanger's), Thea's mother approached Mr. Upjohn with the intention of repaying him. He wouldn't take a penny, insisting that instead she do the same thing for somebody else. Throughout her career, she was involved in providing free health care for the poor. According to Thea, "She was on the staff at Bellevue. And she was required to spend three months of the year 'on service.' That was twenty-four hours a day, seven days a week, for no pay. And she considered it to be the greatest honor that she ever had."

Thea idolized her mother and was determined to become a doctor herself. However, she first wanted to have children, out of the belief that medical commitments kept her mother from spending enough time with Thea when she was very young. The doctoring could wait. Indeed, it waited while she had four children. Once her children were in school, Thea applied to medical school. She had distinguished herself as an undergraduate at Cornell, majoring in English but taking the premed requirements. However, the dean of the prestigious school that was her first choice called Thea into his office to explain that they had refused to accept her application. As she stood in shock, the man proceeded to tear up her application, telling Thea, "Our psychiatrist tells me that a mother's place is with her children."

Undeterred, Thea enrolled in Women's Medical College in Philadelphia, where she flourished, going on to a residency at the University of Pennsylvania, a professorship at Temple Medical School, leadership of the largest rehabilitation medicine institution in Philadelphia, and presidency of the

American Congress of Rehabilitation Medicine (all while raising those four children). She attributes her love of medicine and humane approach not only to her mother's powerful example but also to the training she received as a young doctor. "I was taught that you never thought about money in medicine," she states. "You treated the people who needed you. In your mind, nobody was poor."

This lesson was reinforced by a clinic system requiring young doctors who wanted to become attending physicians at teaching hospitals to do substantial volunteer work at free clinics connected to the hospitals. "You couldn't be on the staff of the hospital unless you worked in the clinics," Thea recalls. "For two years, I worked for nothing. You built your practice seeing nonpaying patients in the clinics. You got referrals from other doctors there. That was part of it. But all through my life I have done clinic work because I like it, and you know, it is kind of a payback." It was also "an excellent teacher," she adds, not only of medical skills but of a physician's responsibility to the community. And it was liberating. At the clinics physicians didn't have to worry about the business side of medicine: "Somebody else took care of whether patients were eligible for the clinic," and the doctors could concentrate on seeing patients and providing the best care possible.

Thea Glass chose rehabilitation medicine over obstetrics and internal medicine because it enabled her to have long-term relationships with patients, many of them with spinal cord injuries that required lifetime care. When I asked her what she was proudest of, given her many professional accomplishments, she reflected:

I am just delighted that I was given the opportunity to practice the kind of medicine I loved. To be working with people that I really thought a lot of, including my patients. I have a huge respect for people with disabilities. Animals, when they're badly hurt, crawl off into a corner to die. These are people who fight back and say, "I'm going to have a life. This terrible thing has happened to me, but that's the way it is." I think of one young man who at sixteen broke his neck diving into ten inches of water, because his fellow gang members dared him to. He turned out to have the highest IQ of anyone we ever tested and went on to become a psychologist. He was partially paralyzed from the neck down. But he drove, he worked, he did everything. And when I asked him what it was that gave him so much courage, he said, "I do what I have to do. I don't have a choice. I can live, or I can die."

Volunteers in Medicine amounts to Thea's third career in medicine. After retiring from her responsibilities in Philadelphia, she moved to Florida and spent a decade setting up a residency and serving on the faculty of the University of Miami. Then, after retirement from paid medicine, she began act three—as a volunteer physician in Stuart. In a way, her career has come full circle, in that she has returned to practice medicine in the kind of clinic setting that played such a key role in shaping her earlier career and outlook.

One aspect of Volunteers in Medicine that is most important to Thea has nothing to do with medicine directly. She believes the clinic is sending a message to younger generations that not all older adults are selfish and self-indulgent: "I don't blame some of the young people today for being resentful of all these older people playing golf and sitting around at the nineteenth hole drinking. . . when [the young people] are going out of their minds just trying to keep up." She adds, "I like the young people to see us doing this kind of work."

However, most of all, her enthusiasm about this third phase of her medical career centers on the continued opportunity to interact with patients and be part of a community providing care. "Everybody at the clinic is here because they want to be here," she says, adding emphatically, "And they aren't harried."

The visit to Stuart, Florida, made it clear that the Hilton Head clinic was no accident. The Martin Memorial Volunteers in Medicine was every bit as impressive—with lessons of its own to impart. However, the question remained, could a clinic of this sort take root someplace that wasn't an affluent retirement area? On the one hand, places like Hilton Head and the Palm Beach coast offer access to remarkable medical talent—people like Harry Nelson, Oliver Crawford, and Thea Glass. On the other hand, clinics in these settings have to contend with special out-of-state licensing (it took Thea eight months to get her license). These clinics also must deal with the reality that many of the area volunteers are seasonal residents who spend six months of the year elsewhere. This creates enormous problems in terms of providing patients continuity of care.

After leaving Stuart, I set out on a quest for similar clinics in year-round communities. Although no national network of these places yet exists, I found a scattering in Maine, Pennsylvania, Indiana, and elsewhere. The most compelling example turned out to be a half-hour drive from my front door: the Samaritan House Clinic, in the town of San Mateo, an ethnically and economically mixed city of 85,000 on the peninsula between San Francisco and San Jose.

This remarkable effort made me realize that a free clinic based on the involvement of retired doctors, nurses, dentists, and others not only could survive in an ordinary city (as opposed to an upscale retirement destination) but is probably easier to operate in such a locale as well. In most urban areas of this type, (1) the number of retired physicians is quite large; (2) extraordinary resources are available through medical schools and teaching hospitals; and (3) people live there year-round, which makes for greater consistency of scheduling, enables continuity of care, and facilitates building on already existing relationships the physicians have with local colleagues, hospitals, and insurance providers. There is no need in these situations either for obtaining special out-of-state licensing or for locating new malpractice coverage.

In addition, an institution of this type might actually become a reason for local doctors and others *not to relocate* in retirement, a factor that could help to stem the exodus of human talent from so many communities (and perhaps even help to alleviate the sprawl connected with older adults moving to retirement communities in so many parts of the country, especially the Southwest).

Good Samaritans

San Mateo was bustling on a sunny October afternoon. A string of impressive 1920s buildings—a post office, library, city hall, bank—line the main street. However, the old stamp and coin shops and five-and-dime stores are giving way to trendy cafes and new branches of expensive San Francisco restaurants. This stretch equidistant between Silicon Valley and the Golden Gate is fast becoming one of the most expensive areas in which to live in the Bay Area. A modest house now costs a half million dollars; the median housing price in 1997 was $341,000.

By the time I arrived at the First Watch diner, Dr. Bill Schwartz was waiting for me by the window. A balding but youthful sixty-something with tufts of gray-brown hair, he waved enthusiastically from the table. Even though Schwartz lives in the especially affluent area of Hillsborough, he is utterly unpretentious. He drives a middle-aged Nissan. His clothes are casual. He doesn't seem like a Californian; I immediately suspect that he is from somewhere in the Midwest. In fact, he grew up in Cando, North Dakota—pronounced "can do" (a sign, "You can do better in Cando," greets motorists entering the town). His family settled there as part of a little-known Jewish migration in the late nineteenth century; his grandfather was a homesteader and a farmer, and his father owned a local business. Where he grew up, Schwartz tells me, volunteerism was just what everybody did. It wasn't even called volunteerism, it was assumed—"Everybody took care of each other."

Although there is no trace of the physician's ego in Schwartz, the man's career is impressive. He took the train in 1949 from Cando to attend Berkeley and returned to the Bay Area a decade later to practice internal medicine. Schwartz spent thirty-two years in private practice as an internist in San Mateo while also serving as clinical professor of medicine at the University of California at San Francisco (UCSF), one of the country's most prestigious medical schools.

Bill Schwartz's passion about the free clinic he started almost a decade earlier—but for which he refuses to accept credit ("It was a group effort from the beginning," he is quick to assert)—is immediately evident. He tells me that throughout most of his life, he has been one to avoid conflict and controversy. In the context of his work with Samaritan House, however, he finds his personality transformed: He has become a fighter, not for himself but for the clinic's patients.

The patients get the worst of two worlds, he explains. On the one hand, they make little money as gardeners, laborers, fast-food workers, and the like, and they receive no health insurance for their efforts. On the other hand, they pay exorbitant rents as a result of the overheated real estate market in the area. "A typical family may have a combined [annual] income, husband and wife working, of $12,000, and to help make ends meet, they may share a $1,200-a-month apartment with another family." They are barely able to feed themselves. In this context, health care becomes a luxury, and other than the emergency room, the free clinic is the only place in San Mateo they can turn for medical care.

The Samaritan House Clinic is located on Doctors Row, the string of medical practices that lead up to modern Mills-Peninsula Hospital on San Mateo Drive near the business center of the city. The idea for the clinic came not from Schwartz but from John Kelly, a former priest and Latin teacher who is now director of Samaritan House, a nonprofit community organization. Samaritan House shelters the homeless, feeds the hungry, provides clothing, and offers programs for impoverished adults and youth out of three trailers located in the low-income section of town. Kelly wanted to add medical care to Samaritan House's services in 1989 and put a notice in the county medical society's bulletin asking for volunteer physicians who might help start a clinic. Bill Schwartz, fifty-seven and an active internist in private practice in San Mateo at the time, saw the notice and responded.

It was not just Schwartz's upbringing and early exposure to volunteerism that made him receptive. He was a product of the same training system as Thea Glass. When Schwartz first completed his residency in the early 1960s, there was an expectation that physicians perform pro bono work at a well-developed network of free or minimal-cost clinics operating out of medical schools and teaching hospitals. In fact, when he first started practicing medicine in 1960, Schwartz went down to the local teaching hospital and asked for a volunteer clinic assignment. However, the creation of Medicaid and Medicare—although unquestionably, on balance, major advances—in fact led to a decline in these clinics, partly out of the false assumption that everybody was now being served. Over time, the clinic system was largely dismantled and the pro bono expectation in medicine weakened considerably. (This is a story told by every one of the doctors from this generation I interviewed in Hilton Head, Stuart, and San Mateo.)

Before Schwartz could begin seeing patients in the context of Samaritan House, the clinic needed to be licensed by the state. Schwartz thought that the best route would be to work through the county hospital. For three long years the hospital was polite and seemingly supportive—the check was in the proverbial mail—but nothing happened. Eventually, Schwartz learned that the hospital had no real interest in making the clinic happen but was simply delaying in hopes that the physician would give up. This realization left him furious but all the more dedicated to making the free clinic a reality. (He remembers thinking, "I'll show them.")

Working with an eighty-year-old retired physician, Walter Gaines, Schwartz successfully secured a license for the clinic, generated a range of donated medical equipment, and opened for service as the Samaritan House Clinic in the summer of 1992. In Gaines, Schwartz found the perfect complement. Gaines was a doctor who loved paperwork; a retired radiologist, he was the partner in his medical group who was always selected to handle financial and management duties. But Gaines also had a strong social conscience and had spent significant time abroad running a volunteer medical clinic in Ethiopia.

Initially, the volunteer physicians operated out of the conference room at Samaritan House, in one of the community group's trailers. One night a week, Schwartz, Gaines, and several other volunteers—most of them practicing middle-aged physicians—saw patients. For hours beforehand, Schwartz would scurry around transforming a meeting room into a medical facility. Soon demand for the clinic's services caused the volunteers to increase their time to six nights a month, then to eight. Schwartz was present every time the clinic was opened—while simultaneously recruiting other doctors to volunteer and generally functioning as the glue behind the operation.

Unlike Jack McConnell, Schwartz never set out to start an operation of the scale Samaritan House Clinic has become. He was more of an *incremental entrepreneur*, almost an accidental one. Little by little, as he came face-to-face with the tremendous need for care on the part of individuals and families in San Mateo and saw tangibly that he and other physicians could make a genuine difference in meeting that need, Schwartz simply couldn't look away. Instead, increasingly, he took on leadership and more responsibility.

So when Schwartz "retired" from private practice, he moved quickly into a forty-plus-hour-a-week volunteer job guiding the clinic through an expansion that moved it out of the conference room and into its own dedicated facility. (Nearly a decade after John Kelly's ad first appeared, the clinic regularly receives calls from physicians who hope to "retire" to practicing at the clinic as opposed to "retire from" medicine. They feel they can end their for-profit practice because they know they will still be able to keep a hand in medicine through Samaritan House—and do it in a fashion that promises to be more satisfying than what they're currently experiencing in the world of managed care.) Over time, Schwartz has reduced his role, cutting back his hours to provide more freedom for the current leaders of the clinic and to return to his original retirement dream—learning to paint.

In tracing the origins of the Samaritan House Clinic and discussing Bill Schwartz's incremental entrepreneurialism, I found it significant that organizing the clinic around a group of retirees was never part of the original conception. Things simply evolved in that direction. Initially, with the exception of Walter Gaines, Schwartz and the bulk of other volunteers were still in active practice. The turning point came when the new facility was leased and the clinic set out to be open during normal business hours. In their efforts to expand, they could find few active physicians in private practice who were available during the daytime.

In part, this situation was prompted by the growth in managed care. As the *New York Times* recently reported, "The uninsured are finding that their last resort—charity care—is being threatened by the rapid expansion of managed care, which is putting tremendous financial pressure on doctors and hospitals to focus their resources on insured patients." All across the country doctors are trying to see more and more paying patients to offset reductions in income. Repeatedly, Bill Schwartz heard this message from the practicing physicians he approached: I believe in what you're doing—and I might be able to spare an hour or two in the evenings every once in a while—but I am simply too squeezed to do charity care during the day.

That response led Schwartz to think about who might have the time. He didn't have to look far. Newly retired himself and with Walter Gaines as a powerful role model, he turned his attention to recruiting peers who were at a similar stage. The response was overwhelming.

The Samaritan House Clinic is just a few minutes from the center of San Mateo, and after lunch Bill Schwartz is eager to pay the bill and show me the place firsthand. I follow him a few blocks, past the impressive Mills-Peninsula hospital building and into a parking lot next to a low-slung, drab 1950s building with aluminum windows, weathered siding, and a flat gravel roof. Although there is clearly nothing fancy about the facility, it also is indistinguishable from all the utilitarian-looking private doctors' suites that run up and down San Mateo Drive. A standard sign with a caduceus sits at the entrance to the driveway, soberly listing all the M.D.'s, Ph.D.'s, and other professionals operating out of the clinic.

Once inside the clinic, there are also similarities to the typical doctor's office. Patients make appointments and receive callbacks to confirm their times. There is a sliding glass window where the medical secretary logs in patients. The office has the same magazine subscriptions that adorn the typical doctor's waiting room—although here, as in Hilton Head, patients are urged to take the magazines home in an effort to encourage the largely Latino and Pacific Islander patient group to read in English.

It is immediately evident and quite striking that this operation is thriving, even as Schwartz scales back his involvement and passes on leadership to the next generation of volunteers and staff. The hallways are filled with doctors, nurses, and other workers of all ages, speaking English and Spanish, obviously and thoroughly engaged. I am reminded of one of Bill's comments at lunch—which I dismissed at the time as a bit euphoric: "You know, we're having more fun than we have any right to." In fact, these people look as if they are having a great deal of fun. The caption that keeps forming in my mind is "the joy of medicine."

Scott Smyth, Bill Schwartz,
Anand Mehta, and other volunteers
at the Samaritan House Clinic

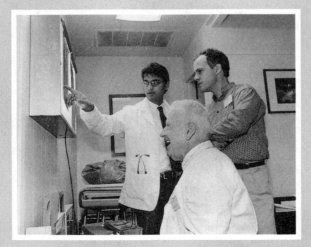

The Samaritan House Clinic began operating a full schedule in its Doctors Row facilities in March 1996. The 1,850-square-foot building is a third as large as the Stuart clinic and a quarter the size of Hilton Head's Volunteers in Medicine (although with only a quarter the space, Samaritan House serves more than half as many patients—largely because its volunteers work year-round).

The clinic recently explored the possibility of buying the building, but at a cost of $700,000 the administrators have decided to continue renting. Nevertheless, the structure is far from ideal, especially compared with the other clinics I'd seen—which, if anything, have overcapacity. At Samaritan House, the waiting room is cramped. Most of the equipment is donated secondhand. Overall, it is much more of a shoestring operation than either Hilton Head or Stuart.

Despite modest quarters, the range of medical services offered at Samaritan House is extensive. Mornings are reserved for subspecialties and afternoons for general medicine (as is Monday evening). In addition to primary practice and internal medicine, the clinic provides care in pediatrics, gynecology, orthopedics, surgery, psychiatry, dermatology, neurology, endocrinology, cardiology, neurosurgery, urology, ophthalmology, and numerous other subspecialties. The facility also has a dental clinic and even offers psychological and social work services.

The major difference between the clinic and its Doctors Row neighbors, of course, is that all services are gratis. However, one would be hard-pressed to find any drop in quality of care. The more than forty individuals who volunteer as doctors are absolutely top-notch. Like Bill Schwartz, many were or continue to be faculty or attending physicians at UCSF and Stanford and affiliated with highly rated Mills-Peninsula Hospital. (On my last visit to the clinic, Bill Schwartz was aglow: Samaritan House was closing in on recruiting the just-retired chair of the Ear, Nose, and Throat Department at UCSF.)

The clinic is staffed by doctors who have spent much of their life caring for well-to-do patients and teaching bright young medical students. Now they are applying these decades of experience to the care of indigent patients. The doctors are screened by Schwartz not only for medical skill but also for attitude and personality; Samaritan House is dedicated to assuring that all patients are treated with the same dignity. As Adriana Valdovinos-Campa, the medical director, points out, this is care that only significant sums of money could buy in today's environment. For most people, "there is no longer access to this kind of care—with doctors of this level of skill spending an hour or more with patients—no insurance company would ever pay for it."

(When some of Bill Schwartz's well-to-do patients, upset when the doctor announced he was retiring from private practice, inquired about continuing to see him through the clinic and simply paying out-of-pocket for the services, Schwartz told them he would be glad to continue treating them at no cost. All they needed to do was donate their homes, cars, and all but $10,000 in annual income to charity and they could qualify for all the care at the clinic they could ever need.)

The volunteer physicians, dentists, and nurses—about 90 percent of them retired—work with two paid MDs: Valdovinos-Campa, who is on the staff at UCSF and who serves as medical director, and Cabilia Williams-Chen, who serves as clinic administrator. Both of these young women, in their thirties, were born in Latin America and are native Spanish speakers with a strong commitment to serving Latino patients. In addition, there is a half-time paid dentist. Bill Schwartz serves as a special adviser to the clinic now, after functioning as the volunteer director for years.

As with Volunteers in Medicine, the Samaritan House doctors, nurses, and dentists are but one—if a central—tier in the mix of volunteers helping to operate the clinic. The facility has a retired pharmacist who organizes medications and assists in applying for free prescriptions that many drug companies offer through programs for indigents in need of medicine. There are also a number of translators, who interpret between doctors and patients, as well as volunteer secretaries, most of them retired. There are medical students and students from a local community college. There is even a group of "room stockers"—four older volunteers—who take turns showing up a half hour before the clinic opens to make sure all the examining rooms have syringes, gowns, pap smear materials, tongue depressors, and other essentials.

In addition to locating a reliable group of highly committed, highly skilled volunteers, a medical license, and a place to practice, the clinic has worked out the potential obstacles to providing care. The indigent prescription program is one example. The close relationship with Mills-Peninsula Hospital is another. The hospital provides all laboratory and radiology studies for the clinic free of charge—again with the goal of reducing emergency room visits that result from inadequate earlier intervention.

The most important relationship is with the Samaritan House community organization. It screens patients for eligibility and is the chief source of referrals. The fact that the clinic grew organically from Samaritan House has been critically important in ensuring its legitimacy from the outset. The larger organization has been instrumental in fundraising for the clinic's operations, including locating support for paid staff and the cost of malpractice and liability insurance (provided by the same carriers that covered the doctors when they were in private practice, on a prorated basis averaging $15 for each two-and-a-half-hour stint by a doctor). The bulk of these resources comes from local private sources, with the David and Lucile Packard Foundation and the Peninsula Community Foundation as the leading donors.

The Art of Medicine

My pilgrimage from Hilton Head to Stuart to San Mateo began out of a desire to show how the sophisticated skills possessed by older Americans could be harnessed on behalf of communities. The Samaritan House Clinic and Volunteers in Medicine are vivid examples of just how this can happen in the context of an area of undeniable need.

Still, the common-sense logic and obvious efficiency of these clinics have prompted some, like former South Carolina governor Carroll Campbell, to misstate their importance, portraying them as a panacea for the nation's health care woes. Campbell refers to Volunteers in Medicine as "a model for the nation. . . this is people, not government, solving the problem." In fact, these clinics will never come close to "solving the problem," to serving the estimated 50 million people who currently are uninsured. If all the nation's retired physicians were suddenly to come forward and start practicing full-time for free, we would still be far from a solution. Any illusions to the contrary will only slow our progress toward finding a viable way out of our current dilemma.

More accurately, efforts like Samaritan House and Volunteers in Medicine are, in the words of one volunteer doctor, "an answer, not a solution." However, in the process of stepping into the breach that currently exists, in *answering* as opposed to *solving*, the clinics have much to say about what a solution might entail. In part, they are a reminder that regardless of the ultimate arrangement, there is probably a valuable role that physicians and other medical professionals in the third age can play in extending the reach of a reformed health care system—should we ever muster the good sense to put one in place.

However, the greatest significance of the medicine being practiced in places like Samaritan House is not primarily about numbers—that is, about finding more trained human bodies to provide medical care to those lacking it. Rather, it can be located in the kind of medicine that is being practiced. These clinics offer a compelling example of what health care can be—both for the recipients of care and those providing it. Indeed, if we ever do manage to reform the health care system, the architects of such an effort should be required to spend a month at places like the Samaritan House clinic.

A Matter of Time

It is ironic that Sidney Wolfe, director of the Public Citizen's health care advocacy group, dismissed the Volunteers in Medicine Clinic when it was first proposed as an example of second-class health care for the poor. Wolfe is right to be concerned about the development of a two-tiered system. However, if any gap in care is illustrated by places like Samaritan House and Volunteers in Medicine, that gap highlights the inferiority of most medicine being practiced outside the clinics.

In part, this discrepancy exists because the doctors volunteering in San Mateo, Stuart, and Hilton Head are at the top of their field (who else could afford to live in these places?). However, the more significant reason is that these clinics have become magnets for doctors who simply love medicine, who want to keep practicing because, in Thea Glass's words, "it is the most interesting thing I've ever done." Over and over again in my visits to the clinics I heard about—and witnessed—a love affair with medicine that one rarely encounters among practicing doctors today.

Indeed, most of the doctors I interviewed had been driven out of medicine by the changes that had occurred since they began practicing. Years ago, when they first hung out their shingle, relationships with patients were an important part of their work—some even performed housecalls! They could practice medicine, in the words of one Samaritan House volunteer, "in three dimensions." They abandoned their practices not because they no longer were interested in helping or healing but because they'd had it with the harried, profit-driven world of medicine today.

Because the doctors receive no pay at the clinics, the result is a self-selected group of volunteers who—in a phrase that I heard so many times from so many people in the three clinics that it began sounding like a mantra—"all want to be there." They derive so much intrinsic pleasure from practicing that they find the recognition they get for this work amusing. As Thea comments, "The thing about the clinic is you get a lot of encouragement and accolades for something that you just love to do."

But the clinics deserve more credit than simply being magnets for caring and committed doctors. Bill Schwartz and his social entrepreneurial compatriots in Stuart, Hilton Head, and elsewhere have cleared away all the debris interfering with the ability of the doctors to practice the best medicine possible. In the words of Scott Smyth, an orthopedic surgeon practicing at Samaritan House, these pioneers have eliminated the "anvil" of corporate medicine, systematically removing all the encumbrances "to practicing medicine the way it should be practiced." Doctors can use their judgment about ordering lab tests, consultations, prescriptions, or special examinations without having to seek permission. They no longer have to wade through insurance forms or handle other paperwork, other than to write up their evaluations of patients and progress notes. Malpractice insurance is taken care of for them by the clinic. In short, Schwartz and his compatriots have created something akin to a medical utopia—for doctors and for patients. As a result, the doctors need only show up and concentrate on seeing patients.

At the core of the clinics' strategy for both transforming the quality of care and bringing back the joy of practicing medicine is the same notion that Bernie Nash talked about in the context of the Foster Grandparent Program, that of *time*—and the retirees bring this asset in abundance, especially compared with their previous schedules. At the Samaritan House clinic, for example, the doctors are able to spend up to two hours performing a history and initial examination of a new patient. In his previous practice, Schwartz recalls, that examination was squeezed into ten or fifteen minutes, at best. There was no time for delving deeply into a case, much less building a relationship of trust with the patient, seeing that individual as a whole person, or getting to the bottom of things.

In fact, in reaction to his experience with the encroachments of efficiency on medicine, Schwartz has made something of a virtue of "inefficiency" at the clinic—principally through scheduling more doctors than are needed to see the number of patients scheduled. Schwartz takes seriously the need to see a large number of patients in a community where they have few other options, but he is also aware of the downside of efficiency and productivity when it is taken too far—how it distorts the nature of medical care and undermines the fulfillment in practicing medicine.

The end result is that doctors feel they can take the time necessary to go beyond treating the immediate complaint in an effort to get to root causes. For example, a man in his late twenties recently came to Samaritan House complaining of muscle spasms in his upper back and neck. Rather than simply prescribing muscle relaxants or physical therapy, then rushing off to the next case, the doctor at the clinic was able to dig deeper, eventually discovering that the man and his wife were living in their car. At night, his head would fall back over the seat as he slept. And because of the clinic's connection to the Samaritan House community organization, the physician was able not only to treat the symptoms but also to help find a place for the couple to sleep.

The clinic environment also provides opportunities for the volunteers to connect with each other, free from the concern that sociability is the enemy of productivity and profits. This interaction contributes to the strong sense of community that one feels at Samaritan House (as well as at Volunteers in Medicine).

When I last visited the Samaritan House clinic, two retired dentists were sitting in the clinic lounge in easy chairs, having just completed their volunteer hours. They were drinking coffee and telling jokes (according to the other doctors, the same jokes they always tell!). Over the course of fifteen minutes, several other doctors and nurses wandered in and out of the room, exchanging pleasantries.

I asked Bill Schwartz if sometimes the doctors, dentists, and other volunteers take advantage of the lounge, spending too much time socializing when they should be treating patients. He told me that hasn't been a problem—that the people who come to the clinic have a well-developed work ethic. However, he added that it was his hope that more retired doctors, nurses, and dentists would come to the clinic lounge simply to hang out—as if the clinic was a community center for retired doctors. "Maybe some of them will choose to become involved after they see all the good things happening around them."

Bill Schwartz told me a story that underscores how important simply having a place to go, a role in life, can be. During one of our interviews, I asked him to tell me about his biggest disappointments during his involvement with the clinic. He explained that several years ago a retired eye doctor he knew wanted to volunteer in the clinic. Schwartz was eager to provide eye examinations at Samaritan House but lacked the necessary equipment. This was especially frustrating, because he knew the man to be a superb practitioner—although he had experienced some psychological problems over the years, these difficulties had not affected his professional performance. Eventually, it seemed that Schwartz was about to secure donated optical examination equipment, but the contribution fell through. Shortly afterward, the retired doctor committed suicide.

For Schwartz, the suicide was devastating. He is still haunted by the sense that had he been able to get the eye clinic up and running, his friend would have thrown himself into the work, found a new sense of community, and strengthened his will to live.

One especially humane aspect of the clinic that Schwartz has been able to implement is a strong commitment to finding a place for the volunteer doctors who, for reason of advanced age or failing health, are unable to perform clinical work to required levels. He is now developing a lecture series that will enable these individuals to talk with both volunteers and medical students about their areas of expertise.

"People Get Better"

The middle-class, mostly white, retired doctors, nurses, and dentists who volunteer at the Samaritan House are by no means the entire community. The clinic is very much a multiethnic environment. The medical and administrative directors who run the clinic on a day-to-day basis are Latino women. Furthermore, there are many Latino translators. It is also a multiage community—thanks to not only the two younger paid physicians but also the volunteers who are middle-aged doctors and nurses (about 10 percent), the translators, the patients, and two groups of students. In the first group of students are medical office assistants in training from the College of San Mateo. They are studying primarily with the retired nurses, who tutor them in both the technical and interpersonal aspects of their job.

In the other group are medical students from UCSF who rotate through the clinic in their third and fourth years as part of their clerkships in community medicine or internal medicine. They are joined by first-year residents from UCSF.

The students and residents rotating through Samaritan House see patients, perform workups, and receive grades from the retired physicians, who are still affiliated with UCSF and Stanford Medical School. This is a favorite rotation for the medical students, in large measure because they are lavished with one-on-one attention from the older doctors at the clinic. Just as these retired physicians have more time for the patients, so too do they have more time for the medical students. In fact, a significant proportion of the students end up coming back on their own time to volunteer in the clinic after finishing their rotation.

Dr. Richard Aulwurm, himself a graduate of UCSF and a volunteer who spends five days a week at the clinic, believes that Samaritan House is the one place where the medical students learn "the art of medicine." They learn "that there is a person behind the ailment, that compassion is essential, that a superior attitude is no help."

Anand Mehta, a twenty-four-year-old in his third year at UCSF, agrees with Aulwurm. "I was really pleased to see all these doctors over sixty-five," he comments. "Most of the older patients I normally see are sick, cranky, and tired." Mehta talks about learning "the art of medicine" from Scott Smyth, a seventy-year-old orthopedic surgeon. "Most of the people I encounter in medicine are young, ambitious, trying to get somewhere, and they want to show you how much medicine they know. Everybody's running around. Unless the [patient's] condition is exciting or especially interesting, you're supposed to get rid of it fast."

Mehta describes Dr. Smyth as "someone who has reached his prime" and who "is not trying to prove anything. . . . He doesn't care about what's the fastest or the cheapest way to do things." Mehta explains, "From the very beginning, he taught me the patient is first. When you walk into an examining room, always ask the patient about themselves, about their life."

Mehta has also learned a great deal about what it means to be a doctor from Scott Smyth: "He told me, once a doctor, you're always a doctor—it's like being a parent. He doesn't need to be doing this, he doesn't need the money. It's not an obligation. He just truly enjoys seeing patients. He says, 'I've done this too long to stop.' And to see someone his age so interested in learning—always wanting to know about new techniques, new prosthetics—it's phenomenal. He has more energy than I do!"

Bill Schwartz describes Smyth as a "master teacher." For forty years Smyth practiced in San Mateo, taught at UCSF, and played an active role in civic affairs. For two of those years he was president of the county medical society. Now in retirement he divides his time among serving at the Samaritan House Clinic, playing tennis three times a week, serving on the County Aging Commission, and tending his garden. And he continues to teach part-time at UCSF.

Upon meeting Scott Smyth, one is struck immediately by two things: his physical presence (he is broad-shouldered and towering) and his great

warmth and openness. And when the topic of conversation turns to medicine, Smyth's great love of the profession is evident. He, like so many of the
other physicians I talked to, was driven out of active practice by the paperwork, insurance companies, and fear of malpractice suits. Smyth also despairs
about the degree to which medicine has become a business. When he first
decided to become a doctor, his father, who was chancellor of the UCSF
Medical School, gave him a speech about not going into medicine to make
money. "He told me, 'If you want to make money, become a salesman or a
lawyer.'" Rather, Scott Smyth's dream of medicine was to serve, and despite
his being a surgeon, it was also to care for patients—to build relationships
with them.

One of his great joys now is having sufficient time to build these bonds
not only with patients but also with the medical students: "I've always believed that the best way to teach was one-on-one, and I'm able to do that in
the clinic—to spend the time." But despite his affinity for teaching, Smyth is
concerned about the future of these medical students and of the profession
they are entering. I asked him whether he thinks about their future opportunities. "You know, I try not to think about it. If I did, I think I might cry."

This uneasiness, in fact, was exactly what Dr. Adriana Valdovinos-Campa
was feeling before coming to the clinic. A vital young woman, fluent in English
and Spanish, she is also an attending physician at UCSF, where her husband is
an assistant professor of medicine. "When I was going through my residency, I
wondered whether I had made a mistake. I felt so burned out. All the joy of
practicing had been stripped away," she recalled. Valdovinos-Campa went to
medical school for idealistic reasons, to help people, she explained, as well as to
have a career with some professional autonomy. What she found in the world
of contemporary medicine was quite different. "But when I came here, I was reminded about why I wanted to be a doctor, about what medicine could be. At
the clinic, you have enough time to do things the right way and enough room
to use your judgment." The clinic has a budget and certain constraints, of
course. "But the decisions are yours. And people get better. They come back.
Anytime you come here, you see flowers. Patients bring them. They bring
food. They care about the doctors as much as the doctors care about them. This
is the most cohesive and compassionate practice I've ever seen."

A New Stage

According to Bill Schwartz, he and the others at Samaritan House are doing nothing new. They're "reinventing the wheel," essentially reproducing the kind of clinic experience that was such an important part of their introduction to medicine. These clinics do appear, in certain respects, to be throwbacks to the way medicine was once practiced in its best and most noble form.

Yet at the same time, these retirees provide a glimpse of the future, of new roles for older Americans that defy the stereotypes of not only endless leisure and total disengagement but also the tame kinds of envelope-stuffing assignments so often associated with "senior volunteerism." These doctors are doing real work and making a significant difference in the lives of many people in their community.

In the process, however, the Samaritan House retirees and their peers elsewhere are threatening to do something further: to transform the profession of medicine. They are carving out something akin to an emeritus phase in doctoring, one that has two key aspects. The first is a return to practicing medicine for its intrinsic, essential value, to be a healer—unencumbered by either the business and bureaucracy of medicine or the status pressures that are so much a part of the profession.

Second, they are actively involved in passing on this vision to the next generation of physicians, in this case the medical students and residents from UCSF. They become intensive mentors for these individuals in imparting not just the technical skills of medicine but also something more important than technique—a quality hard to underestimate in a field where all too often we have traded wisdom for narrow expertise. They are instructors in the soul and spirit of the profession and role models of doctors who have returned to what is most important about medicine.

In taking on this role, the physicians I interviewed made me realize how false was my dichotomy between older adults involved in programs like Foster Grandparents and retirees participating in high-skill initiatives like the clinic. At every turn at Samaritan House (or for that matter, among the Stuart Volunteers in Medicine or at the Hilton Head clinic) are relationships: between patient and doctor certainly, but also between doctors and medical students, among physicians, and between the paid staff and the volunteers, including the greeters like Jeanette Mayer.

To be sure, nobody is likely to mistake Bill Schwartz and Scott Smyth for

Aggie Bennett and Louise Casey—the height difference alone is a guarantee of that—but for all their differences in education and medical skill, the similarities in what the doctors in San Mateo and the women in Portland are doing outweigh the divergent tasks they perform. In the process they are beginning to articulate a fresh purpose and definition of success for the third stage of life. Just as the social entrepreneurs chronicled in the next section are building the institutions we will need for a new generation of retirees, these role models are showing how the third age can truly be a compelling and distinctive stage of life.

The New Social Entrepreneurs

The stories about Samaritan House Clinic and Volunteers in Medicine bring with them considerable irony. Given the role physicians have played historically in defining aging as an "incurable disease" and older people as a drain on society (one need only recall William Osler's comments in "The Fixed Period"), it is striking to watch a group of doctors challenging so fundamentally—with their own lives and actions—the notion that older Americans are washed up. The irony is all the more pointed when we consider contemporary debate about the aging of America, so much of it focused on the so-called failure of success—on the dramatic increase in health care costs resulting from improvements in longevity. The clinics offer a radically different vision in revealing physicians who, while providing free health care for younger generations, are contributing to their own well-being in the process (many of the retired doctors invoke the phrase "use it or lose it" to refer both to their medical skills and to their mental and physical health).

These clinics also exemplify a new and no less radical phenomenon: the social entrepreneurism of individuals, many in later life themselves, who are fashioning new and necessary institutions that reinvent retirement by reimagining society. In a recent article entitled "The Give-Back Years," *Time* magazine profiles a half dozen of these institution builders, including retired University of Nebraska football coach Tom Osborne (creator of a mentoring program called TeamMates); a trio of retirees in Kennett Square, Pennsylvania (founders of an after-school program staffed by older adults and focused on drama, computer science, and dance); and an eighty-four-year-old former associate justice of the California Court of Appeals, Leonard Friedman (who formed ACE—Aide Corps for the Elderly—recruiting and placing older and younger volunteers in thirty-five agencies that serve frail seniors). These individuals are but a tiny fraction of the hundreds of new entrepreneurs and entrepreneurial start-ups who have appeared in recent years.

These new social entrepreneurs are reminiscent of Del Webb in creating—as the master developer/marketer did—"something out of nothing." At root, they are closing the gap that exists between the changing nature of the older population and the institutions that exist to enable these individuals to continue contributing to society. In short, they are attempting to replace the institutions that hold us back with creative new ones that contain the potential to carry us forward. So much of the fate of America's aging rests with these entrepreneurs and their inventions—the institutional inheritance, to borrow historian Peter Laslett's phrase—that we will bequeath to the next generation of third agers.

And their timing is right, occurring as it does on the brink of the baby boomers' retirement. As even Pete Peterson argues in his most recent exercise in alarmism, *Gray Dawn*: "It is high time to establish institutions that can help us manage the transition to a much older world."

In fact, today's institution-building ferment aimed at enabling older Americans to play an expanded role in civil society marks the first real surge of innovation in this area since the days of Foster Grandparents. Unlike in the earlier era, however, the primary impetus for the current round of institutional invention is neither the government nor professionals in the field of aging (although public policy in a variety of forms does continue to play a key role). The new inventions also tend to be far more sophisticated than their predecessors—which themselves have evolved considerably over the years. If programs like Foster Grandparents were the "first rough drafts" of the kinds of institutions we will need, then new efforts like Samaritan House and Volunteers in Medicine can be seen as significant revisions—if not yet final products.

For the most part, the new entrepreneurs are individuals—like Jack McConnell—who have made their mark in other fields of endeavor. Now they are adapting previous experience from the for-profit world or from academia to new uses. McConnell's odyssey is illustrative. His previous career was not primarily as a physician or even as an inventor. McConnell was an expert in taking promising ideas in the field of health care—such as the MRI—and turning them into products that could be used widely and affordably for practical purposes. What he has achieved with the Volunteers in Medicine clinic is, in key respects, an extension of this expertise—but with the new goal of meeting urgent social needs rather than serving Johnson and Johnson's shareholders.

Although McConnell's story is becoming better known (he is the subject of a flattering chapter in *Courage Is Contagious* by Republican congressman John Kasich), for the most part, the great entrepreneurial upsurge aimed at harnessing the time, talent, and experience of older Americans has been overlooked. This is striking considering how much attention has been accorded to young social entrepreneurs such as Wendy Kopp, the founder of Teach for America program, and Alan Khazei and Michael Brown, who created City Year.

In fact, there is a parallel movement at the other end of the age spectrum. Three representatives of this new surge in creative activity are Hope Meadows, Troops to Teachers, and Princeton Project 55. Like Samaritan House and Volunteers in Medicine, these institutions suggest the myriad possibilities that exist to create new roles for retirees that fully use their skills, address pressing social needs, and provide genuine fulfillment in the process.

Hope Meadows

You could be in Sun City—the original Sun City. The one with single-story utilitarian houses aligned in close proximity, the one that looks part suburban subdivision, part golf course, and part military base (after all, Del Webb cut his teeth building military bases throughout the West). There was once a guard gate as in Sun City, and everything appears consistently manicured in the manner Webb insisted upon. And there are plenty of older adults living in Hope Meadows, individuals who have consciously relocated in retirement to be part of this community. Even the Illinois climate is no tipoff—Sun City recently opened its first northern retirement community outside Chicago.

However, the similarities between Sun City and Hope Meadows extend no further. The older adults who have picked up and moved to this former-military-base-turned-foster-care-village have not come to escape the younger generation and school taxes but to become part of a new community where the much overworked slogan "It takes a village to raise a child" is a central operating principle of day-to-day life.

Hope Meadows was created by a child development scholar and social entrepreneur, Brenda Eheart of the University of Illinois. Eheart grew up in a small town in upstate New York in the 1940s and 1950s and remembers vividly the neighborliness and nurturance of that community. The immediate impetus for creating the project was thinking about her own two children, one adopted and one biological, and the kind of environment she would want for them if she and her husband died suddenly.

The idea for the foster care village came also from decades of research. She knew that the population of foster care children had reached 400,000 by the early 1990s—when she was first considering the idea—an increase of 60 percent in ten years. Today the number of foster care children is 25 percent larger still, over a half million. In Illinois, where Eheart is based, 1,000 new children enter the state's foster care system each month. (These numbers are even more foreboding when one also considers that 80 percent of the inmates in the Illinois prison system had once been in foster care.) And the number of foster parents is dropping precipitously, down 25 percent nationally during the same period. According to Eheart, "I had been complaining about the system for fifteen years, about how the system was broken. In the meantime the numbers were getting worse and worse. I knew I had to do something about it."

The rest of her story is a testimony to common sense and persistence. Eheart's research on foster families showed that one of the principal reasons placements failed—even placements that on the surface made great sense—is that families lacked sufficient support. The addition of a difficult foster child simply overwhelmed them. So, Eheart reasoned, why not put families together and let them help each other.

In her conception, Hope Meadows would build upon this insight to provide an alternative to foster care, focusing on the adoption of children who had "no place to call home"—in other words, serving as a place of last resort for children under the age of nine who had been abused, abandoned, and appeared headed for deep trouble. It would also pay foster parents a stipend of $18,000 a year to stay home with these children (usually two or three young people per household) and provide families free housing. Overall, the entire community would center on the needs of the children who live there, not only the adopted and foster children but the biological children of the foster parents as well. And because half the children at Hope Meadows are biological children, it is difficult for outsiders and many insiders to know who is biological and who is adopted.

However, from nearly the outset, an essential ingredient in the Hope Meadows community—which consists of thirteen families and thirty-five children—has been the adults age fifty-six and older who receive reduced rent in spacious apartments in return for living within the community and volunteering to help the young people. These individuals function as "honorary grandparents" for the children. Officially, they are asked to do six hours of volunteer work per week, tutoring children, serving as crossing guards, and acting as crafts instructors.

Although not unimportant, these activities are mostly a pretext for the informal contact these older adults have with the children—who are their neighbors—as well as the foster families. The "grandparents" provide advice, support, and nurturing for the parents and the children. They also spend time at the Intergenerational Center, which functions as the main community center for the development and its social hub. The center contains a library, computer room, playrooms, and an open area. The older adults come there to provide homework assistance or simply to have fun playing with the children. Hope Meadows also helps foster a sense of community among the older adults who live in the development, providing the opportunity to be among a group of agemates who share a great love for children.

Throughout Hope Meadows, one encounters the older residents engaged in the activities of daily life, much as occurred in the town where Brenda Eheart was raised. As one observer notes: "They're at the school crosswalk, ushering kids across the street, or they're. . . trimming hedges and mowing the lawn. At night they're baby-sitting. During the day they're repairing kids' bicycles in a carport or tossing a ball with a child on the sidewalk."

Eheart got the idea for involving older adults from a lecture she heard Maggie Kuhn give in Philadelphia in 1989. The ninety-year-old Kuhn was touring the country to stump for intergenerational housing, having lived that way herself for several decades. Kuhn's idea was that by taking in younger boarders—in particular college students—older adults (often house-rich but income-poor) could help pay their property taxes while alleviating the housing difficulties faced by many young people. In the process, they would set up the context for an ongoing exchange between the generations .

Inspired by Kuhn, Eheart set out on the same journey as Bill Schwartz and Jack McConnell, one that also led quickly to the political realm. In this case, the politician was Democratic Senator Paul Simon of Illinois; Eheart approached him in 1990, winning his strong support. The next big turning point came in January 1992, when Eheart began acquiring housing on the Chanute Air Force Base in Rantoul. The base, which was being closed, provided a good environment for the project, in part because the military had designed the residential areas of Chanute to help families from disparate areas form a new community.

By the summer of 1993, Eheart convinced the Illinois state legislature to appropriate $1 million to purchase the rest of the housing and renovate the facilities, as well as $500,000 a year to cover operating costs. Today the state pays for 75 percent of these costs, while the rent from the older adults supports another 20 percent of the budget. Private contributions account for the balance. The first Hope Meadows families moved in at the beginning of May 1994, and the Intergenerational Center opened a year later. Now, just five years after the doors of Hope Meadows opened, it is embarking on an effort to expand the program to new locations around the country, beginning with Cleveland.

Troops to Teachers

J. H. "Jack" Hexter was mandatorily retired as the Charles Stille Professor of History at Yale in 1978. Unwilling to halt his academic career prematurely, he accepted an endowed chair at Washington University in St. Louis and in his late sixties began work on an eighteen-volume history of modern individual freedom spanning the late sixteenth century to the present. He and a fellow historian completed the first two volumes before Hexter decided to retire from academia for good at the age of eighty.

However, Hexter still had, to invoke Robert Frost, "miles to go." Impressed with the American troops during the Gulf War, who maintained their demeanor despite dreary and spartan lives in the desert for months, Hexter wondered what would become of them when they returned, knowing the Army alone was cutting its troop levels from nearly 800,000 to less than 400,000 over the coming three years.

Many of these individuals had spent their entire careers in the armed forces and would soon be retiring in their forties. They were an even more extreme version of the downsizing phenomenon leaving so many Americans in their midfifties to ponder how to spend the remaining third of their lives. Most of these retired soldiers would have not a third but a full half of their lives left to live. Furthermore, with a military pension to take with them, they would have a measure of financial freedom in choosing their next move.

Hexter also knew that many of these soldiers were sergeants—individuals expert at taking adrift and alienated young people and teaching them self-discipline and self-respect. He reasoned that they might possess some of the most needed skills for inner-city schools, which were desperately short of teachers, in particular male teachers and teachers who could relate to young people from tough urban neighborhoods. Furthermore, Hexter knew that the teacher-shortage numbers were as staggering as those for troop reductions.

Overall, the nation will need 2 million new teachers over the next ten years, with the largest gaps predicted in inner-city schools. Estimates of the shortfall range as high as 200,000, and the teacher shortage is expected to be particularly acute in California and Texas.

Efforts to find young, inexperienced recruits and quickly train them for classroom duty have sprung up across the country, with predictable results. As David Haselkorn, president of Recruiting New Teachers and a leading expert on the subject, states: "It's not healthy—and it's not sufficient or realistic—to just replace the next generation of teachers with only twenty-three or twenty-four-year-olds from the suburbs who don't have much life experience."

In this context, Hexter was convinced that the life experience of sergeants and other noncommissioned officers—many of them African American and Latino and from inner-city neighborhoods themselves—was just what was needed in many schools. He developed the idea into a paper that he delivered at an American Philosophical Society meeting. He also presented the idea to the chancellor of Washington University, William Danforth, who urged him to "carry it as far as you can." Danforth suggested that Hexter see his brother John, who happened to be the senior U.S. senator from Missouri.

By all accounts, Hexter—like Brenda Eheart, Bill Schwartz, and Jack McConnell—was unwaveringly persistent. According to the *Los Angeles Times,* "Hexter's idea became Hexter's obsession." However, he did not have to badger John Danforth into pursuing the idea; the senator was an instant convert, and he put one of his top aides on Hexter's proposal with the charge to make it happen.

To their great surprise, Danforth's staff discovered that a bill had been passed in 1992 with this purpose in mind. The proposal was called Troops to Teachers and was designed to help men and women coming out of the service become certified as teachers. However, no funds had been appropriated for the program. Furthermore, the legislation effectively shut out noncommissioned officers by restricting assistance to college graduates.

Senator Danforth championed an amendment that enabled retired soldiers to receive up to $5,000 in assistance to gain teacher certification, so long as they returned to school and earned their college degrees. In addition, the amended version provided an incentive of $50,000 over five years for low-income schools that hired these ex-soldiers, to help offset their salaries.

Colin Powell, then chairman of the Joint Chiefs of Staff, rallied behind the bill and it passed the Senate in twenty minutes. The result was a $65 million appropriation in the defense budget.

By August 1998, four years after Hexter's program was launched (and two years after he died at age eighty-six), more than 3,000 retired veterans had become teachers through the initiative. There were placements in forty-eight states, although nearly a third ended up in Texas, California, Florida, and Virginia. In fact, the success of the program prompted no less an observer than Richard Lyman, former president of Stanford University and of the Rockefeller Foundation, to comment in the *New York Times*: "I have never seen a more dramatic example of what a single individual can accomplish, despite handicaps, armed only with a good idea and boundless determination to see it put into effect."

A study of Troops to Teachers by the National Center for Education Information found that 91 percent of the retired soldiers were highly satisfied with their new jobs, while a companion evaluation of nearly 400 school principals using these second-career teachers found that 75 percent ranked the veterans "among the best," "well above average," or "above average." Best of all, most were from underrepresented backgrounds. Overall, 90 percent of the Troops to Teachers participants are male in a teaching field that is 74 percent female, and about a third are from minority groups, compared with 10 percent nationally. A full 40 percent of the first class of ex-military teachers were African American men. And retention rates, at 85 percent, are five times higher than the norm for urban teachers.

Certainly, Troops to Teachers is not the only program working with retirees to train them to become teachers. AT&T has funded an Urban Teacher Corps in a variety of cities, and many of its recruits are older adults. Polaroid also created a program concentrating on retired scientists and technical staff to retrain them for urban teaching. Another significant effort is the United Negro College Fund's "Second-Chance Teachers Program," underwritten by the Ford Foundation and involving a coalition of historically black colleges in the South.

Troops to Teachers, however, is undoubtedly the largest such effort, and it was also the partial inspiration for another federally funded initiative—the $5 million Scientists to Teachers program aimed at retraining laid-off scientists and engineers from the defense industry to teach math and science in inner-city Los Angeles high schools. Run by the National Research Council, the program is in part an attempt to alleviate the desperate shortage of math and science teachers in that school district. Bruce Alberts, chair of the National Research Council, sees another agenda as well: "This is a lot more important than just producing some more teachers," he explains. "We hope the Scientists to Teachers will become leaders and advocates for science and math reform."

Princeton Project '55

The examples of Volunteers in Medicine, Hope Meadows, and Troops to Teachers are just a few of the hundreds of new entrepreneurial ventures aimed at reinventing retirement in a way that blends personal fulfillment with social renewal. As Ralph Nader commented in a piece written for the 1995 White House Conference on Aging, "A generational stirring is rumbling among those who grew up in the 50s when America was number one in just about everything and who now find their land in deep trouble on almost all domestic fronts. With their children raised and some financial security achieved, more of them are looking outward to help solve the country's problems."

Nader should know, having helped to create another new institution to give shape to that stirring and turn it into tangible action. In April 1989, seventy-five members of Nader's Princeton class of 1955 met in Washington, D.C., to hear their rabble-rousing classmate keynote a weekend dedicated to the topic of public policy.

Although Nader worried that his classmates would roll their eyes and think "there goes Ralph again!" he used the speech, essentially, to tell them that the time had come to give back to society. One of the members of the audience, Stephen McNamara, paraphrases Nader's challenge: "Hey, guys, you're successful. You've made money, sent your kids through school, done well in the rat race. . . . Now what? Is it really good enough, for you or for the world, to spend the rest of your lives lowering your golf scores?" Nader urged them to leave a legacy they could be proud of, contending that the best way to commemorate their thirtieth anniversary as a class would be to found a center at Princeton aimed at guiding more undergraduates into public interest careers.

The classmates were polite as Nader made his appeal. When he finished, however, instead of rolling their eyes, they leaped to their feet and gave him a standing ovation. One after another they offered personal testimonials of support. Finally, Charles Bray, the president of the Johnson Foundation, issued a protest: "For once, Ralph, you are not being sufficiently ambitious." It wasn't enough to assist young people to be more public-spirited, the class members wanted to get involved more directly in the act themselves.

Within two months, Princeton Project '55 was incorporated as a nonprofit organization with 250 members, a board, a full-time staff, and a headquarters on Nassau Street in Princeton called the Center for Civic Leadership. The center oversees student internships aimed at protecting the environment, helping urban education, and supporting other public-spirited projects.

Just as important are the activism and involvement of the '55ers and their spouses. Through this work the group hopes to influence the causes of poverty and to effect "systemic change," which one member argues can get them much further than "Band-Aid" projects. Another, Peter Milano, adds: "We don't want to lend a hand in soup kitchens. We want to understand how people end up there in the first place and how to get them out."

Part of this strategy has focused on mentoring, an attempt to steer inner-city kids in promising directions before it is too late. In Trenton, New Jersey, '55er Gary Turndorf has started a mentoring program at the Cadwalader Elementary School in conjunction with the Big Brothers/Big Sisters program involving thirty-two volunteers who are connected with third graders. Another member of the Princeton class, Donald Brigham, is heavily involved in the Mentor Program of the Norwalk Public Schools in Connecticut.

Not content to confine their mentoring efforts to school children, the '55ers also have also created a Public Interest Program through which young Princeton University students and recent graduates can do internships in the public sector while being mentored by alums from the class of '55. In addition, the class is undertaking an effort to combat the reemergence of tuberculosis, and another to expand the "time dollars" notion, a barter system involving "service credits" in which older adults receive credits for performing service for others (such as driving them to doctors) and can cash in the credits for services they need (for example, minor home repairs or lawn mowing).

Lessons from the New Entrepreneurs

Princeton Project '55, Samaritan House, Volunteers in Medicine, Hope Meadows, and Troops to Teachers are potent reminders of the wealth of resources in the population entering the third age—from Ivy Leaguers to Army sergeants—and of the many new roles and institutional arrangements that are possible as we set out to forge a new kind of retirement. They also reveal the critical role social entrepreneurs—who are often, in Richard Lyman's words, "armed only with a good idea and boundless determination to see it put into effect"—can play in the process of reinventing the third stage of life. These entrepreneurs all display an ability to identify hidden opportunities, build wide support for them, raise substantial funds, cultivate policymakers, and negotiate the difficult transition from conception to implementation.

Several additional implications suggested by these entrepreneurial initiatives are also worth highlighting. One is the role universities can play in this process. Hope Meadows and Troops to Teachers demonstrate the resources present in university faculties and the prospect of transforming their bright ideas into new social ventures. Princeton Project '55 exhibits the potential role of alumni groups. The Princeton classes of '66 and '68 have followed suit and started projects of their own, while Yale and Notre Dame alums are adapting the project to their groups.

Meanwhile, Hope Meadows shows how housing can help bring together the generations in a natural, informal, mutually supportive context and serves as a concrete counterexample to the many ways residential segregation separates the generations and contributes to age-based conflict. It also exemplifies how the public sector (in this case, the state of Illinois) can play a key role in demonstrating an important idea.

Troops to Teachers is a reminder that in creating new public interest roles in retirement, we are not confined to unpaid volunteerism. As we will see in the next chapter, there is immense value in Peace Corps–like opportunities involving modest stipends aimed at helping cover the costs associated with an intensive commitment to service for a defined period of time. But as Troops to Teachers reveals, there is also considerable promise in salaried, market-rate second (or third or fourth. . .) careers doing work of pressing importance to society—particularly in areas where acute human resource shortages exist. The program also underscores the potential contribution residing in young "retirees."

However, despite so many impressive accomplishments, the new wave of entrepreneurial activity aimed at reinventing retirement brings with it the challenge of moving from a loose collection of inspiring pilot projects—and some small-scale attempts to reproduce their success—to a national movement enabling millions of older men and women to become involved in the kind of essential and fulfilling work occurring at places like the Samaritan House Medical Clinic and Hope Meadows. In other words, the challenge will be to achieve a scale that matters—and do so in time for the arrival of a vast generation of retirees looking to find new roles and new meaning in the third stage of life.

PART FOUR

THOMAS ROMA

Harold Allen, sixty-eight, grew up in South Philadelphia, one of a small number of African Americans in an overwhelmingly white neighborhood. After being denied a college scholarship rightly his, Allen was swept up in the civil rights movement and became a community organizer in the 1950s and 1960s, before settling down into a more conventional life as a city water department worker. After retiring from his career with the city, Allen moved into a new phase teaching prison inmates the skills they would need to find work after being released. Finally, in his early sixties, he retired for a second time, before joining the Experience Corps, a new initiative mobilizing neighborhood retirees to help transform struggling inner-city schools. Allen is part of a team of fifteen

Experience Corps members at the Taylor Elementary School in North Philadelphia.

·

I came up at a time when we thought we were going to change the world.
And you dedicated your whole life to that. But at a certain point, there was
just the feeling that nothing was happening anymore. It just stopped, everything stopped. But when I heard about Experience Corps, it was like a wake-
up call.

For thirty years I worked for the Philadelphia Water Department, in waste
water treatment. I got in at the right time, because in the 1960s they started
to become ecologically conscious, and the job was upgraded from semiskilled
labor. We received training and certification, learned lab processes. So it became a challenging job—and it gave you a feeling not just of making a living but
of doing something you could really feel good about.

When I retired from the city in 1988, I wasn't ready to retire. When I was
working, I was involved in decisionmaking There were certain standards to
meet. All of a sudden you don't have a specific time to get up. You read the paper . . . do crossword puzzles. People look at you and say things like, "I can't
wait until I can retire so I can sit around like you." But in reality, you wake up
in the morning and wonder why.

So I took a job with the state, working with guys who were in prison, helping them develop a trade so they could go back into society. I taught them
about waste water treatment. A number of guys got their license.

But it's sad to see life in prison. Most of the prisoners were not professional criminals. And none of the guys I was working with were any threat.
They made stupid mistakes. It taught me compassion. One of the guys I was
helping was scheduled for early release. Just before you're released they give
you a drug test. When they checked him he tested positive. I realized he did
not want to go out! He didn't have one visitor the entire time he was in
prison. Here's a guy who had no family to go home to. Prison inmates were
the closest thing to a family for him.

There are children, just like this, who have given up. They feel like there's no
point. They don't know how to overcome adversity. That's where we—the Experience Corps members—hope we can help. We may not be able to do

anything about this parent generation, but we can help these kids feel some sense of worth, some sense that "I am somebody."

For me, the work in Experience Corps has a special significance. It deals with the problems of the inner city. The family has been just about demolished in our neighborhoods, and the young people considered just about expendable. They're supposed to be our future—but they have literally been cast aside.

I was drawn to Experience Corps by the possibility of being able to effect some kind of positive change. Like most of the people here, I heard about it through AARP. But once I got into the program, and into the classroom, and began to relate to the children one-on-one, I began to really see the depth and scope of the issues—to become aware of the enormity of the task. So many of these kids have tremendous potential—their natural abilities are unquestionable—but they live in such negative environments that they have already given up on themselves.

One kid I was working with was put into a program for slow learners, which he is not. But the system cannot deal with a kid that doesn't read and refuses to try. He lives with a single mother. And when you meet that mother, when you're finally able to break through and communicate to her, you see how negative she feels. In a lot of cases, the parents take out their frustrations on the child—particularly if it's a young mother who feels her life has been terminated by this child.

And the children are so starved for attention that they just latch on. When you arrive, they run to you, and when you miss a day, right away, it's "why weren't you here?" They are practically writhing for attention.

In general, we are able to supply two main things the children are missing: that family tie they are not always getting at home, and the individual attention that's impossible for the teacher to give in the classroom of thirty—and in so many of the classes now, you have even more, because they're not putting the necessary money into the public schools. We also teach the children respect, especially respect for the teacher. I like to tell the children that when I was coming up, the two people I could not talk about were the teacher and the preacher.

I graduated from South Philadelphia High School in 1947, and at that time there were college scholarships from Coca-Cola. You had to have certain grades to get them. I remember one day, this guy sitting behind me asked if I applied for the scholarship. I told him I didn't get my grades. He said, "I got the scholarship, and your name was ahead of mine on the list." So I went to the counselor and I said, "I didn't get my grades back. I understand that I'm on the scholarship list." He said that he thought the only colored boy in the college curriculum was another student, and he didn't make the list. So I asked if I could put in for the scholarship then, and he said it was too late. I was about seventeen years old then.

But things have changed. In 1971 my son graduated from high school, and he went on to Yale. Besides, I don't regret what happened with me. By not going to college in 1947 I got involved in civil rights and the Progressive Party, and that changed my life. Henry Agard Wallace, Roosevelt's Vice President, was the head of it. It was an interracial party. One of the main speakers at the convention was Paul Robeson, and I was part of the honor guard when Paul Robeson came in to the convention here in Philadelphia.

Later I became an organizer in Easton, Pennsylvania, and here in Philadelphia. One time I was leading a picket in front of the Woolworth's in Point Breeze—we were trying to get them to hire blacks. The police picked me up and took me to the station house. In those days, if they arrested you they were supposed to take you to the jail downtown, but instead they took me to the basement of the police station. They put me in the middle of a circle of cops with nightsticks, and the captain yelled in my face, "Let me hear about all your rights! You were talking a lot about your rights in front of the store. Why don't you tell me about your rights now!" I was no dummy, I said, "Right now, I have no rights" [laughs].

When I was younger, I had no patience. I was intolerant. You had to be ready to stand up and change the world. Everybody else was a compromiser or a sellout. But by the time you reach a certain age, you realize real change requires time, work, and patience.

Patience does come with age. You realize that things don't happen as fast as you'd like. When you're young, things are supposed to happen tomorrow. It seems the more time you have, the less time you want to take—and the less time you have, the more time you are willing to take!

Now, you're less self-involved. You're able to look back in retrospect and understand better what happened. And death is something that you come to realize is part of life. It is not something you dread, think about. But you want to leave good memories of yourself, and you hope to leave something behind that's worthwhile.

With Experience Corps, there are good relationships among all of us. It's that same feeling you used to have with your co-workers on the job. That's nice. You can talk about the things you have in common as well as things you don't have in common. And all of us in Experience Corps, we get much more out of this program than we put into it. It just blows you away.

When we started out, it was just to be involved, to participate. It was something you wanted to join. Now there is an awareness that we can do more. I have started a program after school, the "A-Team." What triggered it was this one kid who was very quiet, always completed his assignments, never raised his hand. I remember when if a child knew the answer to something, he or she would be the first to raise a hand. But there was no challenge for this child, or for a number of the students. We have kids that are behind, but we also have kids that need to be moved up. So in the A-Team we give them more challenging things to do. While the other kids were beginning to learn the alphabet, and do sound and letter recognition, these kids were ready to do problem solving. So we started picking them up. We have about twelve kids who made the cut, who made the A-Team. And once the kids started coming, especially the guys, they really wanted to come everyday.

I try to reach out to every child. You get involved with them, and you find out about their personal lives and you're aware of what's really going on with them. Sometimes you're the only one that these children can talk to . . . tell what's going on in their lives. You need to ensure them that they are all right. Children think that they are to blame in a lot of their situations. They need a lot of praise and love and recognition.

We also need to take the steps necessary to bring about more systemic kinds of change. The school system here has no money. Kids don't even have books. If more people were active and created a new awareness of these conditions, there would be a change. There has to be a rebirth of involvement. This is basically a struggle for survival.

In the meantime, we'll take the one-to-one approach—to help one child, or a small group of children, at a time. Hopefully, they will remember this group that got together to help them. These kids are the potential organizers for change in the future.

CHAPTER 5

Leaving a Legacy

The great use of life is to spend it for something that will outlast us.

·

William James

In 1988, after returning from my encounter with Nick Spaneas and the other Work Connection mentors, I sat down and wrote a thin volume suggesting that older adults had special gifts that made them particularly well-suited for connecting with young people—even tough kids like those targeted by The Work Connection. However, these conclusions did not propel me toward a new career dedicated to reengaging the time, talent, and experience of the older population on behalf of society. Rather, I began a decade-long inquiry into the potential of mentoring and the question of how we could create more relationships with caring adults for kids who needed them—regardless of the age of the mentors themselves.

What did I learn from all those years studying the value of mentors? In some ways, not much that Nick and his colleagues at The Work Connection hadn't already told me a decade earlier: that kids need adults who care about them (in Nick's words, "adults with patience, adults who feel about them," not "bluffers"), and that when kids have such adults, these young people are not only happier but tend to be less vulnerable to the pitfalls of growing up today, including drug abuse, alcoholism, smoking, violence, and truancy.

All of these common-sense insights were confirmed by a major national study of the Big Brother/Big Sister program that I helped develop, and by hundreds of interviews I conducted directly during the late 1980s and early 1990s. In the end, we knew not only that mentoring mattered but also that the mentors who succeeded were the ones who put in the time and who were there for young people consistently. They showed up, and it paid off.

And although this news was enormously encouraging in some ways—we now knew from careful social science research that you don't need to be a charismatic superhero to reach young people on the edge—it also underscored that most mentoring efforts were running into a basic paradox. Those middle-aged volunteers being targeted for programs like Big Brothers/Big Sisters were the same ones battling the "time bind," working long hours and struggling to spend enough time with their own children. How many people had two or three days a month to dedicate, one-on-one, to somebody else's kid? No wonder there were nearly half as many children on the Big Brother/Big Sister waiting list as were being mentored through the program.

Yet programs such as Big Brothers/Big Sisters—like most nonprofit organizations—had historically overlooked the segment of the population where the untapped time in our society resides: older Americans. This disconnection was on dramatic display when I served as a delegate to the President's Summit on America's Future, the 1997 rally in Philadelphia intended to produce caring adult mentors for two million additional children by the year 2000. It was exasperating to sit in the audience and watch a procession of retired U.S. presidents well into their third age, led by the sixty-something retired general Colin Powell—who that same week told *Time* that he was delighted to have finally reached the stage in life when he had the time to give back to society—exhort the middle generation to spend more time on behalf of poor children. Why weren't these individuals turning to their peers, calling them to action and reminding them that they were the one group in society with the time and numbers to actually approximate the summit's ambitious goals?

The Father of Invention

In fact, by the time I attended the summit in Philadelphia, my foray into the world of mentoring had already ended up steering me right back to The Work Connection and its lesson that there are extraordinary untapped human resources present in the older population, even in seemingly ordinary people like Nick and his fellow mentors.

The specific impetus for this return came in the same way the original opportunity to study The Work Connection had come: without much warning and from over the transom. I was asked by AARP—which had been asked by a special Commission of the Carnegie Corporation of New York—to help write a background paper for a report the Carnegie Commission was preparing called *A Matter of Time*. The Carnegie Commission was not focused on the untapped free time of older adults but rather on the unsupervised after-school hours for children and youth. My assignment (added at the eleventh hour by the soon-to-retire Carnegie president, David Hamburg) was to analyze what the older generation might do to help improve the circumstances of young people when they were not in school. It was during this writing project that I first met Aggie and Louise and John Curtis and began developing an appreciation for the Foster Grandparent Program as the country's one existing infrastructure for enlisting a segment of the older population on behalf of children.

Six months later, having sent off my piece to be part of the larger Carnegie report, I headed to Washington to participate in the event heralding the release of *A Matter of Time*. Despite a midwinter storm in D.C., I was intent on making it to the conference—in part because the keynote speaker was scheduled to be Carnegie's former president, John W. Gardner.

I had long admired Gardner for his contributions to American civic life. In 1964, at age fifty-two, he was awarded the Presidential Medal of Freedom, the highest civilian honor an American can receive—largely in recognition of his work at Carnegie. For most people, that would constitute an appropriate culmination to a distinguished career. But Gardner was just getting started. He would go on to serve as Secretary of Health, Education, and Welfare at the height of Lyndon Johnson's Great Society, to found and lead Common Cause and Independent Sector, and to initiate a host of other important new institutions. In 1965 the *New York Times* called Gardner "the most powerful behind-the-scenes figure in American education today"; twenty-five years later the paper simply labeled him the "father of invention," acknowledging his entrepreneurial success in so many areas of civic endeavor.

His address to the Washington gathering was going to be about "Reinventing Community," and I was particularly interested in his perspective on this subject. I had written about mentoring as a vehicle for building community and strengthening the social fabric, even quoting Gardner in the final paragraphs. So as waiters started clearing the lunch plates and David Hamburg began his introduction of Gardner, I could feel my anticipation build.

Eighty years old at the time, Gardner moved with ease to the podium, slowly arranging his speech as the crowd of several hundred waited silently. A full minute passed. Then, he began speaking, deliberately at first, each word measured. I didn't catch the first few sentences. I was mostly struck by the man's voice, resonant but quavering ("the voice of God," a usually staid social policy professor at my table quipped). We were all mesmerized, and the conclusion of Gardner's remarks were followed by an extended standing ovation.

But for all the man's oratorical gifts, Gardner's speech that day was far from an elementary exercise in eloquence. He was there to impart an unsentimental honesty about community. What we heard was an appeal, from a man beginning his ninth decade, to reject nostalgia in all its guises.

True, he declared, both family and community had suffered devastating blows; in fact, "to be blunt about it, neither will ever be wholly reinstated in its old form." But it was time to face reality, dispense with longing for a mythic past, and move forward in pragmatic and innovative ways—to "stop lamenting the loss of old patterns, and ask what steps must be taken toward new patterns." (Besides, Gardner added—with characteristic dry wit—it was generally unwise to be nostalgic about anything unless you were absolutely certain it wouldn't be coming back!)

Gardner's perspective hit home for me that day, and it is one that underpins this book—a belief that American society is remarkably resilient, and that although community is always breaking down, new opportunities to rebuild and fortify the social fabric are constantly emerging. The task for us is not to retreat into the sentimental longing that, for example, David Galernter displays with respect to restoring women's former roles, but to muster the insight and ingenuity required to identify these new sources and patterns. And to cultivate them, in particular through the creation of innovative social institutions.

Gardner's speech alone would have warranted battling the snow to get to Washington. However, I emerged from that conference with more than an intellectual framework for how we might rebuild our communities.

An hour after the speech I found myself, by pure chance, heading straight toward Gardner in a crowded corridor. He was alone, and I mustered the courage to introduce myself. Talking fast, I also managed to interject that I had written a background paper for the Carnegie Commission on the role older Americans might play in assisting the younger generation. He listened patiently, nodding occasionally and looking down at the ground. Because of his silence, I was beginning to regret having imposed myself, especially at such an awkward location (people were streaming past us in both directions through the corridor).

Just as I was convinced that Gardner was simply being polite, he reached into a brown leather briefcase, rummaged about, and fished out a typewritten three-page paper from 1988 labeled "The Experience Corps." (This scene would repeat itself again and again over the coming years, as we began working closely together: I would raise an issue, convinced that I had happened on some formidable insight, and John would produce, as if by magic and with no fanfare whatsoever, a beautifully crafted treatise fully vetting the subject.)

John Gardner's notion of Experience Corps was for the creation of a new institution that would unleash the time, talent, and know-how of older Americans to revitalize civil society: "We believe, without being immodest," he wrote in the paper, "that the large numbers of us over age 65 constitute a rich reservoir of talent, experience and commitment potentially available to the society. . . . We know the conventional view is that society owes its older citizens something, and we would be foolish to quarrel with that. But we owe something, too, and this is in one sense our 'operation give-back.'" However, giving back hardly precluded getting back, and Gardner envisioned Experience Corps as an opportunity for continued learning and growth in later life—as "a great adventure."

For Gardner, the Experience Corps idea built on insights that first became evident when he launched the Older Americans Act and Medicare as secretary of HEW. When he came to Washington to join the Johnson administration in 1965, he "was pretty well fixated on the idea that the economic problems and the health problems of the later years were the whole story." However, the more he traveled around the country and talked with older adults, the more he "encountered a cluster of important issues, nestled under those big, widely publicized ones. There was loneliness, boredom, a need to be needed." Further, he was aware from his other duties overseeing education and human service efforts at the federal level that society needed these people too.

After leaving government, he first put some of these observations on paper in his 1968 book *No Easy Victories*, which suggested that the third stage of life might be the time when people made some of their most important contributions to society and to the well-being of future generations. Twenty years later he was still refining the notion, incorporating into the Experience Corps paper the rough contours of a national initiative that might make this ideal possible for millions of Americans in the third age.

Although I didn't realize it at the time, the encounter with Gardner would be a turning point for me—one that would lead not only to a focus on the potential role of older Americans as a source of social renewal but also to a shift from analyzing the actions of others to a new role striving to make things happen on the ground. Specifically, it marked the beginning of an effort to launch—with Gardner acting as counsel, mentor, and friend all along the way—an Experience Corps aimed at mobilizing older Americans on behalf of our communities.

Launching Experience Corps

Eugene Lang, the founder of the "I Have A Dream" project, observes that the best ideas are rarely the ones that you come up with. Rather, Lang reflects from his own experience as an entrepreneur first in business and then in the realm of civil society, "they seem to come up with you in mind."

As I reflect on my own path toward helping to create Experience Corps, Lang's observation rings familiar. Like Bill Schwartz, my entrepreneurial activities have been incremental, roundabout, even a bit accidental—and far from a solo course. In fact, other than intercepting John Gardner in the hallway that day in Washington, my involvement in Experience Corps progressed through a procession of unsolicited opportunities (mostly papers that, in turn, led to people who, in turn, became partners)—including the original study that introduced me to Nick and The Work Connection, and the second that put me on a course heading, quite literally, toward John Gardner.

And then several months after completing the Carnegie study, good fortune in the form of another chance to write a paper (which would ultimately lead to new partners) presented itself yet again. The phone rang and it was The Commonwealth Fund in New York requesting a study about the role older Americans could play in the realm of "community service." Commonwealth was wrapping up a commission on work by Americans over age fifty-five, focusing on promoting the value of older workers and removing barriers to work in later life (such as age discrimination). However, as the commission was drawing to a close, its members realized that the analysis was primarily focused on private-sector employment. Karen Davis, former dean of Johns Hopkins' public health school and then executive vice president of the Commonwealth Fund, felt there should be more attention paid to other kinds of contributions by Americans in later life.

Davis's interest was timely. Bill Clinton, starting his first term, was in the midst of launching a national service program focused on young people, AmeriCorps, and much attention was focused on the untapped resources in this segment of the population. Unfortunately, older adults seemed to come up in these deliberations only as a needy group that might be ministered to by idealistic youth.

Remarkably, at the same time consideration of a "domestic Peace Corps" through AmeriCorps was under way, the fastest-growing group within the Peace Corps was older adults, and Peace Corps officials were singing the praises of these volunteers. Indeed, the definitive study on the subject of national service, by Richard Danzig (who would go on to become secretary of the U.S. Navy) and Peter Szanton (a former Kennedy School professor), had recently appeared with similar conclusions. In their Ford Foundation–funded book, *National Service: What Would It Mean?* Danzig and Szanton argued that although national youth service had some potential, older Americans "may have more to give and more reason to benefit from national service than any other age group."

On the Road

The Commonwealth assignment seemed the perfect opportunity to explore what a national service program for older Americans might look like— a national Experience Corps capable of doing for this population what AmeriCorps was hoping to do for young people. From my earlier research, I knew that devising such an initiative wouldn't require starting from scratch. There were important lessons present in solo projects such as The Work Connection as well as in long-standing efforts like the Foster Grandparent Program.

So I hit the road in search of innovative ideas that might be integrated into the next generation of opportunities for older Americans to contribute more substantially to society. And the more I traveled, the more impressed I was with how many of these innovations were already being pioneered in Foster Grandparent Programs (even, in some cases, in contradiction of the program's official rules and regulations).

One example of this innovative "rule breaking" was in Portland, Oregon, and the perpetrator was Cherry Hendrix, a seventy-year-old African American grandmother living across the street from Woodlawn Elementary School. After retiring from her job as an aide in Portland's public schools, Cherry set up shop on her porch, keeping an eye on neighborhood children and trying to provide them with both love and guidance. However, as the lower-income neighborhood became increasingly dangerous, she started searching for other routes to perform these community-building functions. Her quest led her to the Foster Grandparent Program and to an assignment inside the Woodlawn school.

I first encountered Cherry in the school's vast gymnasium. She was standing at the front of the room, which also doubles as the lunchroom. Along one wall of the gym, leading up to the woman, were nearly a hundred third graders. On her other side, three cafeteria workers in white uniforms and hairnets prepared to serve lunch from a steam table. However, before the students could get their food, they had to make it past Cherry, and that meant two things: first acquiring a set of utensils, and then receiving some word of encouragement, a high five, or even a hug from the Foster Grandparent. (It was amusing to watch the flat midmorning demeanor of the children transformed, one by one, as they reached Cherry and burst into laughter or succumbed to big euphoric smiles.)

The woman was undoubtedly having an impact working with Woodlawn students in the cafeteria and two classrooms, providing them personal attention and helping them with their assignments. However, after several years of this activity, she was ready for more. In part, she believed that many students still viewed her as an authority figure, and she was interested in finding new ways to break through and connect with them. She was also aware that many of these young people had no place to go after school.

Cherry came up with the idea of creating an after-school bowling program for the children. This idea was not a great stretch; other than children, her great passion in life was bowling. Two nights a week she anchored a coed team, the Jacks and Jills, at Interstate Lanes a few miles from the school. Why not take the kids to Interstate after school? She could teach them how to bowl, get to know them in a less formal setting, keep them occupied during a time when they might well get into trouble, and possibly even work in some practice frames herself.

So Cherry Hendrix handwrote forty-three permission slips to the parents of the children she thought might benefit from after-school bowling. She even convinced the management at Interstate Lanes to provide the kids free shoes, while she paid for the lanes out of her $9-a-day Foster Grandparent stipend. Soon she was overseeing a thriving youth bowling project (all of this as Robert Putnam's "Bowling Alone" argument was rising to prominence, suggesting that the great decrease in American bowling leagues was emblematic of the overall decline in civic engagement in America.)

Yet at the same time, Cherry was worried that she was going to be ousted from the Foster Grandparent Program for violating its dictate that all participants engage exclusively in one-on-one, direct service activities with children. As I watched Cherry at work, it was obvious that what had to change was not the woman but the Foster Grandparent Program. The kind of initiative and leadership potential that Cherry displayed needed to be not only legitimated but also celebrated, developed, and supported.

Another idea that would become central to Experience Corps came from the other Portland, the Portland of Aggie and Louise. While I was visiting the two women at Maine Medical Center, Susan LaVigne, the local Foster Grandparent director, suggested I check out what was under way at Reiche Elementary School. At Reiche, located in one of the city's toughest neighborhoods, eight Foster Grandparents had accumulated in the school of several hundred students. This concentration was unusual. In an effort to "spread the wealth," most Foster Grandparent programs tend to distribute the small number of volunteers among a wide number of institutions—a practice that helps enlarge the constituency for the programs but dilutes the impact at any given setting.

At Reiche, the eight Foster Grandparents (each serving 20 hours a week) meant the equivalent of 160 person-hours a week at the school, all of it focused on supporting and enriching the lives of the children. In fact, these individuals were everywhere at Reiche—in the classrooms, the library, the hallways, the cafeteria. It was telling evidence of their importance that the principal every morning on the school's public-address system welcomed the school's three major presences: the students, the teachers, and the Foster Grandparents.

At the same time, they were reaping significant benefits themselves. Because all eight individuals ate lunch at the same time, they evolved into an informal team. Every day at 11:30 they would go to lunch and catch up on each other's lives, as well as spend time talking about the children at Reiche and the issues confronting them. (These sessions were strikingly reminiscent of those where the Work Connection mentors sat around a table and discussed the kids they were working with.)

The group had also become like a second family for the members. When one of the Reiche team developed Alzheimer's, the other seven banded together, taking turns picking her up in the morning and taking her home in the afternoon, convinced that the best way to preserve her functioning was for her to remain active and engaged through the school.

From Promise to Practice

After many months of background work—collecting ideas like those suggested by Cherry Hendrix, the Reiche volunteers, and others within and outside Foster Grandparents; wading through the research literature on successful aging; and attempting to integrate information from these sources with insights in John Gardner's paper—I concluded the study for The Commonwealth Fund both with a call for an Experience Corps and a set of recommendations about how this initiative might be structured and operated. In the end, the key ingredients boiled down to a set of common-sense ideas—a little more elaborate than Tom Breen's three-element "activity, economy, and individuality" memo that served as the underpinning for Sun City, but still a fairly straightforward collection of guiding principles:

- *Impact:* To start, Experience Corps would be serious. It would strive to attack real problems of real significance to the community, putting the skills of third agers to full use.

- *Commitment:* Joining Experience Corps would be a bit like joining the Peace Corps ("the toughest job you'll ever love"). It would entail a major commitment for a defined period of time, and as such it would constitute a significant part of every volunteer's life and identity.

- *Critical mass:* Experience Corps members would be deployed in sufficient concentration to be a presence wherever they were serving, in much the manner of the volunteers at Reiche. It was my hope that over time this kind of critical mass might exist not only within the walls of a particular institution—such as a school—but in entire neighborhoods as well (for example, in all the schools of a geographic area). This level of participation would enhance the prospect both of providing valuable service and of changing community perceptions and expectations regarding third agers' roles.

- *Leadership:* Like Cherry Hendrix, Experience Corps members not only would provide direct service but also would be encouraged to use their initiative, creativity, and leadership to become social entrepreneurs within the context of the program. Ultimately, it was hoped that the members would take on an increasing responsibility in setting the priorities of the Corps and actually running the operation.

- *Community:* Experience Corps would consciously strive to develop teams like the one that had formed naturally at Reiche. Given the challenges of making a difference in so many settings, creating a built-in vehicle for mutual support seemed to make sense. It also seemed like an express route for those involved to make new friends during the transition into a new phase of life.

- *Learning:* John Gardner's longtime belief in the notion of renewal contributed to an emphasis on ways Experience Corps might promote not only *expending* experience but also *acquiring* new experiences in the process. Thus, members would have opportunities to learn new skills and to engage with others around important issues.

- *Diversity:* Experience Corps would be open to everyone over age fifty, not just low-income individuals in the manner of Foster Grandparents. And through marketing and other means, the Corps should also work hard to improve on existing efforts to recruit older men (Foster Grandparents has fewer than 5 percent men) and should strive to draw the younger group of third agers rarely recruited by "senior volunteer" programs (especially given so much early retirement).

- *The name:* One of the most important features of an Experience Corps would be that it was an "Experience Corps." John Gardner's label astutely sidestepped any reference to chronological age or, for that matter, any of the other appellations so often associated with being older: senior citizen, grandparent, retired, and the like. Furthermore, Gardner had also been careful to avoid the label "Elder Corps" or anything that might sound too exalted. Rather, the Experience Corps name was a deliberate attempt to honor a sturdy, widely possessed, and unintimidating asset present in so many older Americans: experience.

The call for a new Experience Corps built around these principles was issued at a Capitol Hill briefing sponsored by The Commonwealth Fund following the spring 1994 publication of my report. Hundreds of people showed up to listen to a procession of dignitaries, including Eli Segal (head of the Corporation for National Service, the Clinton creation to oversee AmeriCorps and run the National Senior Service Corps projects) and Arthur Flemming (HEW secretary under President Eisenhower and a longtime advocate for the aging), describe older Americans as an important and un-tapped resource for society. Flemming, almost ninety at the time, recalled his own experience as a young man sitting in the crowd as FDR announced the passage of Social Security, at the same time asserting that older Americans today "needed a dream every bit as much as a memory."

Overall, the day in Washington was uplifting, but afterward I harbored few hopes that it would lead to anything. As with "Partners in Growth" and the Carnegie paper—and indeed most of what I had ever written—my as-sumption was that the Commonwealth Study and its call for an Experience Corps would now be placed on the shelf to begin collecting dust.

And that certainly would have been the case had it not been for Tom Endres.

Raised in a small mining town in Pennsylvania, Tom Endres had dedi-cated much of his adult life to service. After college, the handsome former basketball player embarked on a tour of duty with the Peace Corps in Colombia, then stayed on to train new volunteers for assignments in Latin America. Upon returning to the United States, he shifted to the VISTA pro-gram, directing that incarnation of a domestic Peace Corps in Oregon, be-fore moving to Maine to oversee the full collection of federally sponsored service programs in that state (including not only VISTA but the Foster Grandparent, Senior Companion, and Retired and Senior Volunteer Pro-gram (RSVP) programs).

Those were lean years for social programs, but Endres showed skill at making the most of increasingly scarce resources, all the while continuing to advocate for expanding the efforts under his jurisdiction. On the strength of his reputation as a gifted manager, Endres was eventually invited to Wash-ington to lead the Senior Companion Program. Soon he was elevated, first to deputy director (under former St. Paul, Minnesota, mayor Jim Scheibel), then to director of the National Senior Service Corps (NSSC)—the first person to hold this top position who was not a political appointee.

In his leadership role with the NSSC, Endres quickly established himself as a reformer and a bona fide social entrepreneur (a reminder that such crea-tures can exist in the context of a government agency). Although a champion of Foster Grandparents and the other NSSC programs, Endres also believed these efforts would need to be substantially retooled to move beyond mar-ginality and capture the imagination of the advancing wave of boomers.

Out of this conviction, one of Tom Endres's first projects at the NSSC was to develop an initiative to increase the social impact of NSSC programs.

Eager to begin concrete steps in this direction, Endres (with Scheibel's strong backing) convinced Congress to appropriate $1 million to an existing but obscure—and never before funded—line item in the federal budget earmarked for innovation through the use of "demonstration projects." Furthermore, Endres had sent out copies of the Commonwealth study to each of the 1,200 NSSC projects across the country and was determined to put the entire new appropriation into turning the Experience Corps idea into reality. Suddenly, in response to Endres's urgent request, I found myself working (a la Bernie Nash) around the clock to develop a blueprint for a new Experience Corps pilot project.

As this plan was being completed, another unanticipated development occurred: Tom and I were approached by Dr. Linda Fried of Johns Hopkins School of Medicine. A humane physician in the mold of Thea Glass, Fried was also dreaming about a national corps aimed at engaging more older Americans on behalf of communities.

Linda Fried's interest in a new corps grew primarily from her scientific research on how to promote the well-being of older adults, but it was also supported by her experience as a practicing physician. Through her geriatrics practice at Johns Hopkins—where she is also professor and vice chair in the Department of Medicine—Fried was treating a great many older patients who, she felt, had little wrong with them other than a lack of purpose and few connections in their lives. They were visiting their doctor, Linda Fried, because they had all day to worry about what might be going wrong with their aging bodies. And many were coming simply because they were desperate for somebody to talk to.

So nearly a century after Dr. William Osler used his bully pulpit as chair of the Department of Medicine at Johns Hopkins to argue that older people were useless drains on society, Fried was concluding from her research and experiences in that same department that many older adults were declining precisely because of the circumstances Osler had done so much to promote. Indeed, Fried wanted to "prescribe" for her patients meaningful opportunities to contribute to society but was at a loss about where to send them.

One of Fried's most important contributions to the emerging Experience Corps derived from another source of direct experience. As not only a longtime advocate for quality public education but also the mother of two boys in Baltimore elementary schools, Fried knew how starved for human resources these educational institutions often were. She urged Tom and me to concentrate the Experience Corps demonstration in these settings.

I agreed with Fried from my own work on mentoring, which had left me convinced that we should move beyond one-on-one volunteering to more systemic forms of change. My hope was that we might someday turn our schools into "mentor-rich environments" where young people had opportunities to connect with a variety of caring adults during the school day—not only Big Brother/Big Sister–type volunteers but also teachers, coaches, counselors, and other adults close at hand and with the time and inclination to support young people.

Emerging information from educational demographers further supported a focus on public schools. Fed by an "echo boom" of boomers' children as well as by immigration, school enrollment in the mid-1990s had already surpassed a twenty-five-year-old record dating to the height of the baby-boom years. According to projections, this record was likely be broken every year for at least the next decade. The result would be even more overcrowded classrooms and more impersonal school environments—at precisely the juncture when young people would be facing more stresses than ever before.

In the summer of 1995, with the parameters of an Experience Corps model in hand, a focus on urban public elementary schools established, and our team in place (and John Gardner chairing the project's advisory board), Endres asked all fifty state directors overseeing his network of NSSC programs to nominate one innovative Foster Grandparent or RSVP project to apply for new funding to run an Experience Corps. Working quickly, we pared these recommendations down to eight finalists, before selecting five projects to be the first Experience Corps pilots. These were in the South Bronx; North Philadelphia; Minneapolis; Portland, Oregon; and Port Arthur, Texas. (Port Arthur, birthplace of Janis Joplin and Jimmie Johnson and a city of 50,000 in the part of Texas where oil was first discovered, was the big surprise.)

Each of the five pilot projects agreed to place teams of fifteen half-time Experience Corps members in inner-city elementary schools, usually two schools the first year and four the second. They were also to work in the most needy schools in their communities. In the South Bronx, for example, the project was concentrated in the poorest congressional district in the country; across the five sites, the schools selected were ones where virtually all of the students qualified for the free/reduced lunch program.

In return, each project received funding to cover two years (primarily to hire a full-time paid project director and to provide stipends of $100–200 per month to individuals committing a minimum of fifteen hours a week), along

with a last-minute bonus. Just as we were launching Experience Corps, Elderhostel volunteered to provide free classes plus room and board, anywhere
in the United States, to Experience Corps members who served a full year.
Not only did the organization donate the equivalent of $50,000 in free
classes, but it also printed certificates honoring Experience Corps member
for their efforts to leave a legacy on behalf of the younger generation.

Experience Corps in Action

In early 1996, as the six-month planning period for the Experience Corps
projects was drawing to a close, our team felt a little as Tom Breen and his
associates must have felt just before Sun City was launched. We had spent a
great deal of time in preparation, we had tried to cover all the bases, and we
had put forward our best guesses about what might work—but would anybody really take us up on this proposition? Would anybody actually show up
for Experience Corps?

Bastions of "Social Capital"

It must have been exhilarating for Breen and the other Webb lieutenants
to stand in front of Sun City on New Year's Day 1960 and watch 100,000
people come streaming through the gates. There was no such immediate response to Experience Corps, no twelve-mile traffic jams, no thousands clamoring to participate. To some extent, the lack of pandemonium was probably
a good thing; after all, this was a pilot project looking for just under two
hundred people overall.

However, even by those standards, initial recruitment for Experience
Corps was slow, with individuals trickling into the program one at a time.
Where were all these hordes of older adults we'd been promised, wondered
the teachers and principals excited about the program and counting on an
influx of new human resources? We, meanwhile, were learning firsthand how
hard it can be to create "structural lead" from scratch, to diverge from what
the prevailing culture was telling people about appropriate ways to spend
one's "golden years." Furthermore, we were peddling an untested project:
Nobody in the community had ever heard of Experience Corps; there was no
stockpile of moving stories to regale potential recruits. Just as important, we
lacked a coterie of existing volunteers to pass on the message directly to
friends and neighbors via word of mouth.

Furthermore, we were using "retail" techniques in trying to find people to participate in Experience Corps. The projects were too small to justify a major marketing blitz—resources were sufficient to support only thirty people in each city—yet in the absence of such a campaign, recruitment became a laborious process. Recruiters can go to senior centers, senior housing, and other "senior" enclaves—which the Experience Corps projects did with limited success—but we were looking particularly for a group of third agers unlikely to be found frequenting those places, a group of individuals who tended not to think of themselves as "senior citizens."

In some cases, these initial recruitment woes were rectified by simply hiring more energetic and skilled recruiters. But the great structural break occurred in New York, where the AARP state office agreed to give the Community Service Society of New York, the group running Experience Corps in the South Bronx, mailing lists for its members in the zip codes immediately surrounding the two schools where Experience Corps was to be located (P.S. 154 and P.S. 156). This was the first attempt to recruit "wholesale," and the results were encouraging. The South Bronx might not be considered a hotbed of AARP membership, but in fact the mailing triggered a substantial response: In all, 200 individuals from the neighborhoods surrounding the two schools expressed interest in the thirty slots.

The objective was never to accept just anyone who came through the door, and the South Bronx Experience Corps ultimately accepted candidates at about the same rate as Princeton or Stanford admitted students. As a result, project directors were in a position to be selective about the skills and experience of the volunteers (who continued to think the program was an AARP project long into their involvement, since that was the way they first heard about Experience Corps).

Soon recruitment success followed elsewhere, in some places due to the AARP connection—that's how Harold Allen found out about Experience Corps in Philadelphia—in others after the project had sufficient time to establish its reputation in the community. And once the inaugural group of volunteers had found their way to Experience Corps, the good news was that the project managed to attract individuals not usually found in "senior volunteer" programs. They were young (two-thirds in their fifties or sixties), healthy (two-thirds assessing their health as either excellent, very good, or good), not engaged otherwise (only one-third were currently volunteering in another program), and, very happily—in the context of nearly all-female-staffed elementary schools—nearly a third men.

The most significant discovery, however, was socioeconomic. Nearly 70 percent of the Experience Corps members across the five cities were African American (and another 11 percent Latino), and most of these were working-class and middle-class individuals who had long been living in the neighborhoods surrounding the schools. The men who volunteered tended to be retired city workers or postal employees, while the women most commonly had backgrounds in nursing and teaching. Across gender, these careers reflected the opportunities available to educated African Americans of their generation. These individuals had much in common with Foster Grandparents I had interviewed, but their pensions and other income would have rendered most ineligible to participate in that program.

Who were these people? Experience Corps drew men like Harold Allen, the former Philadelphia Water Department supervisor, or Jesse Davidson, a retired postal worker in the Bronx who had once studied philosophy at NYU on the G.I. Bill. Davidson left NYU before graduating (too many philosophical differences with his stodgy professors) and went on to work the night shift at the post office for many years. He chose night work so that he could be at home for his kids during the day. At the same time, Davidson and his late wife ran a local youth program through their church.

Maude Galloway, a Port Arthur volunteer, is typical of many of the women who joined the Experience Corps. Galloway left Texas to head east after graduating at the top of her class from the single black high school in segregated 1940s Port Arthur. After working as a secretary in wartime Washington, she enrolled in the nursing program at Harlem Hospital and practiced as a registered nurse for many years. Later, she relocated to Los Angeles, returned to college, and became an English teacher at the first high school in that city named for an African American. Galloway returned home to Port Arthur after retiring from her career in the Los Angeles Unified School District.

Most significant, Jesse Davidson, Harold Allen, Maude Galloway, and so many of their fellow Experience Corps members are people who—according to the reigning orthodoxy in sociology—are not supposed to exist any longer, at least not in low-income, inner-city neighborhoods. Yet when the call was put out for Experience Corps members, they were the individuals who volunteered to be part of this effort (which for many functioned, in Harold Allen's words, as a kind of "wake-up call").

These older adults recall the individuals chronicled in Mitchell Duneier's ethnographic study *Slim's Table*, a powerful account of a half dozen African American men, most in their fifties, sixties, and seventies, living on the

South Side of Chicago. Duneier's book is a useful corrective to the argument that there has been a complete exodus of working- and middle-class African Americans from many inner-city neighborhoods, leaving those enclaves utterly isolated from role models for stability, responsibility, and hard work. Although there is certainly a trend in this direction, a raft of studies such as Duneier's—indeed, the response to Experience Corps as well—suggest that social scientists may overstate the extent to which this transformation has already occurred. Slim and his buddies, like Harold Allen and Jesse Davidson, continue living in the same houses, on the same blocks, in the same neighborhoods where they have lived for decades.

The main problem currently is that these individuals are all too often living in exile within their neighborhoods. Duneier shows how violence and other changes have caused members of Slim's group to abandon their former role of mentoring and socializing unrelated young people on the street corner, setting up shop instead in the separate sphere of Valois's "See Your Food" Cafeteria, elsewhere on the South Side. Duneier makes it clear that the problem is not that these individuals have abandoned the neighborhood, but rather that many of the old opportunities for being an essential part of its social fabric have broken down.

Experience Corps members like Harold Allen, Jesse Davidson, and Maude Galloway remember those former roles, having grown up in racially segregated but class-integrated African American neighborhoods in the 1930s–1950s period. They all recount that in these areas it was common for adults—in particular, older adults—to be stationed on their porches as children played on the block, providing a watchful eye over the activities of the block and intervening when young people violated community norms.

Today, however, it is often too dangerous to hang out on the porch in many inner-city neighborhoods, much less to intervene in the behavior of other people's children. That is why Cherry Hendrix took her nurturing activities down the street and inside the doors of the Woodlawn school (and eventually into the bowling alley). That is also the reason many of the Experience Corps volunteers signed up to participate in the project. They were looking for new ways to do old things.

As I traveled to the South Bronx, Portland, Port Arthur, and the other Experience Corps pilot sites around the country, it was clear that the individuals who responded to the Experience Corps call had what it takes to do these "old things." They were bastions of social capital, individuals who had worked hard all their lives, raised families, were active in their church, and cared a great deal about what was happening in their neighborhoods. Many talked about trying to revitalize some of the values and practices of the settings they grew up in.

The number one reason these individuals gave for deciding to join was concern about what was happening to children, particularly the next generation of African American children (overall, 93 percent of the Experience Corps volunteers said that helping children was their primary reason for volunteering). In interviews, many also spoke of the desire to "give back." As one volunteer in Portland stated: "Basically, life has been good to me, and it's my way of giving back a little bit."

"I'm retired, and how do I say this," reflected Jesse Davidson, "I've got beans in the fridge, bread in the fridge, I have no needs." His goal now is to meet other objectives, ones more rooted in the soul than the material world: "I don't have that many more years left in this life," he continued, adding that his girlfriend hates it when he talks this way: "I want to get some things done." Helping children is at the top of that list: "I think that as we age we have something the younger generation needs: love, understanding, and responsibility. This is what we bring to the children, something that's missing in their life."

Richard Russell, one of Jesse's teammates in the Bronx Experience Corps, agrees with all those reasons, but admits that he joined to break out of the rut of retirement. A barrel-chested, soft-spoken man with iron-gray hair and a neatly sculpted goatee, Russell too is retired from the postal service. He and his wife successfully raised four children, one of them a prosecutor in the Bronx courthouse not far from P.S. 156. "I retired about ten years ago," he recalled. "A couple days out of the week, I'd go down to the church and do something. Basically, I stayed more to myself. I was getting dormant. My wife got bothered. 'You can't go on like this,' my wife would say. 'How can you spend your life like this?' I'd say, 'Who am I bothering? I'm not bothering nobody. I'm happy doing what I'm doing.' But truthfully," he continued, "you wake up to the same old thing every day. So this is an outing. Gives me something to do. I have something to look forward to. And I have kids that are counting on me."

Several of these individuals also explained that they came forward as part of a recent development in their neighborhoods, the reemergence of older persons as a last line of support for many families. This trend is most obvious in the large number of grandparents in the African American community who are stepping into emergency situations to raise grandchildren and other young relatives. It is a trend that, in certain respects, runs counter to the drying up of informal opportunities to socialize young people in many inner-city neighborhoods.

As Ken Comer, another Experience Corps volunteer in the Bronx commented as he motioned toward the front entrance of P.S. 156: "Come to this school any morning at 8:00 a.m. and watch who is dropping these children off. It's us, the older generation in the neighborhood. We're the ones who are raising the next generation of children."

Making a Difference

The individuals who joined Experience Corps provided a promising foundation from which to build. But would the project succeed in translating their abundant skills and social capital in ways that benefited kids and schools? Furthermore, despite general enthusiasm for the idea of Experience Corps, the schools were not without some concerns in signing up for this experiment. Most had been burned before by volunteer programs in which individuals showed up sporadically, requiring more work than they were worth. The last thing these educational institutions needed—we were warned—was a bunch of older people who required baby-sitting when the schools were already understaffed and overwhelmed.

From the side of the Experience Corps members, we worried about just how open these settings would be to the involvement of outsiders. Public schools are notoriously inhospitable to community involvement, often even the involvement of parents. Would they provide opportunities for the Experience Corps members to contribute that were fulfilling and offered a real chance to make a difference? (I remembered the beginning of the Foster Grandparent Program, when local agencies promised in their funding applications to connect the volunteers with children in need and then proceeded to assign the Foster Grandparents to changing bedpans and taking out the trash—leaving Bernie Nash to run around the country threatening to revoke their grants.)

I ultimately had to do a small amount of troubleshooting along these lines, reminding a couple of wayward principals that Experience Corps was not developed to ease their photocopying needs. But in reality few concerns of this type materialized. Indeed, the inner-city public schools we were working in—like so many similar institutions around the country—were so desperate for responsible human beings to help that the Experience Corps members were embraced from practically the moment they entered the building.

In reality, so overwhelming was the need on the part of schools that we found ourselves with considerable margin for error in implementing Experience Corps—operating in an environment that might best be described as "forgiving." That was an advantage, because we were working at breakneck speed to get this new initiative off the ground (for budgetary reasons, the Corporation for National Service had to get the dollars out the door by the end of the 1995 federal fiscal year).

How did the Experience Corps volunteers help meet these schools' overwhelming needs? To start, Experience Corps members did what many of the Foster Grandparents I had met were doing: They reduced the ratio of adults to students in the classroom and in the school. As one teacher in Port Arthur explained, this wasn't rocket science: "When there is only one of me and thirty kids, it is hard to get around to everybody's needs." This was a comment I heard repeatedly from teachers at the five pilot projects.

In fact, many of the retired teachers who signed up to participate in Experience Corps joined for precisely this reason. After years of frustration at not being able to give their own struggling students the personal attention they desperately needed, these educators came to Experience Corps with a desire finally to rectify this situation.

The rectifying that they and their fellow Corps members performed had two components. First, they were able to provide direct and intensive support to the cadre of children in the class who were behind and in desperate need of more one-on-one assistance. Second, in the process, they were able to free up teachers to do the job they were hired for—teaching a class—and thus liberating them from spending disproportionate time with the three or four children who might have easily absorbed half their energy in the past.

Overall, most of the Experience Corps members spent at least part of their day working one-on-one with children. Some of this activity was dedicated specifically to helping with schoolwork—going over lessons, reading with students, helping them catch up with the rest of the class. But much of their effort was in pursuit of E. M. Forster's famous dictate "only connect"—getting to know the students, supporting them emotionally, and becoming their mentors.

Through this connection, the men and women in Experience Corps brought something akin to a grandparent's unconditional love for the children—praising them, acknowledging talents, fussing over their accomplishments. It is the kind of pride that, for example, infused Jesse Davidson's description of one of the girls he was working with: "We got a little girl in here—she is one of the smartest little kids I've seen in a long time. You can see the brain turning around. She's a dynamo. I say, if you can control that mind, you've got an Einstein!"

Along with recognizing the latent talent in many of the children, the Experience Corps members were also alert to their basic needs as human beings. They paid attention to the small things, from celebrating birthdays to noticing subtle signs that something might be awry. In much the same way Thea Glass described the doctors at her Volunteers in Medicine clinic, these men and women made for "fewer cracks" that students might fall through. In fact, Maude Galloway used similar language to describe the value of the Experience Corps members in Port Arthur: "I just feel that some children are falling through the cracks. It's not that they're not talented, it's not that they aren't motivated. But there's just nobody picking up the little pieces."

Maude Galloway's observation reminded me of a story I heard when visiting one of the volunteers in Philadelphia, a retired nurse mentoring a small boy whose home life was in turmoil. Sitting in the Taylor School's library, a few weeks after Valentine's Day, she recounted this event:

We were making Valentine's cards. We were to make them for a special person, so I said, "Your mother's going to like your Valentine." He said, "No!" So I asked why not. "Because I made one yesterday, and I gave it to her when I went home, and she threw it in the trash." I said, "Well why don't you make me a card?". . . He didn't have a card, but he picked a lot of the red pieces of paper that had little hearts on them out of the trash and put them on another piece of paper. He said, "This is for you. I forgot to give you a Valentine."

The incident made her realize how important a role she'd come to play in the child's life, and it moved her. "I still have the card," she told me.

Willie Douwes, another volunteer at the Taylor School, went searching all over the section of North Philadelphia known as the "Badlands" to find one student she'd been working with. He had been absent from school for several weeks, and she was trying to give him some books and assignments he'd missed. When she eventually found the apartment where he was living, it was virtually uninhabitable—no electricity, running water, or even windows. It made her understand what this child was facing and gave her a new perspective on the modest progress he'd been making academically.

For the volunteers, these experiences were chastening—even for those

Experience Corps members living in the same neighborhoods as the young people. They realized that many of their victories working with the children would be small ones (more often than not "an answer, rather than a solution"). Still, most of the Experience Corps volunteers interviewed felt that they were stepping into an important void, and that some children's prospects would be improved dramatically through their work together. "I have been around long enough to know you can't change the world," reflected Harold Allen. "If you can change one or two lives, that is a tremendous feeling."

For me, having spent so many years studying mentoring relationships, I was struck by how many powerful bonds formed between the Experience Corps members and the children. It was unlike anything I'd seen before, even in excellent programs such as Big Brothers/Big Sisters. One of the messages of my book about mentoring had been that this endeavor is hard. Yet the connections I witnessed between older persons and elementary school–aged children defied that characterization. The rare exception was the bond that didn't take.

I think the connecting success resulted in part because children that age are receptive, often open and eager for love, much more so than adolescents a few years older. However, an equally strong factor is the special qualities that older men and women bring to the mentoring process, qualities that are a close fit with what we know about high-quality mentoring.

Research shows that the best mentors are the ones who take their time, who listen to children, who are more intent on building a relationship than racing toward some preordained goal. Conversely, mentors in a hurry—"efficient" mentors bent on transforming young lives—usually fail. For example, a study by Public/Private Ventures found that those Big Brothers or Big Sisters who arrived with a prescription for turning around a child frequently found that there was no express route to making this kind of difference, no shortcut to building real trust. In these situations, kids voted with their feet—91 percent of these "prescriptive" relationships had ended within nine months. The young people just stopped showing up. Meanwhile, 70 percent of the mentors in the Public/Private Ventures study who were relationship-oriented—"developmental" mentors—were still going strong after nine months and in the end made a vast difference in the lives of children not only in terms of enhancing the quality of their life but also in areas of great value to society.

Through their "inefficient" approach to mentoring, the older adults in

Experience Corps were raising a similar point to the one demonstrated by Bill Schwartz, Thea Glass, and many other doctors at Samaritan House and Volunteers in Medicine. Their point is that certain things are best done at their own pace, without shortcuts and free from the dictates of expediency. Mentoring is surely one of them. It is best performed patiently, and patience is one of the great virtues of age.

Over and over again, as I crisscrossed the country talking to Experience Corps volunteers and other third agers about how they had changed from their younger selves, I heard few claims to wisdom. Rather, the invariable, immediate response to my question "Are you able to do what you are doing now in a manner different from twenty or thirty years ago?" was "I am more patient." They spoke about having more time but just as powerfully about having a different relationship to time. They described the perspective that comes with having lived a certain amount of time. But mostly they talked about patience.

In a typical remark, Shirley Juarez, a retired bookkeeper in the Port Arthur Experience Corps, explained: "The special thing that I bring is patience. At this age, you take more time. You don't expect the kids to do everything right the first time. I'm not in such a hurry anymore." Richard Russell had been relatively patient as a young man, but even he detected a difference: "I could always listen, but now I understand."

Yet for all this patience and perspective, there was a way in which the Experience Corps volunteers were *impatient*—they were loath to waste their time on matters perceived as unimportant. (That sometimes included being interviewed for my book, when children were waiting for them, counting on them, and needing them.)

At a time of life when we are so often told that the ideal is to be frivolous, to enjoy a second childhood built around play, they were heading in the opposite direction, paring their lives down to the things seen as most meaningful and most essential. They seemed to believe, as Dr. Oliver Crawford's comments likewise indicate in the last chapter, that "now is later," that there are some things best not put off to an uncertain future date.

Harold Allen commented on this seemingly paradoxical combination of patience and impatience in later life. "It seems the more time you have, the less time you want to take—and the less time you have, the more time you are willing to take!" But in reality there was no paradox for Harold Allen, Shirley Juarez, and the other Experience Corps volunteers I interviewed. They had simply reached the conclusion that now was the time to tackle tasks that mattered most, and to do this essential work free from compromises.

Alongside their one-on-one connections directly with children, the Experience Corps volunteers contributed to the schools in another manner, one harkening back to the example of Cherry Hendrix and her bowling league. Within the context of the program, a great many of the volunteers were becoming social entrepreneurs, using their ingenuity and initiative to help fill significant gaps that had opened up in the schools.

Like Harold Allen's creation of the "A Team," most of these efforts came after the program was established for some time and the volunteers had developed a feel for what was impeding the education and development of students. In the process, the Experience Corps teams began an ongoing conversation with the principal and the teachers around two basic questions: "What do you need, and how can we help?" When good fits were identified between what they had to offer and the school's answers to these questions, the Experience Corps members began devising new strategies for taking them on.

These Experience Corps–initiated projects tended toward straightforward, common-sense activities. Some were simply attempts to get aspects of the school functioning properly. At the Lent School in Portland, Oregon, for example, Doris Bowman, a retired music teacher, and Lorie LeMay, a piano-playing former deputy sheriff, started a before-school choir for children—resurrecting an activity that had previously existed before Oregon voters cut funds to the schools. Across town, at the Kenton School in Portland, Richard Anderson, a retired engineer, wired the school's computer system and set up Kenton's Internet access, enabling the school to meet a state requirement that all students have access to computers. (The problem Anderson helped solve is one that many schools today face: They have plenty of computer equipment but little expertise in how to use or maintain the hardware.)

Another compelling example demonstrating how individuals' previous work experience might be reconstituted comes from Taylor Elementary School in Philadelphia. There, John Rudd, a retired postman, thought that a schoolwide, in-house mail system might be a clever way to get more students to write. So, after working to develop the idea with the Experience Corps director in Philadelphia, Rob Tietz, Rudd hauled a mailbox into the school and devised a scheme in which children write letters to fellow students, then "mail" them to each other's classrooms. The students simply deposit the letters through the big blue "U.S. Mail" box Rudd positioned outside the school office. Then every Friday Rudd dons his old postman's uniform and delivers the letters—frequently accompanied by a group of students he has deputized as junior letter carriers.

When Arnita Murray was interviewed for Experience Corps at P.S. 154 in the South Bronx, the lithe, elegant woman with flowing gray hair (and a fondness for berets) told the project director in New York that she had nothing to offer. Recently widowed and just retired as a customer-service representative for Brooks Brothers, Murray confessed that she hadn't been in a school since her daughter was a child. Nevertheless, the Experience Corps decided to accept her, and she turned out to be a committed tutor and mentor for students at the school.

Later, however, after Murray had been at the school for over a year, one of the teachers learned that the woman had not always been a customer-service representative. Well before her Brooks Brothers days, she and her late husband toured the country as tap dancers and afterward started the first African American–owned tap dance school in the Bronx. When their daughter (now a singer in Montreal) was born, Arnita Murray stopped dancing, stopped teaching, and focused on raising her child and running the business side of the school.

Excited about Murray's artistic past and what it might contribute to P.S. 154, the teacher urged her to consider creating an after-school tap program. Although reluctant at first, Murray agreed to try after convincing her friend and Experience Corps teammate Ruth Meyers to join her in the adventure. Together the "M and M" sisters developed a thriving dance program that doubled as an African American heritage class, with children flocking to participate.

Another ingenious project initiated by an Experience Corps member was the work of Harold Ford, a retired industrial arts teacher in Port Arthur, Texas. Ford, a prominent figure in the local civil rights movement, wanted to be an architect when he was growing up. However, for someone starting out poor and black in east Texas in the 1940s, there were few opportunities to pursue this dream. So he did what seemed the next best thing—he became a draftsman and industrial arts teacher. However, Ford maintained his interest in architecture, over the years designing most of the African American churches in town.

A member of Experience Corps at Franklin Elementary School, Ford observed that because the cafeteria had only a single lunch line, hungry students often waited twenty or thirty minutes to eat. Frequently, this was the time they landed in fights or started acting out. Ford determined to re-design the cafeteria to incorporate two lines, enabling students to get their lunch twice as quickly. He first went to city hall and pulled the architectural drawings for the school, studying them until he could come up with a practi-cal reconfiguration. Then he located unused school cafeteria equipment (Port Arthur was closing several schools at the time.) Finally, working with the school principal, he oversaw implementation of the project until it had be-come a reality.

As these examples help to convey, the Experience Corps volunteers' con-tribution to the schools frequently extended beyond providing kids more personal attention, for all the merits of this nurturing work. In the words of one teacher quoted in the *Philadelphia Inquirer*, "The Experience Corps has fit in niches we didn't know were there." And in the process of caring for kids and filling these important niches, the men and women in Experience Corps often become an essential part of the fabric of the schools.

The degree to which these individuals become integrated and essential is reflected in numerous ways, such as the willingness on the part of principals and teachers to set aside a room for Experience Corps volunteers in schools where space is at a high premium. Other signs are more subtle. For example, during a visit to Harold Allen and his teammates at the Taylor School in North Philadelphia, I passed by the faculty and staff mailboxes while leaving principal Wendy Schapiro's office. Out of the corner of my eye, I could see that the first mailbox belonged to Harold Allen. Upon closer inspection, it became evident that mailslots for all the Experience Corps members were there, alphabetically and seamlessly interspersed among those of teachers, counselors, and other full-time school personnel.

Schapiro explained that the reason for this fully integrated status is the steady presence of the Experience Corps members, who are staff-like in their commitment, reliability, and professionalism. "From a teacher's point of view," contended one New York City educator working with the program, the consistency of the Experience Corps volunteers is "all-important." She added, "We've had other volunteer programs—or we've had parents. They come in, then they don't come in—and they have valid reasons—but it's very difficult." Another teacher commented that the older adults bring not only reliability but also "a real sense of wanting to be here," echoing a phrase I heard frequently about the doctors of Samaritan House and Volunteers in Medicine. The decision to serve was a choice, not an obligation.

As these comments suggest, much goodwill developed between the Experience Corps members and the schools. Through their direct involvement, the volunteers became not only sympathetic to individual teachers but informed champions for public education as well. In Portland, for example, three of the Corps members at the Lent School organized a meeting with the mayor to plead for more public education funding. Diane Rothery, a retired lab technician and one of the Lent volunteers, explained that seeing public education from the inside out left her galvanized. "Once you are in here and see what is going on, I don't think the teachers will ever get paid enough. . . . As painful as it is, I vote for everything that would help the schools."

In many instances, the Experience Corps volunteers provide support to the teachers directly, becoming mentors for them as well as for the students. At Franklin Elementary School in Port Arthur, for example, Shirley Juarez served in the classroom of first-year teacher Monica Lopez. Lopez began her position midway through the year with little in the way of preparation for the new job. Because Juarez had worked closely with the preceding teacher in that classroom, she was the person who provided Lopez's makeshift orientation to teaching. Lopez recalled: "When I first started, I asked Shirley, 'What did the former teacher do? Is this the way he does it?' I was asking her, 'You run the show for a while. Let me observe you!'" The bilingual Juarez also translates between Lopez (who is third-generation Mexican American and speaks little Spanish) and some students' parents who are recent immigrants from Central America.

"Over the Rainbow"

During my travels, I witnessed one of the most dramatic examples of this mutual appreciation between Experience Corps volunteers and school staff at the June 1998 dinner celebrating completion of three years by the Philadelphia Experience Corps.

The Philadelphia project started slowly, and was dangerously close to squandering early enthusiasm for the idea on the part of the local teachers and principals. But with help from AARP, a change in project directors, and the simple passage of enough time, the trickle of volunteers eventually turned into a torrent. By the end of the initial pilot stage, a waiting list for the program was accumulating (and three years later, with new funding from foundations and local schools, the Philadelphia project had more than tripled in size—with more than a hundred volunteers serving in ten schools, and the Philadelphia school district urging further expansion).

By the June 1998 dinner, this momentum was apparent. Held in the basement of Temple University's faculty club, the event drew the Experience Corps members and their families and an equal number of teachers, principals, counselors, and school administrators. I was struck not only by how many people had turned out for the recognition—on a weeknight at the end of a long school year—but also by how much people seemed to be enjoying themselves. In fact, it was often difficult to distinguish the Experience Corps members from the school staff. In part this was due to significant overlap in age. (For example, one of the Corps members, Leo Jones, a fifty-seven-year-old recently retired teacher, was younger than some of the teachers and principals attending.) But mostly it was difficult to sort out the groups because they were so thoroughly immersed in socializing with each other, as integrated as their mailboxes at the Taylor School.

After dinner, the group of well over a hundred adjourned to an a neighboring conference room, where local jazz singer Juanita Holliday (well into the third age herself) was already singing "Over the Rainbow." I sat down in a row that included John Rudd, the former postman who initiated the writing program at Taylor, and Willie Douwes, the volunteer who went searching all over North Philadelphia for her missing student.

By the time we were seated, Juanita Holliday was finished singing, and the program quickly moved to a succession of endorsements from various high-ranking school district and community officials. I was asked to say a few words on behalf of Experience Corps nationally and about the role older adults could play in communities.

Finally, we arrived at the real purpose of the night. One by one, delegations from each of the schools came to the front of the room, with teachers and principal taking turns bragging about their Experience Corps volunteers and presenting them with awards highlighting their contributions over the past year. As each new group came forward, I could sense the friendly competition building. The contest culminated in a command performance by James Forte of Morrison Elementary School's Experience Corps. The six-foot-three-inch Forte, a retired EPA administrator with thick glasses and a rich baritone voice, was already renowned among the Experience Corps members for his gospel singing. At first he feigned embarrassment as calls of "Sing!" came from several volunteers in the audience. Then with little real prompting, Forte launched into an a cappella version of "He's Got the

Whole World in His Hands" soon joined spontaneously by Juanita and her accompanist on the keyboard.

The crowd—Experience Corps members, teachers, and principals alike—were now clapping along and swaying with Forte. Steadily, almost imperceptibly, the evening was being transformed from a recognition banquet into something akin to a revival. As James Forte and the Morrison contingent returned to their seats to whoops of approval and a standing ovation, the stage was set for the evening's concluding speaker, Harold Allen, to send the group home with a message that might carry them through the summer and into the next school year.

Head shaven, sporting Pierre Cardin glasses and a sweatshirt proclaiming "Retired CEO of Diddly-Squat," Allen looked as ageless as ever. A gentle, soft-spoken man with a wonderful sense of irony (Philadelphia's Experience Corps director Rob Tietz called him "the most humble person I've ever met"), the old organizer in Allen is also unmistakable. And once in front of the crowd he was in his element. In fact, "in his element" is too staid a characterization. As I listened, it was not hard to imagine Harold Allen in front of the Point Breeze Kresge's in his civil rights days, rallying the marchers to stand up against discrimination.

"This is going to be about us," he began, speaking without notes, improvising to develop themes raised in earlier testimonials. "The impression always is that if something gets old—it deteriorates." (Harold's South Philadelphia accent turns the last word into "deteriates.") "But no more. We are talking about fine wine!" As the crowd burst into laughter and calls of "Amen," Harold smiled, his voice growing raspier and more impassioned: "The older it gets, the better it is! Without further adieu, I have this to say: We, the members of Experience Corps, are America's greatest asset!"

By now the revival was in full swing, and Harold in full form: "And we are denied that fact by being told to sit down, get out of the way, pushed to the side. 'You're a liability.' 'You're the reason health care cost is going up.' Over here is a young man who says, 'These people are our asset.'" As Harold looked toward me, I felt a twinge of embarrassment at having been singled out.

"Let's get that. Because we have within us the best of this country." Now he was pointing to Juanita Holliday, the jazz singer:

When Juanita opened up, she sang a song, "Over the Rainbow." That's the dream. We remember that dream. Judy Garland. *1939!* You remember what else from 1939? Depression. Hard times. Open, vicious discrimination. You were told you weren't going to be anything! [Amens from the crowd]

But we kept that dream, kept looking for the rainbow, and the key to that dream was *go to school!* The one thing every family was teaching—the one thing—was education. Education was so paramount. Remember the night schools? [moans of assent] The poor teachers never had time off! They had more adults in night school than they had children in the daytime, because everybody knew the way out of that deep, dark hole—that depression—was education.

Today is almost sixty years later. Sixty years since we went over that rainbow. And we've hit rock bottom again. But I know some of you hear another voice, a voice that our youngsters can relate to. *"I believe I can fly!"* It is the same dream, in their language. That was thirty-nine, this is ninety-eight, but we survived and we can tell them, "We are going to help you climb out of this hole. And, yes, you *can* fly!"

So all I want to say today is we have been given a great opportunity to give back this rich experience that we have. So let's not be modest: We *are the* most talented, *the* most gifted, people around nowadays.

We *are* America's greatest asset.

So let's put it to work!

The room erupted as Harold finished, with volunteers and teachers stomping their feet, laughing and clapping. Harold glided back to his seat—a wry grin tucked in the corner of his mouth. Without missing a beat, Juanita was up again, thanking everybody for coming and singing Louis Armstrong's standard, "Wonderful World."

A half hour later, the music ended, and soon the room was virtually empty. But Harold was still hanging around, still animated. When he saw me the first thing out of his mouth was "This is about rejuvenation! It's all about rejuvenation"—about a rebirth of activism, about a return to the community, about the older generation coming back to help out the children who needed it most.

He had been there once before, and he could taste the old feeling again. For him, the Experience Corps had become something of a new beginning—"a wake-up call" stirring idealism long dormant and providing a glimpse of new possibilities yet to come.

Operation Get Back

A year after the Philadelphia celebration, the *New York Times* featured a story on Experience Corps highlighting Harold Allen, accompanied by a color photograph of him tutoring a young girl at Taylor. Although delighted about the attention the program was getting, Harold told the *Times* reporter that he should not be portrayed as a hero: "I get a lot of credit because of the time I give," he confessed to her. "But, you see, this is a fulfillment thing for me. It fulfills me and gives me a sense of purpose."

Although there can be no dismissing the importance of what Harold is accomplishing in the schools of North Philadelphia, his comments reflect the widespread view among Experience Corps members that they are getting much more than they are giving. There is almost a collective sense of guilt among these individuals about how much of a "fulfillment thing" this work ends up being.

This lesson was driven home to me again while I was interviewing one of the Port Arthur volunteers. I had somehow wandered into describing the origins of the Experience Corps name and its emphasis on the asset so many older adults bring to their roles, when the woman, looking surprised, interrupted me: "I thought it was about all the *experiences* I was having," she exclaimed. Her perception was that the Corps was where older Americans went to have experiences. At that moment I realized, once again, the genius of John Gardner's name for the program. (Later I encountered some volunteers who were convinced the name Experience Corps was selected because the goal of the program was to provide "experiences" for young people—adding yet another layer of richness.)

Regardless of interpretation of the program name, there was virtual consensus among the Experience Corps volunteers I interviewed that the reliable basis for sustaining these efforts and expanding them to involve many more people is the powerful match that exists between giving and getting. Just as Experience Corps proved to be a "forgiving" model in terms of meeting the approval and needs of schools, it appears to be the same as far as the volunteers are concerned. Their involvement does not depend on great self-sacrifice. They are getting so much back themselves that they can accommodate many of the frustrations and ambiguities that often accompany working in the realm of inner-city schools.

So what is it exactly that Experience Corps volunteers get back in the course of their efforts? The answer is the usual suspects, pretty much the same collection of benefits described in previous chapters and in other programs, ranging from Foster Grandparents to the Samaritan House Clinic. It appears that waitresses and doctors, bus drivers and teachers, carpenters and computer engineers, all reap approximately the same benefits from making a substantial commitment to service in the third age.

The most basic of these benefits is simply building back some structure into their lives, after losing the day-to-day routines that came with previous work. Lorie LeMay, serving at Lent Elementary School in Portland, retired in her late fifties from her career as a deputy sheriff. "At first, it was great, planting my yard and stuff. I kept up with all the soaps. But that grew real old."

Sometimes, Experience Corps also helped the volunteers get back on their feet after losing a spouse. When she received the AARP letter calling for Experience Corps members, Marian Chambers in the Bronx was still recovering from her husband's death. "It was a year ago in April that he passed," she remembered. "And I said, 'Gee, this is something to get me out of the house,' because I was really grieving, and at the same time, I could help somebody."

As with Chambers, for most of the volunteers, new structure alone was only part of the allure of Experience Corps. They were looking to do something both valuable and valued. Martha Jones, one of Harold Allen's teammates in Philadelphia (known on the team as "Little Martha," in contrast with her more robust colleague, Martha Chew), told a story that shows the interrelationship among these objectives. Jones recalled waking up on a particularly bleak February Philadelphia morning and not wanting to get out of bed. If not for Experience Corps, she would have stayed under the covers, the drapes drawn, for most of the day. But she knew she was expected at Taylor, so Jones pulled herself out of bed, got dressed, and climbed into her car.

When she arrived at Taylor, the seventy-year-old woman still wasn't feeling lively—wondering whether, in fact, she wouldn't be better off back in bed. However, as Jones was hanging up her coat on a rack in the classroom, she felt a faint sensation from behind and looked down to discover "these two little arms" wrapping themselves around her. "I'm short and they can reach me—and I was surprised," she chuckled. "I got these two little arms around me. It just caught me off guard, but I was really moved by that. I said, 'Hey, somebody likes me!'"

Many other Experience Corps volunteers recounted variations on this story, such as being mobbed by adoring young people waiting for them when they arrived at school, as if they were rock stars or human magnets. They also talked about the children's response when they took a day off or were out on vacation. According to Richard Russell: "When I don't show up, right away with the children, it's 'Where you been? We were looking for you!'"

Overall, the close, caring, and reciprocal relationships formed with the young people were, in the opinion of most Experience Corps members, the paramount benefit they derived from participating. They talked about how these relationships provide a chance to be generative, to leave a legacy with the next generation. Harold Allen articulated a sentiment felt by many of the volunteers: "You want to leave good memories of yourself, and you hope to leave something behind that's worthwhile." Victory Story, a volunteer at the Lent school in Portland, visualized this kind of impulse reverberating into the future: "What we do here makes a circle back around so that others can go out and do the same thing." In particular, she expressed hope that the kindness the children receive from Experience Corps members will inspire them one day to serve the next generation.

These feelings of attachment to the children and concern about their future do not always make life easy for Experience Corps members. As Lorie LeMay admitted, "I have a couple of kids . . . some nights I go home and I cry because I feel so helpless to do something about their lives." But most of the time she feels that her contribution brings some hope desperately missing in the children's lives. Richard Russell in the Bronx maintains a similar perspective: "Sometimes, I'll be sittin' there, my wife'll say, 'What's the matter?' I say, 'Lord, I don't know what I got myself into!' But most of the time, it makes me feel that I have accomplished something."

In the study of Experience Corps volunteers conducted by Dr. Linda Fried and other Johns Hopkins researchers, 68 percent of the men and women in the program stated that they had learned new skills, while 74 percent responded that they had grown personally. The Hopkins study on Experience Corps also revealed health-related benefits as well as significant improvement in volunteers' perceptions of being emotionally supported.

In interviews, the Experience Corps members attributed these improvements in support primarily to being part of a team. One stated, "If I had been doing the same things here, but with no team, I would have quit. The problems in the school are too overwhelming, and I would have felt I couldn't make any difference all by myself." Another, who lost her husband before joining, said: "I was talking yesterday afternoon with a teacher [and] I was saying, 'You lose your own family, but through this program, it's like you gain another family,' because we joke, we work together, we support each other, and you know, we share a lot of experiences."

Jean Burnside from the South Bronx (who went on to become a New York City public school teacher after a year in Experience Corps) also described her team members as a second family, speaking of their role with a kind of reverence: "It was like I had a dream and then it came true, to be among people who want the same thing from their hearts—to help the children." I met Burnside at P.S. 154, in the converted locker room that is headquarters to the Experience Corps there. Windowless, airless, lined with cinder-block walls and broken gym lockers, the room nevertheless is home for the team. A group of parents and teachers volunteered their time to paint the room, which includes an out-of-tune piano in an alcove toward the back. At the other end sits the coffeepot, focal point for impromptu conversations among the team, next to a brand new microwave presented as a gift by school staff after the Experience Corps team's second year in the school.

Visiting the Experience Corps in their P.S. 154 headquarters is a bit like dropping in on a family reunion. The atmosphere in the room is usually festive, despite the austere space. It is a place where the volunteers can take a breather, laugh, tell stories, even complain about frustrations without having to worry about being overheard. They celebrate each other's birthdays in the room—much as they celebrate the children's outside it. The oldest member of the team, Ernie Wilder (cousin of former Virginia governor Doug Wilder), even has his own special chair reserved for him out of deference to his age.

Getting involved in Experience Corps conferred a variety of benefits on the men and women who came forward to participate—adding structure to their lives, providing a sense of purpose, expanding their social networks, and enhancing health—but for many of these volunteers, the whole added up to something more than these individual parts. They found in Experience Corps a source of renewal—the beginning of a new life.

Alfreda Horn joined the Experience Corps project at the Highbridge Community Life Center in the South Bronx looking to start a new chapter after years employed in a toy factory ("mainly I was putting dolls' heads on backwards," she recalled to Constance Casey of the Newhouse News Service). Horn described the Experience Corps as the most satisfying work of her life, although the satisfaction also has been bittersweet: "Sometimes I feel sad that I had to wait till this time in my life to find something I enjoy so much."

One of the most compelling stories about finding a new life through Experience Corps belongs to Edward Blystone. A truck driver with the *Chicago Sun-Times*, Blystone quit his job after his wife lost her battle with cancer. Alcohol had been a problem for him in the past, and he started drinking heavily. Aware that he was in real trouble, Blystone deeded the Chicago triplex he owned to his children. He then headed to Portland, Oregon, essentially to drink himself into oblivion. After being thrown out of a skid-row hotel for launching a television set through a window during a bender, Blystone ended up living for nearly five years on the docks of Portland.

"Sometimes I enjoyed it because I love the outdoors, being outside," he recalled, "but it's not a life. It's just an existence, that's all it is." Staying clean was one of the most difficult parts of being homeless, and virtually every penny Blystone could get his hands on went toward alcohol.

One freezing night he was nearing the end, dying of pneumonia, with a fever of 105. He couldn't even move. Although not a religious man, he began praying, promising that if he survived he would sober up and spend his remaining time helping other people. Later that night the man was rescued by a homeless outreach group, Blanket Coverage. After he was released from the hospital, Blystone started spending most of his time volunteering for Blanket Coverage, later joining Experience Corps at Lent Elementary School.

Meeting Blystone at Lent one would never guess that the man was living on the streets just a few years earlier. In fact, for the first six months I knew him, I had no idea of his homeless past. Ed looks the Teamster he once was: stocky frame, pot belly, round face, and a smile missing several prominent teeth (attributable to his rabblerousing *Sun-Times* days). The last time I saw him he was wearing a "Love Is Ageless" T-shirt presented to him and the other Experience Corps volunteers by the teachers at Lent.

Along with mentoring half a dozen children at Lent, Blystone started a film night to involve more parents in the school and designed a button that Experience Corps volunteers sell in the community. He is also a fierce advocate for children. As he watched students storm down a Lent corridor, he commented, "I know it sounds corny—but right out there in those halls is the future of our country."

Lori LeMay described Ed as "the rock of Gibraltar," the backbone of their Experience Corps team, and one of the backbones of the Lent school. He reminded me of Nick, another one who battled alcohol but managed to pull through. On the docks of Portland, Blystone was known for his kindness, someone who always shared an extra blanket or would help out a friend in trouble. That same sense of caring is evident with the children. "You get hooked, you really do," he confessed, taking pains to explain that at this point he's hardly a sentimentalist.

In addition to Blystone, the Lent team is anchored by Victory Story and Laurie Chilcote. The trio and the team they lead (which includes Lorie LeMay, Diane Rothery, Doris Bowman, and seven other volunteers crossing a wide socioeconomic spectrum) have long amazed me. The Lent school is in the heart of the Lents neighborhood, an all-white, impoverished section of Portland known locally as Felony Flats because it has the highest proportion of parolees of anywhere in the Northwest (it is also a skinhead enclave). The Lent school has the lowest reading scores in the state, despite an excellent principal and committed teachers. The needs at the school, in a state where education dollars have been cut back drastically, and in a neighborhood where poverty rates are exceptionally high, are monumental.

In the midst of Felony Flats, the Lent Experience Corps team is led by three individuals who can only be described as outcasts in the context of that neighborhood. The trio includes the recently homeless Blystone; Victory Story, an African American cable TV minister serving in a neighborhood that can be fairly characterized as inhospitable to African Americans; and Laurie Chilcote, a disabled gay activist in an area where a person is gay only at great personal peril.

Story, who has a master's in social work, was formerly a social worker in Topeka, Kansas. She moved to Portland to attend graduate school in religion, in the process changing her name from Elsie to Victory. Today, in addition to spending half-time serving in Experience Corps, she produces (and hosts) "Community on the Move," a spiritually oriented television show focusing on good works happening in Portland's communities.

Chilcote, named for one of the few male characters in *Little Women*, helped found the Portland Gay and Lesbian Archive. He grew up in the Lents neighborhood, where his sister now edits the local newspaper, but left Portland after college. He was working in Los Angeles when he was run over by a hit-and-run driver in the early 1990s. After the accident, in too much pain to work, he returned to Portland a broken man, subsisting on disability checks and consumed with self-pity. "For a long time I felt sorry for myself," he recalled in one interview. "Here I was crippled. I was kind of drifting aimlessly."

Chilcote learned about Experience Corps from his mother, who was a

Foster Grandparent. It turned his life around: "It's the opposite of a thread you pull and the sweater comes unraveled. You pull on this thread, and you find yourself connected."

Up the Learning Curve

Nearly forty years have passed since Robert Kennedy issued his call for a national corps capable of capturing the "years of productivity and service" he believed millions of older Americans had to offer. At the time, Kennedy told Congress that he had already encountered so much enthusiasm for a corps of this type, he was convinced America stood on the verge of accomplishing "something unique . . . something undone . . . something still to be done."

As we prepare to enter the new century, Kennedy's dream remains "still to be done." But there is again the sense that we might be on the threshold of something unique. Not only do we have much greater knowledge and experience in this arena than at the time RFK made his case for a corps, but also we find ourselves in the midst of a new wave of innovation in efforts to mobilize older Americans on behalf of society.

And, once again, we hear appeals for a massive new "corps" in certain respects reminiscent of Kennedy's proposal. These calls come from a variety of experts, and the list seems to be steadily growing: gerontologist Ken Dychtwald proposes a large-scale national "Elder Corps"; philosopher Michael Lerner believes we need a new "Senior Corps"; former Brookdale Center on Aging director Harry Moody suggests a "U.S. Wisdom Corps"; Brookings Institution economist Laurel McFarland argues for a "Pepper Corps" (named for the elderly advocate Claude Pepper and focused on older adults providing child care); and journalist Richard Louv envisions a "national army of winter soldiers." The distinguished geriatrician Robert Butler advocated a national corps of older adults in his 1975 book *Why Survive?* and revived the idea in a 1997 *Journal of American Medical Association* article laying out an intergenerational version of such a program.

Despite so many different proposals and so many distinguished champions, most of these recommendations—like Robert Kennedy's earlier conception—raise key questions about what such an institution might actually look like at the ground level. The Experience Corps was—and is—an attempt to put some flesh on the bones of the idea of a national corps while testing out a specific set of "educated" hunches about what might work best in such an arrangement. It is also an effort that has involved some of the most important aging organizations in the country, including the National Senior Service Corps, Elderhostel, AARP, and the Department of Medicine at Johns Hopkins.

The results so far have been profoundly encouraging. They suggest that the right kind of corps can fly, and that it might well be propelled forward on the wings of mutual benefit—a win-win logic that leaves all participants feeling they are getting the better end of the deal. In fact, since the conclusion of the initial Experience Corps pilot, the project has not only survived but has expanded steadily in the original locations, been launched in more than two dozen new places, and moved substantively in a variety of promising new directions.

Along the way, Experience Corps has even managed to capture the interest of some prominent politicians in both parties. Although the project was initiated through the Clinton administration's Corporation for National Service—a favorite target of many Republicans—in delivering his 1996 "State of the State" address, Governor George W. Bush lauded Experience Corps as a model of the "can-do, innovative spirit" that would be required to transform Texas's schools: "Experience Corps," he proclaimed, "has now won private funding and national attention," adding, in reference to the Port Arthur project, "it all started because . . . what Texans can dream Texans can do." A few months later, the First Lady of Texas made Experience Corps a centerpiece of her address to the Republican National Convention.

One-Stop Service

At the same time the Experience Corps idea has moved in new directions and picked up new supporters, the project itself has undergone fundamental revisions. Without doubt, the most significant change has been alteration of the original nature of Experience Corps as a national service program.

When Experience Corps was first launched, "intensive service" was a cardinal tenet. We were essentially looking for "a few good men and women" willing to make a half-time commitment to kids and schools. However, we learned quickly that the half-time role was not for everybody, especially to start. Many individuals responding to our call were unprepared to make such a significant commitment—especially after having not been in a school in many decades and with little sense yet of what they might be getting themselves into.

Sorry, we told them, Experience Corps was not for everybody.

It took a while, but eventually we woke up to the opportunity we were missing and recognized that it made little sense to turn away good people who might make a genuine contribution to kids and schools—at the same time the schools were desperate for more volunteers (some wanted as many as fifty half-time Experience Corps volunteers). So by the second year of the original pilot, we started opening up opportunities for individuals to serve only a few hours a week (usually two to four), so long as they committed to show up on the same days each week and to work consistently with one or two children.

Simultaneously, we started creating opportunities for individuals to make *more intensive* commitments as well (more intensive than the fifteen to twenty hours a week originally envisioned). The immediate impetus was a desire to provide more coordination in the schools—for somebody to be there all day, every day, to serve as a liaison between the school and the Experience Corps—especially as the project was navigating its way through the start-up period in a given location. (Luck also played a part here. As the Experience Corps pilot entered its second year, there was a surplus of VISTA volunteers nationally, and the Corporation for National Service agreed to assign positions in this full-time program to working with the Experience Corps pilot projects.)

As a result of all these developments, the Experience Corps model—which had, in many ways, evolved from long-standing efforts like Foster Grandparents—found itself in the midst of a significant evolution by the second year of the pilot. In place of the original concept, a new approach was devised offering a "one-stop" opportunity for service.

In other words, a person interested in joining the Experience Corps would now find a range of options for contributing—*full-time* (through VISTA), *half-time* (in the original Experience Corps roles), *part-time* (generally two days a week, for two hours each day), or even *some-time*, episodic opportunities (focused on discrete projects lasting anywhere from a few days to a month).

Over time, this arrangement meant that volunteers could move in and out of different options as their life circumstances shifted—with incentives like small stipends and Elderhostel scholarships designed to encourage the major-commitment routes. In reality, some half-time Experience Corps volunteers graduated into full-time positions, as many of these individuals also took on increasing leadership roles in running the program. Others, who started out committing two or four hours a week, signed up for half-time positions after getting inside the school, seeing how much they were needed, and realizing they had what it took to make a significant contribution.

Still others had the freedom to shift in the opposite direction. After putting in a year in a full-time or half-time position, these individuals moved on to other time-consuming pursuits outside Experience Corps (for some, like Jean Burnside, who went on to become a New York City public school teacher, Experience Corps functioned essentially as a sabbatical between their first and second careers). However, having joined the Experience Corps "family," these volunteers jumped at the prospect of staying connected through part-time or "some-time" roles.

Thus, "flexibility" soon came to occupy a central place in our lineup of key Experience Corps elements. This shift also helps to illustrate a larger point: the degree to which we remain in an experimental state with many of the new institutional arrangements being developed. As a result, it will be difficult to rush into place a set of last-minute, large-scale opportunities aimed at enabling the new generation of older Americans to contribute more to society. We need time to test innovative ideas, make some mistakes, experiment with refinements, and go through a cycle or two of informed trial and error before taking all this to the kind of magnitude commensurate with dramatically changing demographics.

And—as the preceding chapters have underscored repeatedly —we don't have forever. The first boomers are fast closing in on the third age. We may be further along the learning curve than when Robert Kennedy first proposed his initiative four decades ago, but we will have to pick up the pace if we hope to shape the coming demographic transformation in its critical, formative stages.

Part of the Solution

According to the prophets of an impending "Gray Dawn," two pillars of the coming intergenerational war are health care and education. When described in the context of health care, older adults are portrayed as a massive and unrelenting burden. But the doctors in places such as Samaritan House and Volunteers in Medicine—like Aggie and Louise on the pediatrics ward at Maine Medical Center—demonstrate that the real situation is more complex and more hopeful. They show that there are many ways older adults can help meet urgent health care needs of society, needs that can only be met by caring and skilled human beings—and that will never be satisfied through the development of new technologies.

To be sure, the fact that older adults can make significant contributions in the area of health care is certainly not to say we don't need to contemplate health care reforms to prepare for the aging society. Rather, their potential is a reminder that with the costs of an aging population come important opportunities as well—even in the places where the most hand-wringing seems to occur. (And, of course, there is reason to believe that the kinds of activities the retired doctors and others are doing to serve in this sphere will likely contribute to prolonging their own physical and mental health in later life.)

Experience Corps makes a parallel point in the other area where older adults are commonly demonized: public education. We've heard that these individuals are "public enemy number one," to quote one newspaper, when it comes to children and their schools. *Newsweek* tells us that "a big loser in the generational tug of war may well be education," while one *New York Times* article quotes a school superintendent in suburban Phoenix, who asserts that the elderly "can generate 3,000 to 5,000 votes for any [education] issue that comes up, and these votes come in at least 90 percent no." The article goes on to present a superintendent of schools in New Jersey who states flatly: "The elderly consistently defeat the budget."

As we have seen, the cases of Sun City West and of Youngtown provide distressing examples that support this perspective. As we move rapidly toward a point when nearly half the voters will be in the over-fifty age group, the prospect of older Americans becoming disconnected from the public education system and the concerns of children is something worth worrying about.

However, as Experience Corps demonstrates, there is another side to this story as well. Operating at "ground zero" of the prophesied generational Armageddon, the Experience Corps illustrates some of the ways third agers might meet the current and future needs of public education—providing more caring and attention to young people, filling essential gaps in the schools, supporting teachers in their work, and helping to humanize the climate of these often impersonal institutions. Furthermore, the opportunity to see schools from the inside out has transformed many Experience Corps members into informed and vigorous advocates for public education in the community.

So valuable was the support provided by Experience Corps volunteers that many of the schools involved began putting their own scarce dollars into continuing or expanding the program. When federal funding ran out for the Olney Elementary School in Philadelphia, for example, principal Henry Barsky decided to put every penny of his school's $13,000 in discretionary resources into Experience Corps, explaining to a reporter from the *Philadel-phia Inquirer*: "Why pursue something else when something we already have is successful?" Barsky's colleague, Morrison Elementary School principal Alan Katz, put it even more starkly, wondering: "I don't know how we survived before Experience Corps."

I encountered a parallel point repeatedly in talking with the men and women in Experience Corps, who often wondered aloud about their own lives before they became involved in this effort. For them, the school had become a kind of renewal center—a place to go in retirement to find purpose, to uncover fresh possibilities, to join a supportive community, and ultimately, for many, to launch a new chapter in their lives. In the process, they were carving out a new relationship between the older population and the schools, one in which the school building, historically an age-segregated enclave, was being transformed into a new institution for intergenerational growth.

PART FIVE

ALEX HARRIS

Marv Welt, age seventy, was born in Chicago. When he was a small boy, his mother, a vaudeville actress, committed suicide in front of him, and his father, a theater agent, abandoned the family. Marv was raised by relatives on the South Side, before going off to World War II, where he was captured and held as a prisoner of war in Germany, eventually escaping. After the war, he attended the University of Chicago on the G.I. Bill, studying literature with Saul Bellow but going on to a career as a management consultant. Upon retiring, he turned his lifetime passion for fishing into an environmental education program (first called the Watershed Program, than expanded into the Waterworld Program) operating in nine low-income Portland, Oregon, public schools. For part of this period, he was also a member of the Portland Experience Corps.

·

When I retired, I was ready to stop working. I had been successful, but a lot of things were getting to me. In consulting it's nothing to work fourteen- or even sixteen-hour days. The pressure is terrible. You're dealing with millions of dollars, and the company expects you to pay for yourself on the bottom line. I was away five days a week, sometimes more. I missed out on raising my own kids.

But after being retired a while, I started getting itchy. I didn't want to just sit. That's when a friend of mine with the Oregon Department of Fish and Wildlife said, "Hey, you've done a lot of fishing all your life. There's an Angler Education Program and we'd like you to be involved." That's really where it started. I started teaching kids living in housing projects how to fish. I'd take them on fishing trips, and I noticed that some kids were in awe of the outdoors, but others were afraid of it or had no understanding of nature.

I enjoyed the kids and the fishing. Really, anything to do with water or marine biology, it's my hobby. It always has been. My happiest times growing up were going with my aunt and grandmother to Lake Geneva, Wisconsin. I would fish and swim, and I'd walk alone at night, coming back along the lakes. I'd see deer. I'd see raccoons. And I would see things in the water, things I knew weren't fish. And I was fascinated. What were they? That's how my interest started to evolve. It was an escape from the city to learn about these different things.

After being involved in the Angler Education Program for a while, I thought, this has been my hobby all my life. Why don't I do something other than just take kids fishing and then drop them. Which is what I was essentially doing. The kids would ask, "Isn't Marv ever coming back?" And that bothered me, so I started thinking, what can I do that is more ongoing?

I decided to go back to school, to Portland State, and started taking courses—entomology, aquaculture—so that I knew more, and that I could do something more. Portland State's got a great deal. If you're a "senior citizen," you can go for free. You don't get credits, but I didn't care about credits—I wanted the knowledge! I took a lot of science, but also other courses I had missed when I was in school. The French novel and Greek mythology, modern poetry, even drama. It was great. I didn't have to submit papers if I didn't want to. I didn't have to worry about grades. I could just go for the fun of it. And I enjoyed being around college kids. I think a lot of them were really surprised at how much we had in common.

By the time I finished at Portland State, the Watershed Program was ready, and the first place I tried it was Portsmouth Elementary School. Somebody gave me the name of the science teacher there. I knew Whitaker Pond, which wasn't too far from the school, and I knew its water drains into the slough. So I started taking groups of kids from Portsmouth School on field trips to Whitaker.

Here was a resource right at their doorstep that the kids were not aware of. Smith and Bybee Lakes are there too, in the same area. Smith Lake has the largest collection of the western painted turtle of any place in the country. Everything is just right for them there, and they've multiplied.

Over time, the word spread, and the program started growing. At one point my son said, "What about teaching the children about water testing?" So I got some kits and I'd say to kids, "Why would we want to test the water? Can fish live in orange juice or battery acid?" I taught them how to use the kits and to test the acidity of the water. But I kept asking them, "Why do we want to know about this? Did you know fish need oxygen, and the water's got oxygen in it?" Kids don't know that. It's a little introduction to ichthyology and to some of the other sciences—and teachers seem to like the program because it helps build vocabulary. It also teaches kids about the life cycle—especially when we're learning about salmon.

It's great to see the kids respond—sometimes I think I could run for mayor if they could vote! Why wouldn't they respond—they have fun. Now I'm not saying everyone. Some of them are afraid of the outdoors. Some figure when they're not in the classroom, it's a holiday. Some are also angry kids. But I can relate pretty well to them because I was an angry kid myself.

But when I was a child, being raised by my aunt and my grandmother, this gentleman took me under his wing, Mr. Riggs. I remember, he said he was going over to the Lincoln Park Casting Club, and would I like to go? (I thought, casting? What's that? Is he making ball bearings or something?) And once I got started I would get backlashes, and being an angry kid, I had no patience. Mr.

Riggs would calmly help me pick out snarls. He taught me patience, and he taught me sportsmanship. But he didn't lecture, he just did it by example. He made a big difference in my life. He was really a grandfather figure, even more than a father figure—he was already gray-haired when I knew him. And something from that is still with me.

In fact, when I retired, I remember thinking back and feeling, don't I owe something? And I felt I did. I felt I owed it to Mr. Riggs, but mainly I think I owed it to myself. Not to sit down, start watching television, drinking beer. That's what my neighbor did, and he was dead within two years. I worried that would happen to me too, that I'd just sort of waste away. I knew I had to keep active. Then it was a question of what do I have to give.

There are some selfish reasons too. The things I love, whether it's the painted turtle or the clean water, whatever it is, these kids are going to decide what happens to our environment. Faster than the blink of an eye. I can't believe how fast the years have gone by since I was forty. How fast it happened. Here I am, an old man. [laughs]

When the program expanded beyond the slough, I changed its name from Watershed to Waterworld. I got into the rivers, asking kids, "What is a river used for? What kind of fish are in the river? What do these fish need?" All these questions. Then it led to the estuaries and to the sea. And of course this tied right in with salmon because the fry turn into parr and they live for a year in the river before they go to sea. And I started talking to them about the wetlands: "What purpose do they serve? What is a flood plain? What happens if water comes to a wetland? Suppose you pave it over?"

I ask a lot of questions and let them give me crazy answers. But mostly they come through. You can't sell these kids short. You just lay the foundation and then, layer by layer, they figure things out. I think sometimes we tend to not challenge children enough.

I'm always pushing them, and when you have a rapport going between you and the class, and a few students start to get into it, and the interest builds, and suddenly the whole class is with you, it's very exciting. To be involved in something that is real, and important, when they're getting it and they're having fun doing it and you're having fun doing it, it's like a symphony coming together in the end. It builds into something very moving.

In fact, I enjoy teaching the kids so much I have regrets. It seems so natural.

Maybe I should have gone into teaching. Maybe I would have had a much happier life. Probably not financially, but overall. I think I would have a had a much more fulfilling life. But you know how you change over the years. If somebody would have said to me when I was in college, why don't you major in education, I would have looked at them like they were crazy.

Before I retired I had no idea I would be doing any of this. I was too involved in what I was doing to be thinking about what's next. But it gives a purpose to life that I think everybody needs. Sitting out in your RV contemplating your navel is, to me, a total waste. What are you doing? Taking up space. You've got to give something of yourself, and I don't just mean paying your taxes. You've got to give something of what you can do.

I have one friend, he has terrible asthma, but he delivers food every Thursday, brings food to people in their house through Meals on Wheels. This is what he likes to do. And he is contributing something. It gives him a reason to get up in the morning, and he feels better about himself. It is a strain on him. We used to take walks by Smith and Bybee Lakes, but he can't do that anymore. He couldn't walk from here to the corner. But he manages to deliver meals by car. He is doing what he is capable of doing.

If everybody could just do that—just give a little bit—what a difference it would make.

CHAPTER 6

If We Build It. . .

There is at bottom only one problem in the world and this is
its name. How does one break through? How does one get
into the open? How does one burst the cocoon and become a butterfly?

.

Thomas Mann

Powerful new conditions are emerging in America today that have the
potential to transform retirement and later life as we know it. Indeed,
changes are appearing much as they were lining up fifty years ago, on
the eve of the "golden years."

Some of these important developments, including the budding movement of
social entrepreneurs, have already been chronicled. But there are other promising signs as well. For example, the *Wall Street Journal* reports a sharp rise in the
number of men in their fifties and sixties becoming physician's assistants, after
first acts in far different fields. Most of the older students composing this
phenomenon, the *Journal* asserts, are accommodating "an overriding desire to
use their remaining years for society's good."

Perhaps the most visible sign of change afoot is the ascendance of a new
group of high-profile role models, individuals who are rejecting through
words and deeds the old notion of aging as disengagement. Lee Iacocca is
one example. After retiring from Chrysler, Iacocca decided to "come clean"
about the auto industry's record on pollution, recycling his skills and knowledge into developing environmentally sound electric bicycles that can go
twenty miles without being recharged. In the process, the former CEO has
missed few opportunities to use his own example to put forward the message
"Don't retire!" He advises anyone over fifty: "Don't start planning your retirement—plan the next third of life."

John Glenn's return to space in 1998, thirty-six years after his first journey, may well be remembered as a milestone in the appearance of a new chapter in America's long experience with aging. Glenn's flight aboard the shuttle *Discovery* captured the nation's imagination, and much focus of public discussion was on the astronaut's age. It led Gene Cernan, the last person to walk on the moon, to observe that Glenn's trip had "probably done more for the senior citizens in the country than Viagra."

In a now famous statement after returning, Glenn proclaimed: "Just because you're up in years some doesn't mean you don't have hopes and dreams and aspirations just as much as younger people do." His message was not lost on the media. Columnist Jonathan Alter wrote afterward that the trip was not merely a reminder that older adults can do adventure travel. Glenn's trip signaled the beginning, Alter wrote in a *Newsweek* essay, of "not just more septuagenarian space travelers but more tutors and child-care workers and counselors, perhaps tens of millions more local heroes as the baby boom retires, in a vast autumn harvest of experience."

Even in this pantheon of impressive second acts, former President Jimmy Carter stands out as the preeminent role model of a transformed retirement. Together with his wife Rosalyn, Carter wrote *Everything to Gain: Making the Most of the Rest of Your Life,* after being turned out of the White House at age fifty-six. In the nearly twenty years since then, the Carters have made good on the title, volunteering with Habitat for Humanity, establishing the Carter Center, helping to bring together rich and poor through the Atlanta Project, teaching Sunday school, serving as an agent of peace internationally, climbing mountains, learning to ski, and writing prolifically about all these experiences, most recently in the best-seller *The Virtues of Aging.*

Throughout, Carter has symbolized a third age that could be the best stage of life, arguing that "retirement has not been the end but a new beginning" and prompting former Georgia Senator Sam Nunn to comment that Carter was "the only man who used the office of President of the United States to achieve a better position." It is striking to witness someone who reached the pinnacle of achievement in midlife yet found greater fulfillment in the next phase—and who arguably is now having even a greater impact on society here and abroad than when he was president.

Coming of Age

The good news is that the impulse toward a new kind of later life—one that is "a new beginning"—does not appear confined to former CEOs, astronauts, and presidents. Growing awareness among Americans that the third age is no longer a brief intermezzo between midlife and drastic decline (a recent study of boomers found that they consider seventy-nine to be the onset of old age) is fueling a reexamination and redefinition among many of what it means to grow older. Indeed, when asked to choose between two different versions of retirement in a 1999 survey by Peter D. Hart Research Associates—the first as "a time to take it easy, take care of yourself, enjoy leisure activities, and take a much-deserved rest from work and daily responsibilities," and the second as "a time to begin a new chapter in life by being active and involved, starting new activities, and setting new goals"—65 percent of Americans age 50–75 selected the latter choice, while only 28 percent embraced the more traditional notion. The numbers were even more dramatic for the group not yet retired, mostly younger individuals in the boomer and preboomer cohorts.

More specifically, what is this emerging new chapter likely to look like? One principal element, research suggests, will be a more education in later life. Enrollment by third agers like Marv Welt in college courses already is soaring, as are the numbers on individuals obtaining new degrees in their sixties, seventies, even eighties. And many want more than classes. We are already seeing what *Newsweek* calls "a golden age on campus," as thousands of third agers flock to live in retirement communities near institutions of higher education. Without doubt, part of the lure is access to the cultural of-ferings associated with universities, but some experts feel there is also a yearning to recapture the sense of community many third agers still associate with their college days. Another reason is the desire to be in proximity to younger generations.

Alongside lifelong learning, another prominent feature of "the new retire-ment" will be continued contribution, of various forms. A 1998 survey by AARP found that 80 percent of baby boomers were planning to work during their so-called retirement years, in contrast to 12 percent of the over-65 pop-ulation in the current paid labor market for full- or part-time work. Most other studies point in a similar direction. For example, research from the Employee Benefit Research Institute indicates that while two-thirds of older

Americans would like to retire from full-time work before age 65, nearly three-quarters still want to do some part-time work in the ensuing decades.

Balance will be a likely watchword for these individuals, who will attempt to assemble lives that include work but are no longer dominated by it. When researchers probe more deeply into why these people want to work at all, it becomes clear that for most the principal motivation is not financial. Whereas about a fifth of boomers (what one study calls the "have-nots") will work because they have to work to stay afloat economically, for most the impetus comes from a desire for meaning and fulfillment. When individuals are asked, as they were in one 1999 study, "How important to you is it that your job involve some type of service or contribution to the community," 64 percent respond that it is either a very or fairly important consideration in the kind of work they choose, and a mere 15 percent indicate that it is not a serious consideration.

Given the strong preference that third-age employment be socially redeeming, it is no surprise that most studies also reveal that the new generation of older Americans is planning to make volunteer work a central part of later life. Next to travel, volunteering is the second highest priority for this group. Many also appear to be well disposed to high-commitment opportunities such as national service projects. When Americans age 50–75 were asked specifically in the 1999 Peter Hart survey about interest in participating in half-time roles resembling those offered by Experience Corps, the results were stunning.

Notwithstanding my patriotism toward Experience Corps, I would have guessed that perhaps 5 percent of third agers might be attracted to such high-commitment roles. (Indeed, that was one of the reasons we created more part-time and "some-time" options in the program.) Ultimately, if pressed, I would have predicted that perhaps 1–2 percent of the older population might ultimately be enticed to join such an initiative. (Still, these are not percentages to scoff at—1 percent of the older population today is approximately equal to the number of individuals participating in Elderhostel each year.)

Instead, 40 percent of respondents to the Hart survey said they were either "very interested" or "fairly interested" in participating in these half-time assignments. Among the segment of the survey not yet retired—principally younger boomers and preboomers—27 percent said they were very interested, while an additional 21 percent indicated they were fairly interested. Taken together, these figures account for nearly half the young-old population. Given that the over-65 segment alone will swell to nearly 70 million over the next three decades, the potential size of this involvement is staggering.

If just 5 percent of the over-65 population could be recruited into such an arrangement—the same proportion of older adults who relocate to retirement communities—the result would be 3–4 million people ultimately engaged in significant service to communities and to the younger generation. That's more than 50 million hours of contribution every week. Furthermore, these calculations do not include the 55–65 age group, an alluring potential pool for efforts combining genuine contribution, income support, and, potentially, health benefits.

These findings suggest that with the right vehicle (really, vehicles), boomers interested in giving back might saturate our neighborhoods, schools, parks, and community organizations with desperately needed human resources—in much the way that same cohort began flooding higher education in the 1960s. We couldn't build campuses fast enough to accommodate these men and women back then, and we may well be pressed to build sufficient service opportunities in the approaching decades. But if that challenge can be met, the result would be an absolute windfall for civil society.

Gold in the Gray

Anyone searching for added affirmation that later life is in the process of being transformed, or that there are significant opportunities that will accompany the aging of America, need look no further than the commercial sector. As one leading management consultant told the *Los Angeles Times* in 1998, "Over the next twenty years, the business community will target everything toward" the aging boomers, whom he termed "*the growth industry of the 21st century.*"

Already there is a profusion of products and gadgets being concocted to ease the transition into later life and lighten the wallets of the new third agers, and the service industry is clamoring to hire more members of the older population. According to Thomas Grass, a consultant with Watson Wyatt Worldwide, "You never saw seniors working at a McDonald's, and now there are two or three at every one." The same can be said for Wal-Marts, Days Inns, and hundreds of other companies looking for a stable and responsible workforce at a juncture when the number of young people is declining.

But within this much broader trend, the financial services sector and the retirement community builders—those same two industries that started selling idealized notions of a leisured retirement in the 1950s—offer the most revealing glimpses of what the future holds. For nearly a half century, the pitch from the pension purveyors has been essentially the same. Ironically, a perfect example of this message can be found in the middle of Pete Peterson's 1996 *Atlantic* article lambasting the older population as a bunch of shiftless freeloaders: a glossy full-page ad from ITT/Hartford depicting a smartly dressed, sixty-something couple dancing on the deck of a boat, kicking up their heels and laughing like a pair of joyous teenagers. Accompanying the idyllic scene is this message: "One day you'll get to act like a kid again . . . but for now, let's discuss your allowance."

Leaving little to the imagination, the appeal continues: "In one respect, retirement is a lot like childhood. You have all the free time in the world. The only problem is that 'free' time is anything but free." After peddling Hartford's pensions and other retirement services, the advertisement concludes: "So if you're interested in one day acting like a ten-year-old again, talk to a company that's nearly 200 years old."

Three years later, the predominant message emanating from the pension industry is a dramatically different one. The first example of the shift I noticed was from American Express, which placed an ad in *Newsweek* featuring an alluring photograph of three attractive sixty-somethings, two women and a man, huddled together, wearing hard hats, jeans, and construction gear. One of the women is sporting her hardhat backward, home-boy style. The trio is the picture of engagement, with barely concealed joy on their faces. Signs make it clear that they are at a Habitat for Humanity site.

The message accompanying the American Express ad is not the traditional "buy our pension so that you can enjoy the golden years." It is, essentially, "buy our pension so you can do something important with this new phase of life." Specifically, it reads: "Do you have the financial security to choose your own path?" And for readers who "see retirement as a chance to volunteer your time," it poses this question: "How do you know you've saved enough?"—enough to be able to make this choice. The tag line at the bottom is American Express's new motto, "Do More."

Shortly after encountering the American Express ad, I began noticing a Paine Webber two-page appeal featuring an attractive father and son, the

former wearing an L. L. Bean fleece jacket, while the younger man to his
right is vaguely reminiscent of Leonardo DiCaprio. The message on the opposite page states: "You're psyched about the future. You're full of new ideas.
You're looking to start a business. You're the guy on the left." Below is a message explaining that Paine Webber's competitors say that retirement is the
end of the contributing years, but "We say plan well—so you can redefine retirement any time and any way you want," whether that be for "a second career. A new business. Or a true labor of love." The ad concludes that
"retirement could lead you to the best job description of all—doing what
you've always wanted to do."

A few days later while waiting in my hotel room to interview Marv Welt
about his environmental education effort in the Portland Public Schools, I
found myself watching a T. Rowe Price television commercial that features a
couple in their early 60s expressing gratitude for the help they've received
from the investment company. As a result of their T. Rowe Price no-load
pension, the couple explained, they were finally able to pursue their dream.
The next scene shows the vigorous duo atop a Sierra hilltop, surrounded by
children of varied ethnic backgrounds, the entire group wearing "Friends of
the Wilderness" T-shirts.

Very quickly my collection of these ads has grown thick. I doubt the pile
results from a sudden outburst of altruism on the part of the financial services sector or from a newfound commitment to ridding American society of
outdated ageist stereotypes. These ads exist because these companies, as always, are doing their homework, conducting hundreds of focus groups and
surveys with the coming generation of retirees and altering their message in
accordance with what they are hearing. And they are hearing that people
want a new beginning in the third age, that they want to continue contributing, and that many of them want to do so in ways that involve giving back to
society.

When it comes to doing homework, no company can compare with Del
Webb—which, according to *Builder* magazine, was the fastest-growing
homebuilder in America from 1986 through 1995. At the heart of the Webb
approach is something that company officials term "the research machine,"
which is fully consistent with the late Webb's obsession with being prepared.
The company has a vast staff of in-house researchers who do nothing but
study the boomer market. They receive direct input every year from between
25,000 and 30,000 older Americans through 25 surveys and 180 focus groups.
(Compare this effort with what goes on to find new roles for older people

aimed at strengthening communities, which is essentially ad hoc and insignificant.) In fact, so extensive are these data-gathering and analysis efforts that the company turns an additional profit selling market research to other industries interested in capturing aging boomers' business.

And what has the research machine revealed about what the boomers will want in their third age? In short, as Ken Plonski, a Webb executive states, "We don't build shuffleboard courts anymore." Now the company builds state-of-the-art fitness centers and new developments wired for the Internet. It has also started building Sun Cities in unusual places, like Huntley, Illinois, outside of Chicago, to key into research showing that many of the new retirees want to remain near opportunities for continued work. (This Sun City, a misnomer if there ever was one, given the area's notoriously foul weather, sold out virtually overnight.)

This research has also caused the Webb Company to overhaul its marketing message. Current press releases sport titles like "Redefining Retirement," "Retire Without Really Retiring," and "Shattering the Myth of Retirement," to cite three examples from 1998—and they are accompanied by statements such as "The myth of retirement—of no longer being an active, contributing member of society—is being shattered by millions of productive mature adults around the country." A major emphasis throughout the revamped Webb marketing and development efforts is on the provision of opportunities for older adults to continue learning and to be able to do volunteer service, along with opportunities for part-time employment.

Webb is not the only developer responding to these new priorities on the part of aging Americans. One of the most interesting new-fashioned efforts in this vein (and an example of the coming "golden age on campus") is the $70 million Academy Village in Tucson, on 168 acres adjacent to the University of Arizona. Created by the university's retired president, Henry Koffler, the community will be centered on lifelong learning and continuing contribution. "Ideally, our residents will continue their research, or continue to write books, or compose music, or volunteer their time," states Koffler, adding, "Who can play golf for 30 years?" The organizational core of the complex is something called the Arizona Senior Academy, which will orchestrate classes for the residents and develop volunteer opportunities, particularly through mentoring students and teachers in the local schools and providing the chance for Academy Village residents to offer seminars for the wider community in their areas of expertise.

Seizing the Opportunity

A s these examples help illustrate, a great many interests are already positioning themselves to cash in on the new aging in America—including the same industries that played such a major role in giving us the notion of retirement as leisure and disengagement that has prevailed for nearly a half century. It is striking that now, as before, they are poised to take advantage of new circumstances, having retooled their message and products in ways that promise to captivate the next generation of older Americans.

Developers and financial services are not the only ones preparing to capitalize on the aging of America. Even a number of states are competing strenuously for the discretionary income of retirees, offering incentives and conducting outreach efforts aimed at convincing individuals to relocate to Alabama, Maine, South Carolina, and other locations that view the migration of graying boomers as a high-priority economic development goal.

Isn't it time our communities also began "cashing in" on the aging of America, doing what it takes to ensure that they get their share of the social capital contained in these individuals and of the civic opportunity presented by this great transformation? The circumstances for doing so could not be more ripe, as we move ever closer to that "vast autumn harvest of experience" that Jonathan Alter describes—not to mention the second coming of the 1960s generation, the first wave of boomers, a group of individuals that could well find a second wind of idealism in their later years.

How might we achieve this goal? Four strategies promise to take us in the right direction, and if we act with dispatch, they might even get us rolling in time for the arrival of the first boomers—who will turn sixty in 2006—into the third age.

Develop a New Vision for a New Age

Not long ago, while thumbing through the Sunday *New York Times*, I encountered a photograph of a grimacing grayed-haired man, somewhere in his seventies, dressed in tennis whites and in the midst of a ferocious overhand serve. Immediately below the photograph, in bold letters, was the headline "The Elderly Are Becoming More Active, and Activity Is Improving Their Lives."

The article is a reminder of just how far we've come in the past four decades. An active new way of life, so radical in 1960, is really just a way of life for older Americans today. And as we have seen, older Americans and society are ready for more.

Nevertheless, we continue to lack a compelling vision for later life in this country, a vision both that reflects the new hopes and dreams of third agers and that is capable of inspiring this group to assume new roles in society. Other than some ads for the insurance industry and Del Webb's new press releases, we are struggling to articulate something that could carry us past the golden years as the reigning ideal for the third age.

So far the most prominent response to this vacuum is the notion that older adults should be more "productive," which mostly amounts to a code word for more years in the conventional labor market. This view often ends up dismissing other forms of contribution as insignificant and essentially attempts to replace the outgoing leisure ideal with one glorifying paid work.

Typical of this thinking is a 1999 *New Republic* essay by syndicated columnist Robert Samuelson, who argues that "We need to reject the platitudes that the elderly can contribute to society by volunteering or offering 'wisdom,'" then he adds, "This may be true, but it is a tiny truth." How then might older adults contribute, according to Samuelson? "The main way . . . is by doing the same thing that other adults do: that is, by working, and not becoming a premature social burden."

Samuelson's perspective is distressing. To begin, it fails to understand that all of this is work—whether it be volunteering, national service, or employment. Some is paid, some is unpaid. Some is full-time, some part-time. The question is not the form—we need to encourage a wide range of forms—but the content. All work is not created equal, and we must resist the economistic-oriented conclusion that unpaid work is inherently less equal. (One wonders how Samuelson would characterize the contribution of American women to civil society over the past century—another tiny truth?)

In reflecting on Samuelson's view, I am reminded of a visit to Minneapolis in 1997 to shadow Yakov Gritchener, a retired mathematics teacher who serves twenty hours a week in the Senior Companion Program. On Wednesdays, then as today, Yakov visits with Harry Dychal, a former postman who is legally blind. Yakov helps Harry with some of the basic functions essential for independent living, but mostly he serves as a bulwark against isolation. Over the years, the two men, roughly the same age, have also become friends.

During my visit, Yakov and Harry took me to lunch at their favorite hangout: Burger King (Burger King is particularly generous with discount coupons for senior citizens, and Yakov and Harry clip them assiduously). Arriving at the restaurant, we were waited on by a tall, distinguished-looking older man—"Dave," according to his plastic nametag—outfitted in an orange and blue polyester jumpsuit and a Burger King beanie, punching in computer icons of shakes and fries alongside giggling fifteen-year-olds acquiring their first job experience.

The encounter at the Burger King was unsettling. Dave surely makes twice as much money as Yakov, but I can't imagine the Senior Companion swapping his daily stipend for the Burger King wage. It would come at a great price in both dignity and sense of purpose. It would also be a loss to the community—in terms of the social fabric and in the expense of prematurely institutionalizing individuals like Harry.

The juxtaposition of Yakov and Dave brings with it fundamental questions about how we will respond to the aging of America. As we proceed further into the postindustrial society, there will likely be growing demand for part-time service-sector employees like Dave—just as there is burgeoning need for the kind of "relationship work" Yakov is engaged in, not only within the older population but between the older generation and young people.

In rethinking the role of older Americans and the nature of later life, we will need to protect the right of Dave and others who either need or prefer to work at Burger King or elsewhere. However, as a society, we must also be cultivating and promoting some options over others, and the ones that hold the most promise simultaneously strengthen our communities and enrich the lives of older men and women—in other words, they constitute the biggest "win-win" situations for individuals and for society.

As many of the examples described in earlier chapters illustrate, these win-win opportunities can include paid, labor-market-wage second careers in the public interest, such as the Troops to Teachers program; paid part-time work doing important things in the community, like The Work Connection; stipended national service, as exemplified by aspects of the Experience Corps; and unpaid volunteering, like the Samaritan House Clinic. What unites these disparate arrangements is the content of the work and the immense mutual benefit entailed.

Furthermore, in thinking about cultivating these win-win situations, it is essential to take into account what is distinctive about the third stage of life and the potential contribution older Americans might make. Inherent in

Samuelson's depiction is the notion of later life as, essentially, a warmed over, part-time version of midlife. But we can do much better than that. We must recognize that the third age can be a unique stage of life—not just a rerun of midlife, or for that matter a second childhood, as the leisure industry has for so long portrayed it.

Cicero wrote that "each season of life has an advantage peculiarly its own" to be "garnered each at its proper time." In this vein, Jimmy Carter contends that the "retirement years are a time to define, or redefine, a successful life, both in retrospect and for our remaining years," adding that this future definition is "likely to be quite different from that of our younger years."

A defining capacity of older adults, exhibited by many of the individuals who appear in earlier chapters, exists in the realm of time: not only in having time to do important work but in having time as well to do that work in a particular way. In other words, the significance is not just that they are doing these tasks but also *how* they are doing them. And how they are doing them has a great deal to do with the qualities of patience and perspective and with the virtue that can best be described as *slowness*. These individuals have an understanding that some things in life—ranging from mentoring to medicine—are best done slowly, and that efficiency, expediency, and productivity have a way of undermining these endeavors. Throughout, there is an appreciation, particularly, of how slowness can nurture and deepen relationships. (At the most basic level, these individuals are demonstrating every day, as the British social scientist Malcolm Johnson observes, that "the essence of human service is not speed and efficiency—it is human contact, it is slowness.")

So in fashioning a new vision of the contribution that older Americans might make to American life, it is essential that we not lose sight of the distinctive qualities of the third age, and that we simultaneously consider which of society's pressing needs might best be addressed by individuals in possession of what Carolyn Heilbrun calls "the gift of time." And as we engage in this analysis, it will be important that these discussions not be confined to the journals of gerontology and social welfare.

We must embark on a major marketing effort communicating that the aging of America is a great opportunity for individuals and society, a massive call to action that replaces the long-standing message that older adults are superfluous ("something that's just hangin' around," in Harold Allen's words) with one that conveys to these individuals that they are not only needed but also have an essential contribution to make.

Build the Breakthrough Institution

As desperately as we need a new way of looking both at the third age and at the role of older adults in American life, the battle against structural lag will ultimately be won not in the air but on the ground. To win the battle, we will need to reform many of our existing institutions so that they do a better job of integrating the talent in the aging population. For example, our civic organizations that depend on high-quality people to achieve their mission will need to wake up to the aging opportunity, to recognize that in the third-age population exists the answer to many of their human resource needs—especially in an era when middle-aged women, the traditional source of volunteer and human services labor, have moved into the general labor force.

Some groups, like Habitat for Humanity, have long been successful recruiting a substantial number of third-age volunteers. Recently, a number of other organizations have started to move in this direction. For example, Big Brothers/Big Sisters—after years of concentrating on twenty- and thirty-something "Bigs"—is now opening up several new initiatives aimed at recruiting older mentors (including an Experience Corps in Indianapolis). The YMCA is another organization operating an Experience Corps (in Kansas City) and starting to respond to the potential upside of the aging society. Millions of boomers already come to the Y's facilities for fitness activities, on a fee-for-service basis. The YMCA would like to persuade more of these individuals to become "two-way" members as they move into the third age—going to the Y not only to swim or lift weights but also to help young people and contribute to the nonprofit organization's mission of building stronger communities.

Hundreds of other organizations might likewise benefit from thinking about how reaching out to third agers might enhance their mission, but they have yet to do so. For example, Bill Bradley suggests that teaching is a prime example, arguing that some of the efforts now focused on bringing young people into this profession could be expanded at the other end of the age spectrum: "Why not open up Teach for America to Third Agers?" he writes. "Surely there is room for our experience and wisdom. We can just as easily go back to school some September, where our most important assignment is learning to teach."

One can think of myriad other possibilities for groups across the civic spectrum, but they will need to be boomer-savvy, realizing that the old roles of answering the phones and stuffing envelopes won't satisfy the new group of third agers. Like Habitat, they will have to "never say senior" and find ways of attracting aging boomers without coming off as organizations for "old people." They will simultaneously need to provide other features that we have seen in successful projects profiled in the previous pages.

In all, we will need to develop literally millions of new opportunities to contribute, to satisfy potential demand on the part of the aging boomers and to begin to have a real impact on the many human resource needs of civil society. However, as we are working to improve the quality of existing arrangements, and to expand their quantity dramatically, we must also remain engaged in intensive innovation.

Despite many interesting new inventions—inventions that deserve to be taken to a much larger scale—I am convinced that we have yet to build the breakthrough institution. We have yet to develop the kind of vehicle that might play for the next phase of America's aging the role that Sun City played in launching the last.

In contemplating what such a breakthrough institution might be structured, it makes sense to begin by considering what the new generation of aging Americans is looking for as they attempt to make the transition to a meaningful third age. Desperately needed is an entity that could speak to these individuals, the 95 percent of the older population who find nothing of interest at the local senior center, who aren't looking for bingo or adult day care (except perhaps for their own parents), and who are unlikely to answer to labels like "the elderly."

Rather, these men and women are in the market for lifelong learning, new opportunities to contribute, the chance to promote their health and well-being (both physical and spiritual), a community of like-minded individuals, and a place to help navigate the passage to this new stage of life. The time has come to develop a new arrangement targeted to these priorities, something that could be the equivalent for third agers of what the senior center has become for the old-old.

Crafting this new entity will require taking the "one-stop" ideal to the next level, creating under one roof—whether that roof be over a downtown YMCA or the campus of a local community college—a new kind of Center (a Center for the Third Age?) bringing together the following opportunities:

- A Full-Service Experience Corps, offering opportunities to serve not only in schools but also in a variety of endeavors (including environmental work, public health, independent living, and other essential spheres);

- An Institute for Learning in Retirement (akin to the institutes affiliated with Elderhostel and based on college campuses), providing
courses taught in the building, offering easy access and registration for
classes at nearby universities, and perhaps even orchestrating regular
lectures, readings, and other symposia on topics of keen interest to
third agers and the wider community;

- A Center for Un-Retirement (a phrase coined by Ron Manheimer of
the University of North Carolina-Asheville) to help individuals prepare
for second careers, with a strong emphasis on public-interest opportunities in areas like teaching and environmental work;

- An internship program operated in conjunction with local corporations, through which individuals phasing into retirement can do micro-
sabbaticals serving for two-week to two-month stretches in local
community-based organizations;

- Quarterly retreats for midlifers (individuals primarily in their forties
through sixties) who are contemplating a third age characterized by
ongoing growth and contribution, to help these individuals begin
thinking through how and when they might act on this desire, and
what they can do immediately to begin their planning;

- Entrepreneurship and leadership training for third agers aimed at helping them develop the tools to establish new projects and institutions
(to become social entrepreneurs), while also providing a support group
and potential colleagues for undertaking these new civic enterprises;

- Health and wellness opportunities ranging from yoga classes to semi-
nars on diet and exercise, including hiking groups and other social activities that emphasize well-being;

- Perhaps even an art gallery displaying the work of individuals involved
in the center through art classes or workshops in areas such as documentary photography.

Along with all of these features, the Center would have a "coffee pot," an
informal gathering place like the lounge at the Samaritan House Clinic

where individuals could come just to be around others engaged in many of the same pursuits. Of course, it is not hard to imagine the coffee pot being a full-fledged café—maybe even organized as a collective and staffed by the men and women using the Center.

The hope would be to array these various features in such a way that the whole transcends the sum of its parts—to create an institution where there is "something for everybody," a variety of hooks to bring people through the door, yet where there is also a conscious effort to link up various elements like the service and learning aspects. For example, individuals participating in Experience Corps would receive free admission to all classes offered by the Institute for Learning in Retirement—as well as free lattes at the Center café. Meanwhile, the institute might be engaged to provide training in contemporary issues in urban education or in whatever subject area helped prepare the Experience Corps members for their service.

Ultimately, an important goal would be to develop a true sense of membership in the Center (free, of course, to those doing significant service), so that it provided both feelings of identity and belonging and also some degree of status—derived from being part of an entity that was so identified with fulfillment and so linked to positive developments in the community.

Create Good Places to Grow Older

There is a role for every sector in fulfilling the aging opportunity and making America a good place to grow older, a place where third agers remain a vital and contributing part of society. Indeed, many examples already exist of how various kinds of organizations and industries might play a constructive role. For example:

- *Corporations* and other organizations could transform their retirement planning efforts so that they more extensively helped employees to make the transition to a new stage of life. These efforts might well encompass more than printing up some new brochures and developing a manual or two. Companies could develop phased retirement options that gave individuals the opportunity to rotate through local community organizations during their last year or two of employment, testing out various options for volunteering or next-act work. In fact, the Washington Post Company has experimented with a project to provide incentives for retirees to get extensively involved in local nonprofit organizations during their first year after retirement (before encountering tax law barriers). Other corporations have also provided funding for service efforts involving their own retirees in the community. One particularly innovative effort is the Stride Rite Company's development in its headquarters of an intergenerational day care center, where older adults provide child care for children of employees and others in the community.

- *Universities* have a critical role to play, and many are already beginning to assume these functions. At the most basic level, they can help impart the knowledge that individuals will need to take on new roles, perform them better, or even start new third-age entrepreneurial ventures in the public interest. Marv Welt's example is a good one. His course work at Portland State—free to older adults—provided the foundation for the Waterworld Program. Universities and other institutions of higher education, including community colleges, could make it easier for individuals like Marv to take this step, through offering course concentrations and workshops with the explicit aim of enabling ongoing contribution in the third age. Other universities have started centers focused on playing a research and development function related to getting older adults more involved in the civic life of the community. The most impressive entity of this type is Temple University's Center for Intergenerational Learning, led by Dr. Nancy Henkin and sponsor of the most successful Experience Corps project and myriad other efforts. The center has essentially turned Philadelphia into a laboratory for innovation focused on pragmatic efforts to engage older men and women in new community-building roles. Another compelling variation is the Center for Creative Retirement at the University of North Carolina at Asheville, run by philosopher Ron Manheimer. The center provides an array of learning, service, leadership development, and retraining opportunities to older adults in the Asheville area and is probably the closest existing entity to the "breakthrough" institution traced in the previous section.

- *Aging Organizations* have an obvious and important leadership role to play in this enterprise, and no organization is better positioned for the job than AARP—whose motto happens to be "To Serve, Not to Be Served." Although AARP often gets typecast as a group exclusively dedicated to the needs of older adults, it has another side as well, as the case of Experience Corps reveals. In this one example, AARP helped recruit members to participate in the program, provided editorial space in *Modern Maturity* for John Gardner to write an essay about Experience Corps, and even launched and helped fund (in collaboration with the Corporation for National Service) a variation of Experience Corps focused on promoting independent living of frail seniors. The organization operates many other projects enabling older adults to volunteer and even administers the Legacy Awards honoring four individuals over age fifty each year who are providing extraordinary service to their community. All this said, now is the time for AARP to play an even more important, catalytic part in this area. To start, the organization might spearhead a Millennial Project on the Role of Older Americans in Society. Held on the eve of the demographic revolution, the millennial effort might aim to raise awareness of the kind of contribution older Americans can make, highlight some of the individual and organizational role models already existing, analyze in more depth the interests and assets of older adults, identify the most sensible routes for channeling this contribution, detail potential obstacles that would need to be overcome, and discuss strategies for translating the most promising directions into policy and practice. Through conferences, talk shows, a Web page, advertisements, opinion polls, and other strategies, the project should strive to engage a wide swath of the American people in debating these issues. In the process, it might not only begin to prepare us for the opportunities inherent in the aging society but also help to reposition AARP in the public mind as an organization as much dedicated to the potential contributions of older adults as to their needs.

- *Foundations* can do many things to promote the aging opportunity, and a number are already engaged in this work. (The Experience Corps, for example, has benefited from several million dollars in foundation support, which helped it expand to more than twenty cities during 1998 and 1999.) In the past, both the Carnegie Corporation and the Commonwealth Fund sponsored important commissions on the aging of America—although neither continues to operate today—and private philanthropy might join together with AARP to underwrite the Millennial Project. Another promising area for foundations is in supporting social entrepreneurs. For example, the Packard Foundation and the Peninsula Community Foundation played a critical role in establishing and sustaining the Samaritan House Clinic, helping that operation move from being a one-night-a-week clinic in a conference room to a major institution in the community. Despite a few examples like the clinic, however, private foundations are doing far too little to promote this movement. One promising strategy is to adapt some of the efforts the philanthropic community is currently underwriting in the area of social entrepreneurship by youth. For example, the Kellogg Foundation has developed a Fund for Social Entrepreneurs focused on initiatives involving young people more fully in serving the community and including both grants and technical assistance. Private foundations are also sponsoring the national magazine *Who Cares?* that concentrates on the good works by young social entrepreneurs serving their communities. Similar support targeted to the efforts of third-age institution builders might stimulate this parallel movement and improve the quality and sustainability of the innovations it is producing.

Overall, some of the most exciting work being underwritten by foundations—and also involving the other sectors mentioned above—is designed to help communities think more systematically, comprehensively, and strategically about how they might make the most of the aging society. These efforts, just being launched in San Mateo (California), Kansas City, and Pittsburgh, extend well beyond supporting specific programs, to exploring a community development strategy that might take full advantage of the assets present in the local aging population, now and in the future.

These efforts vary somewhat in emphasis, with the San Mateo and Kansas City inquiries focusing particularly on service by older Americans, and the Pittsburgh effort oriented more toward learning and cultural activities. (Civic Ventures is undertaking the first two research projects in conjunction with the Packard and Ewing M. Kauffman Foundations; Elderhostel and the Jewish Healthcare Foundation are working in partnership in Pittsburgh.) However, all three entail convening with the major local stakeholders to begin considering how they can best work together to get ahead of the impending demographic changes. And all are hoping to dissuade third agers from relocating in retirement, not only to avoid the loss of financial assets to the local economy but also to avert the exodus of all the social capital that these individuals have accumulated and might be persuaded to plow back into the community. Ultimately, the goal of these three efforts is to transform the local community into a good place to grow old— not just for the benefit of aging men and women but for all generations.

Launch a "Third-Age Bill"

Overall, policy can contribute to unlocking the civic and social resources of older adults at many levels. States, for example, can help underwrite service activities, as Ohio is doing with a variation on Experience Corps, or Illinois in helping to support Hope Meadows. They can even change their laws to facilitate service, as both South Carolina and Florida have done to ease the relicensing of retired volunteer physicians.

Locally, there are interesting examples as well. In Massachusetts and Colorado, a number of cities are experimenting with a program that simultaneously tries to make better use of the talent of the aging population and to help fixed-income older adults deal with rising property tax pressures. In Fort Collins, Colorado, for example, individuals serve in the parks and recreation department, the library, and the performing arts center and receive the prevailing minimum wage for each hour worked as a credit against their property taxes.

Although many creative opportunities in this area exist at the state and local level, federal policy remains critical. There are numerous ways these policies need to be overhauled, both to become less of an obstacle to the contribution of older adults and to help stimulate more substantial involvement. We can reform our tax policies so that individuals are not discouraged from working part-time in retirement (especially in public service careers), and so that we can more easily use creative measures like nontaxable stipends as an incentive for greater involvement in high-commitment, high-priority community projects. We might provide Medicare coverage to individuals between age fifty-five and sixty-five who are involved in half- to full-time service. Obviously, there are many ways in which the federal government could be involved in reforming existing program efforts it sponsors—such as the NSSC—and in underwriting expansion of these retooled operations.

Specific measures such as these would undoubtedly be helpful, but a more appropriate response, I believe, is to develop a policy initiative in keeping with the magnitude of the demographic revolution. This approach calls for more than fine-tuning or piecemeal action. And it calls for more than state and local responses. Indeed, in searching for appropriate policy analogy, I believe the example that comes most quickly to mind is none other than the Servicemen's Readjustment Act of 1944—also known as the G.I. Bill.

The G.I. Bill was devised to help assimilate in a constructive and mutually beneficial way millions of World War II veterans who would need to make a transition back into society after their service overseas. The potential consequences if these individuals were poorly reintegrated were significant—including the prospect of a large segment of the population that was disappointed and disaffected, not to mention a great loss of human resources to the economy and the country. Because of the magnitude of the situation and the stakes involved, the G.I. Bill was both large and comprehensive; it included dollars not only for education and training but also for home, farm, and business loans.

I won't attempt to overstate the analogy, but we would today do well to consider an ambitious, national, multifaceted policy initiative aimed at enabling the transition and integration of millions of individuals who are not crossing a geographic divide, or one from military service to private citizenship, but who rather are traversing a divide along the lines of age and social roles. Like the soldiers of World War II, these aging boomers must be well integrated into society, or the consequences will be dire. Having a dislocated class numbering nearly a quarter of the population, with little or no role in the life of the nation and no connection to the central institutions of society, is a recipe for a sour, gloomy, conflict-ridden nation. Alternatively, the vital involvement of this group might mean something resembling a new golden age.

We need to consider generating a new policy initiative inspired by the G.I. Bill—a Third-Age Bill, or 3A Bill—aimed at enabling the successful transition of vast numbers of aging Americans into new roles strengthening communities and revitalizing civil society. The specifics of such a measure would, of course, need to be debated and developed at much greater length, but the rough contours might include the following:

- A massive new national corps, potentially based on Experience Corps, aimed at involving between 5 and 10 percent of the age fifty-five-plus population over the next decade in areas of highest priority to society. This effort should include administrative grants for operating local projects—with the requirement of a 50 percent local match—as well as vouchers that individuals serving half-to full-time could use to provide a nontaxable stipend along with health and prescription benefits;

- A fund for research and development, stimulating the creation of new approaches to involving third agers (such as the work of the social entrepreneurs) and providing resources, technical assistance, and evaluation designed to help identify and expand successful projects;

- A program to promote training at both institutions of higher education and nonprofit organizations aimed at enabling third agers to make the transition to second careers in high-priority service areas;

- A research initiative designed to identify key niches in society where efforts to tap the human resources of third agers might be targeted— that is, where there is a good match between the talents of older adults and human resource needs of the society—and to examine potential costs and barriers;

- A national report card, issued every three years, to determine how effectively America is making use of the resources in the older population, built around a summit that explores lessons learned, showcases new approaches for involving third agers more effectively, and charts midcourse corrections and promising new directions;

- A set of major awards, given annually and patterned on the Presidential Medal of Freedom (perhaps a much expanded version of the Legacy Awards), highlighting Americans who either themselves are role models for a new kind of third age or who are making it easier for others to contribute to the well-being of society in this new stage of life.

The issue of administering such a Third-Age Bill raises important questions. Could or should it be overseen by the Administration on Aging or the Corporation for National Service? Or might it become part of an entirely new federal agency, a U.S. Department of Aging, that might incorporate through its various parts our efforts both to meet the needs and tap the talents of the vast and burgeoning aging population? This entity might serve as the central impetus for national efforts as America enters the aging century.

Whatever the ultimate nature of such a law or its administration, the most important priority is to begin discussing national policy responses that are of a scale, scope, and potential impact in accordance with the social transformation at hand. Measures that might help realize the silver lining present in the graying of America.

Graying Is Payoff

I f we act quickly and decisively to make the most of the aging opportunity, we can thwart the predictions that America is headed for "a mass leisure class" of older adults living off the labors of the middle generation, a gray dawn pitting young against old and rupturing the social contract. In fact, these predictions were always overstated, but we should be motivated to avoid the prospect that the baby boomers will be poorly integrated into society during their later years. We can't afford to have a quarter of the population at loose ends, dangling outside the mainstream.

However, the principal reason for embracing an agenda aimed at promoting the engagement and social contribution of the older population is far more affirmative. We are poised to create a much more efficient society, one that refuses to waste its most experienced citizens—especially as this group is about to double in size, and at a juncture when human resource needs in civil society, education, social services, and myriad other areas of great significance to the country are massive and dire. Bringing together these untapped resources and unmet needs is very much in the grain of common-sense American ingenuity; the approach essentially turns two problems into a single solution. It also makes ecological sense at a time when we've run short on new resources (not only environmental but also human—as the birthrate throughout the developed world remains low) and must get much better at recycling and renewing older ones.

Thus, if efficiency and ecology were the only issues at stake, we might be inspired to surge ahead with a set of strategies aimed at making full use of what older Americans have to offer. But they are not the only issues, and they may not even constitute the most important ones. At hand is the potential for lasting social and cultural change affecting all generations, beginning with the transformation of the life cycle itself.

Completing the Life Cycle

As the historian Philippe Aries has shown, it took three centuries to transform childhood into a full-fledged stage of life. Previously, children

were regarded by society simply as miniature adults. But over time they acquired their own attire, customs, and roles, and childhood came to be a qual-
itatively distinct phase.

We are in the midst of inventing the third stage of life today and reassessing
its place in society. Erik Erikson observed that lacking a compelling and distinctive ideal for this period, "our civilization does not really harbor a concept of
the whole of life." And although this stage remains a work in progress—one
that hasn't yet acquired so much as a compelling name—we are nearing the
point when the third age will assume equal footing with the ones that precede
it. In fact, it has the potential to become the best stage of all, an age of liberation when individuals combine newfound freedoms with prolonged health
and the chance to make some of their most important contributions to life.
This development is one that will benefit not only those in the third age but indeed all of us—as we can contemplate a life span that includes more opportunities for genuine fulfillment than ever before.

Elevating Civic Life

Another potential payoff of the aging of America is that, once again, civil
society may find a gifted workforce. This is certainly good news, as this essential sector of society continues to reel from the migration of its longtime
human resource, middle-aged women, into the conventional labor market.
However, again this change transcends an issue of numbers and skills. The
prospective entrance in great numbers of third agers into the institutions of
civil society and the social sector will bring with it qualitative differences as
well. To start, it will likely force the transformation of volunteer and community service jobs in these settings. Affected will be not only the kinds of roles
previously reserved for "senior volunteers" but those for all individuals dedi-
cating their time and talent to this work. Gone are the days of busywork and
menial tasks, as the aging boomers demand new roles with real impact and
opportunities for continued growth.

In the process, these individuals are likely to bring about another transformation, one in the value society accords to civic work and to service. For the
longest time we have treated these roles shabbily, as "women's work," or "tiny
truths" in Samuelson's belittling characterization of volunteering. No more.
The aging boomers will not only require the enrichment of these roles but
also will invest them with a prestige they have always deserved but long
lacked. This revaluing of civic work will have positive repercussions for all

who serve in these roles, regardless of age, and for all who benefit from the work being performed.

Rebalancing Responsibilities

At present the responsibilities in our society are wildly skewed, with individuals in the middle generation overworked while older men and women are underused. One group faces a time famine; the other is adrift in a sea of discretionary time (clinging to the "busy ethic" as a way of staving off the persistent sense of uselessness). Transformation of the nature of the third age holds the potential to redress this imbalance, so that the middle agers receive a much needed respite while individuals in later life gain lives with additional purpose, meaning, structure, and significance.

Indeed, one of the principal beneficiaries of this redistribution may be the younger generation. Older adults who take on more responsibility for developing and caring for young people can provide this group with additional support while helping parents lead saner, more balanced lives.

A Revolution in Time

This reallocation of responsibilities is part of a much larger revolution in time that is a promising consequence of the aging society, a potential bonanza that goes well beyond having more people, with more skills, to do more things that need to be done. It is not even simply about having people with more time but rather about what happens when we have a significant segment of the population with a different relationship to time.

This may be the biggest payoff of all from the graying of America: having so many people in the society who have "slowed down," downshifting from the frenetic pace and accompanying values so rampant during the middle years. To some people, this shift might produce nightmarish visions—for example, of all those elderly drivers clogging up the roadways. To commentators like Pete Peterson, it raises the prospect of a stagnant society, one with too few Bill Gates types pump-priming the economy with their restless entrepreneurialism and fast-paced inventions (by 2015, it is estimated that the computer chip will have been speeded up 137 billion times since its invention in 1959).

However, in our whirlwind society where everything seems to be moving faster, the slowness of an expanding population of third agers may well be precisely the counterbalance that is needed. This group promises to become the bastion of those many things in life better done slowly, principal among them the cultivation of relationships and the expression of care. Indeed, from this perspective, we may find ourselves headed not for a "demographic time bomb," in Peterson's terms, but a new "time boom"—one in which older adults become the new role models for balanced lives, the middle generation finds itself with a more manageable set of responsibilities, and appreciation of the virtues of slowness begins to take hold in the wider culture.

Care for the Future

The demographic revolution promises to be a revolution not only in time but across time as well. As Erikson and others have shown, another of the great virtues of later life is an enhanced sense of "generativity"—what University of Michigan psychologist John Kotre interprets as care and responsibility—that moves along the generational chain and links us to the future. We are on the verge of a doubling of people in the stage of life when the principal developmental task will be coming to terms with what it means to be generative, to pass on to the younger generations what we have learned from life. In deep psychological terms, the prospect that we live on in future generations is what, writes Christopher Lasch, "reconciles us to our own supersession—the central sorrow of old age, more harrowing even than frailty and loneliness."

Generativity is a value, much like slowness, that has become increasingly scarce in this immediate-impact society. In fact, as he came into his own old age, Erikson worried desperately that we were on the verge of losing generativity as a cultural value. In a talk with Daniel Goleman several years before his death, Erikson warned that "the only thing that can save us as a species is seeing how we're not thinking of future generations in the way we live. . . . What's lacking is generativity, a generativity that will promote positive values in the lives of the next generation."

Through providing many more opportunities for individuals to leave a legacy and nurture the future, we can turn the aging of America into our best chance at restoring generativity as an ideal in our society and averting the crisis that Erikson described. In this way, potential transformation amounts to not only a revolution *in* time and *across* it, but also one that is just in time.

A New Evolutionary Class

In light of the many ways that the aging society could transform America, one is tempted to conclude with Lester Thurow that the older population is a "new revolutionary class"—although in ways exactly opposite the ones he predicts. When all is said and done, if we play our cards right, the phenomenon that we have been told repeatedly will drag us down may well be the change that lifts us up.

Yet for all this revolutionary impact, it is also possible to see the coming wave of third agers as a "new *evolutionary* class," part of a process that has been evolving and unfolding for decades, generations, even centuries, depending upon one's perspective. Carl Jung believed that "a human being would certainly not grow to be 70 or 80 years old if this longevity has no meaning for the species." Margaret Mead reached a similar conclusion, contending that older adults were critical for the survival of the human community. More recently, Kristin Hawkes of the University of Utah and others have advanced the theory that grandmothers in particular played a critical role in helping humans survive and flourish as a species.

The very long view of Jung, Mead, and Hawkes is a useful one. It helps us see that the survival and expansion of older persons in human societies are an evolutionary adaptation rather than an inherent defect. And it also forces us to ask the long-term question that Jonas Salk raised, namely: "Are we being good ancestors?"

Although thinking in such broad terms is important, this book has been principally concerned about a more immediate trajectory, the evolution of later life in America over the past century from a precarious stage to one increasingly characterized by economic security, independent living, and sustained vitality. By the 1930s in this country, stimulated in significant ways by the passage of Social Security, the rough ingredients of a new stage of life were forming. At first, despite improvements in the material circumstances of older men and women, this phase was characterized by the absence of things: of work, of a role, even of activity. The oldster planted on the porch or on a park bench, living in the state that Walter Reuther called "too old to work, too young to die," was America's answer to the triumph of longevity.

However, as individuals continued to live longer and retire earlier through the 1950s and 1960s, and as this limbo-like stage of life came to approximate the middle years in duration, a set of questions inherent in the advent of Social Security and the growing longevity revolution began increasing in urgency: Secure for what? Independent for what? Vital for what? To sit on the porch and await an increasingly delayed demise? At root was the question that Robert Butler later used as the title for his Pulitzer Prize–winning book on aging in America, *Why Survive?*

As we have seen, it was in this context that insurance companies, eager to boost pension sales, swooped into the vacuum and offered their shimmering vision of later life: a well-earned time of leisure and recreation reminiscent of nothing so much as the life of the aristocracy. No longer an anteroom to death, according to the financial services industry, retirement was a reward for those who worked hard and saved sufficiently.

However, it was left to the extraordinary Del Webb and his fellow developers in the retirement community movement to transform this marketing pitch into a three-dimensional world in which individuals could pursue "an active new way of life." And Webb went after those age fifty-five and up with new and improved marketing pitches, including the brilliant phrase "the golden years." In the process, he turned retirement into a lifestyle.

Today it is time to declare victory with "the golden years." This ideal, for all its negative aspects, was a radical step forward in 1960. The transformation that Webb began by summoning the older population from their rockers forty years ago has come to permeate life today in America, where activity is the norm and many people look forward to retirement as a potentially positive experience.

As we are celebrating the progress we have made over the years, continuing growth in longevity, health, and prosperity among third agers and the impending prospect of the boomers aging make all the more insistent those same questions from the past: Secure for what? Independent for what? Active for what? "For its own sake" is an acceptable answer; after all, this is a society that prizes options, and there is much evidence to suggest that active older adults are healthier and happier than their barca-lounging peers.

However, for a substantial segment of the current and coming third-age population, the old answers no longer apply. These men and women will no longer be content to spend a third of life jogging in place on the sidelines. They are prepared to swap a lifestyle for a life. They want more than the busy ethic. They yearn, in Marv Welt's words, for "something real and important." Indeed, they are beginning to articulate for themselves and for society the challenge that Maggie Kuhn issued when she said, "Our goal is to use our freedom, our experience, our knowledge of the past, our ability to survive, not just for free bus fares" but for something larger. In Kuhn's view, that something larger was "to work as advocates for the public good." And society is beginning to ask the same of them, recognizing that we can't get by without a massive new infusion of the qualities Kuhn extols.

So we are, again, at the threshold of a new era of aging in this country. As we enter a new century, the aging century (the aging millennium?), we are in a position at last to fulfill the promise that Social Security helped elevate in the first place: later lives characterized not only by material well-being but also by a true fulfillment and a meaningful role in society—in other words, a life that still matters. The golden years were a necessary transitional step toward this important achievement. But they could never deliver the real goods.

Will we make it past this threshold, managing to break through to the next phase in the saga of later life in America? Or will we stumble backward, refighting the entitlement battles of the past, stuck in static conceptions of the role of older people and the purpose of later life? I have argued in this book that in the next stage—as with the last—much will hinge not only on the vision we articulate but also on the institutions we invent and the ways we manage to support these new innovations. We must now do for the good of society what Webb managed so brilliantly to achieve for his own bottom line.

My research and experiences over the course of writing this book leave me optimistic, convinced that the mutual benefit involved in this enterprise is simply too great for us to miss this aging opportunity. We literally have, to paraphrase Jimmy Carter, everything to gain. And the gain is for all generations today and for all of us who will pass into the third age down the road. (Much like the passage of Social Security, this effort deserves a broad-based constituency from all segments and age groups in society.)

Indeed, my experiences make me optimistic not only about our prospects as a society but also about my own third age, which should arrive along with the heart of the baby boomers' aging, in about twenty years. When we arrive, I suspect there will be abundant opportunities to contribute in ways that are both essential and rewarding. Engagement in this way will probably seem natural, like the oxygen in the air. And we will probably take it for granted that older adults are an important part in the functioning of society. In fact, as typically ahistorical boomers, we will probably even assume that it has always been so—wondering how we could have ever survived otherwise.

But when future historians do look back and tell the story about where we have come from and how things have changed, they will likely pinpoint the years surrounding the new millennium as a critical turning point, a time when a remarkable group of individuals—people like Thea Glass and Harold Allen, Bill Schwartz and Louise Casey—took matters into their own hands and helped fashion out of a once despised period the new prime of life, in the process transforming a "surplus" population into the backbone of civil society and the spearhead of an unparalleled age of renewal.

Getting Involved

·

A RESOURCE DIRECTORY

Civic Ventures and Experience Corps

Civic Ventures

I founded Civic Ventures in 1998 to expand the contribution of older Americans to society and to help ensure that the aging of America is a source of both individual and social renewal. In pursuit of this mission, Civic Ventures seeks to create more compelling opportunities for older Americans to serve their communities—in particular through Experience Corps; to promote a richer debate about the roles older men and women can play in the life of this country; and to generate public policies and other measures enabling older Americans to be more fully involved in strengthening civil society.

Experience Corps

Experience Corps is now operating in over two dozen cities. As Chapter Five describes at length, the goal of Experience Corps is to provide schools and other youth-serving organizations with a critical mass of caring older adults who: improve the academic performance and development of young people; help schools and youth-serving organizations become more caring and personal places; bolster ties between educational institutions and sur-rounding neighborhoods; and, enhance the well-being of the older volunteers in the process.

For information about Civic Ventures or Experience Corps:
Director of Communications
Civic Ventures
425 Second Street, Suite 601
San Francisco, CA 94107
(415) 430–0141
www.civicventures.org
www.experiencecorps.org

More Service and Volunteer Opportunities

The Corporation for National Service

The Corporation for National Service (CNS) works with community organizations to provide opportunities for Americans of all ages to serve. CNS functions as the umbrella for a number of national service programs, including AmeriCorps, AmeriCorps VISTA, Learn and Serve America, and the National Senior Service Corps. In addition, through the National Senior Service Corps, CNS operates Seniors for Schools and the Experience Corps for Independent Living (in collaboration with AARP), each a variation on the Experience Corps model.

National Senior Service Corps

National Senior Service Corps (NSSC) has a thirty year history of leadership in senior volunteer service and engages nearly half a million Americans age fifty-five and older in service efforts across all fifty states. The Senior Corps is a national network of three projects: Foster Grandparent Program, Senior Companion Program, and the Retired and Senior Volunteer Program (RSVP). The more than 1,200 Senior Corps Programs operate in local communities throughout the U.S.

The Corporation for National Service
1201 New York Avenue, NW
Washington D.C. 20525
(202) 606–5000
www.cns.gov

Volunteers in Medicine

The Volunteers In Medicine (VIM) Clinics provide free medical and dental services to families and individuals who otherwise have no access to health care. The clinics are staffed by retired medical professionals, other volunteers, and a small number of paid staff. Founded in Hilton Head, South Carolina, clinics are now operating in Pennsylvania, Florida, Indiana, and elsewhere.

Volunteers in Medicine
15 Northridge Drive
P.O. Box 23287
Hilton Head Island, SC, 29925
(843) 681–6612
or
Martin Memorial Health Systems
Volunteers in Medicine
417 Balboa Avenue
Stuart, FL 34994
(561) 223–4962

Samaritan House Clinic

Located in San Mateo, California, the clinic is affiliated with Samaritan House, a nonprofit agency providing services to low-income individuals in the community. The Clinic offers free health care to local residents who have no health insurance, through a group of over fifty volunteer doctors, dentists, nurses, and pharmacists, two paid physicians, and a steady stream of University of California at San Francisco medical students and residents who receive part of their training at the clinic.

Samaritan House Medical Center
117 North San Mateo Drive
San Mateo, CA 94401
(650) 347–1556

Elderhostel

Elderhostel is a nonprofit organization providing educational opportunities all over the world to adults aged fifty-five and over. Elderhostel's offerings include educational trips, college and university-based Institutes for Learning in Retirement, and Elderhostel Service Programs, engaging teams of hostelers in short-term volunteer projects in the United States and around the world. Service programs are between one to four weeks in length, and include historic preservation, museum curation, conservation work at national and state parks, environmental research, archaeology, education projects, and construction of affordable housing.

Elderhostel
75 Federal Street
Boston, MA 02110–1941
(877) 426–8056
www.elderhostel.org

North Carolina Center for Creative Retirement

Established in 1988 as an integral part of the University of North Carolina at Asheville, the North Carolina Center for Creative Retirement (NCCCR) has the threefold purpose of promoting lifelong learning, leadership, and community service opportunities for retirement-aged individuals. Most of NCCCR programs are in the Asheville area, but some are carried out in collaboration with other organizations in other parts of North Carolina or across the country.

North Carolina Center for Creative Retirement
UNCA
116 Rhoades Hall
Asheville, NC 28804–3299
(828) 251–6140
www.unca.edu/ncccr

Princeton Project 55

Princeton Project 55 is a non-partisan, nonprofit tax exempt organization established by the Class of 1955 at Princeton University. PP55 was born of the realization that there is a vast untapped resource, available for the public good, among groups of college alumni. PP55 continues to be involved in mentoring, service exchange, and character education programs in several areas of the country. PP55 also works with other classes of Princeton alumni and with alumni groups from other Universities such as Bucknell, Dartmouth, Moravian, Smith, and Williams.

Princeton Project 55
Center for Civic Leadership
32 Nassau Street
Princeton, NJ 08542
(609) 921–8808
http://alumni.princeton.edu/~class55/Project55

Habitat for Humanity

Founded in 1976, Habitat for Humanity International is a nonprofit, ecumenical Christian housing ministry dedicated to eliminating substandard housing and homelessness. Habitat invites people from all faiths and walks of life to work together in partnership, building houses with families in need. Habitat has built some 70,000 houses around the world. A significant portion of short- and long-term habitat volunteers are older adults.

Habitat for Humanity International
121 Habitat Street
Americus, GA 31709–3498
(912) 924–6935
www.habitat.org

The Environmental Alliance for Senior Involvement

The Environmental Alliance for Senior Involvement's (EASI) mission is to promote an environmental ethic among older adults, with the hope that these individuals will expand their knowledge, commitment, and active involvement in caring for our environment.

Environmental Alliance for Senior Involvement
8733 Old Dumphries Road
Catlett, VA 20119
(540) 788–3274
www.easi.org

Hope for the Children

Hope for the Children started in 1994 to provide secure, nurturing adoptive families and caring intergenerational communities for foster care children. Hope for the Children is a licensed foster care and adoption agency located in Rantoul, Illinois, where Hope Meadows, its first planned community, is located. The community offers rent subsidies for older adults in exchange for volunteer work and serving as a community presence.

Generations of Hope
1530 Fairway Drive
Rantoul, Illinois 61866
(217) 893–4673
www.hope4children.org

Peace Corps

Today, more than four hundred older Americans serve as Peace Corps volunteers around the world. Twenty percent of all older volunteers are serving as married couples. These individuals work in all skill sectors, but are primarily concentrated in education (45 percent of volunteers) and business (29 percent). The oldest volunteer ever to serve in the Peace Corps—an English teacher working in Hungary—was 86. There are currently eleven Peace Corps regional recruiting offices around the country.

Peace Corps
1111 20th Street NW
Washington, D.C. 20526
(800) 424–8580
www.peacecorps.gov

Troops to Teachers

The Troops to Teachers (TTT) program was designed to assist former military personnel enter public education as teachers. Since the inception of the program in January 1994, nearly 3,000 service members have made the transition from the military to classrooms across the nation. Troops to Teachers resulted from legislation introduced in the fiscal year 1993 Defense Authorization Bill as a result of military downsizing. The program is managed by the Defense Activity for Non-Traditional Support (DANTES), a Department of Defense agency. The Troops to Teachers program has currently established twenty state Placement Assistance offices in those states that have an interest in attracting veterans as educators.

Troops to Teachers
Old Capitol Building
P.O. Box 47200
Olympia, WA 98504–4720

(800) 743–2357
gwillett@ospi.wednet.edu

SCORE

The SCORE Association (Service Corps of Retired Executives) is dedicated to entrepreneur education and the formation, growth and success of small business nationwide. SCORE is a resource partner with the Small Business Association (SBA). SCORE Association volunteers serve as "Counselors to America's Small Business." Working and retired executives and business owners donate their time and expertise as volunteer business counselors and provide confidential counseling and mentoring free of charge. Local chapters provide free counseling and low-cost workshops in their communities. SCORE was founded in 1964 and assists approximately 300,000 entrepreneurs annually.

SCORE
409 Third Street, SW, 6th Floor
Washington, DC 20024
(800) 634–0245
www.score.org

The Executive Service Corps

The Executive Service Corps (ESC) is an association of retired businessmen and women who volunteer their time to consult with nonprofit and public service agencies. ESC consultants provide advisory services in a variety of areas such as accounting, budgeting and finance, planning, marketing, public relations, personnel administration, board development and governance, organizational systems, and facilities management. There is a network of over forty ESC organizations across the country.

www.escus.org

National Retiree Volunteer Coalition

The National Retiree Volunteer Coalition (NRVC) is a nonprofit consulting organization dedicated to creating corporate retiree programs, through which retirees can serve with former work colleagues under the banner of their former employer. NRVC projects include volunteering in the areas of education, community revitalization, environmental concerns, and public health.

National Retiree Volunteer Coalition
4915 West 35th Street, Suite 205
Minneapolis, MN 55416
(612) 920–7788
(888) 733–NRVC (toll free)
www.nrvc.org

Points of Light Foundation

The Points of Light Foundation works in communities throughout the United States to promote volunteering and community service through the network of over 500 Volunteer Centers. To be connected to the nearest Volunteer Center, call 1–800–VOLUNTEER.
The Points of Light Foundation
1400 I Street, NW, Suite 800
Washington, DC 20005
(202) 729–8000
www.pointsoflight.org

America's Promise

America's Promise—The Alliance for Youth, led by General Colin Powell, is dedicated to mobilizing individuals, groups and organizations to build the character and competence of our youth. At the heart of America's Promise is a set of five basic promises made to every child in America: an ongoing relationship with a caring adult—parent, mentor, tutor or coach; a safe place with structured activities during non-school hours; a healthy start; a marketable skill through effective education; and an opportunity to give back through community service.
America's Promise
909 North Washington Street, Suite 400
Alexandria, VA 22314–1556
(703) 684–4500
www.americapromise.org

Temple University Center
for Intergenerational Learning

The Center for Intergenerational Learning at Temple University was created in 1980 to foster intergenerational cooperation and exchange. Through the development of innovative cross-age programs, the provision of training and technical assistance, and the dissemination of materials, the Center serves as a national resource for intergenerational programming.

Temple Center for Intergenerational Learning
1601 North Broad Street, Room 206
Philadelphia, PA 19122
(215) 204–6970
www.temple.edu/departments/CIL

American Association of Retired Persons

The American Association of Retired Persons (AARP), the nation's largest aging organization, operates numerous volunteer, service, and employment programs, including Connections for Independent Living, The Volunteer Talent Bank, and the Experience Corps for Independent Living.

AARP
601 E Street, NW
Washington, DC 20049
(800) 424–3410
www.aarp.org

The following sections set out the primary source materials I relied upon in writing the book's six chapters, along with selected annotations. Quotations in *Prime Time* are drawn both from my fieldwork (spanning the period 1986 through 1999) and from these sources. I have organized the sources both by chapters and by substantive content within each chapter.

First-Person Narratives

The five first-person narratives included between the chapters of the book were distilled from many interviews with the individuals featured. They have been condensed into a narrative form and edited for clarity.

Chapter One: The Aging Opportunity

The Work Connection

The opening account draws principally on my visits to Work Connection in the late 1980s as well as more recent interviews with Tom Flood. (The story that begins the first chapter is actually a consolidation of experiences during my first and second visits to The Work Connection.) Most of this material can be found in Marc Freedman, *Partners in Growth: Elder Mentors and At-Risk Youth* (Philadelphia: Public/Private Ventures, 1988).

In addition, several quotes are also drawn from a newsletter article about the program, published by the State of Massachusetts: "IUE/The Work Connection, Inc.: Union-Sponsored Program Gives Jail-Bound Offenders One Last Chance." Unfortunately, no additional specifics or the name of the author is available.

The Aging of America

Erik H. Erikson, *Identity: Youth and Crisis* (New York: W. W. Norton, 1968).

Erik H. Erikson, Joan M. Erikson, and Helen Q. Kiunick, *Vital Involvement in Old Age*, (New York: W. W. Norton, 1986).

Betty Friedan, *The Fountain of Age* (New York: Simon and Schuster, 1993).

Robert Friedland and Laura Summer, *Demography Is Not Destiny* (Washington, DC: National Academy on an Aging Society, 1999).

Daniel Goleman, "Studies Suggest Older Minds Are Stronger Than Expected," *New York Times*, February 26, 1996.

Philip Hilts, "Life at Age 100 Is Surprisingly Healthy," *New York Times*, June 1, 1999.

Gina Kolata, "New Era of Robust Elderly Belies the Fears of Scientists," *New York Times*, February 27, 1996.

———, "Pushing Limits of the Human Life Span," *New York Times*, March 9, 1999.

Peter Laslett, *A Fresh Map of Life* (London: Geo. Weidenfeld and Nicolson, 1996).

Kenneth G. Manton et al., "Chronic Disability Trends in Elderly United States Population, 1982–1994," *Proceedings of the National Academy of Science*, 1994.

Phyllis Moen, "Changing Age Trends: The Pyramid Upside Down?" in Urie Bronfenbrenner et al., *The State of Americans* (New York: Free Press, 1996).

Harry R. Moody, *Aging: Concepts and Controversies* (Thousand Oaks, CA: Pine Forge Press, 1998).

New York Times Magazine, "Funny We Don't Feel Old: America Discovers a New Stage of Life—After Middle Age," *The Age Boom*, special issue, *New York Times Magazine*, March 9, 1997.

Demetrius Patterson, "Aging Boomers a Potential Boon to Funeral Industry," Gannett News Service, February 2, 1994.

Thomas T. Perls and Margery H. Silver, *Living to 100* (New York: Basic Books, 1999).

Matilda White Riley, Robert Kahn, and Nancy Foner, *Age and Structural Lag* (New York: John Wiley, 1996).

Sara Rimer, "As Centenarians Thrive, 'Old' Is Redefined," *New York Times*, June 22, 1998.

John W. Rowe and Robert L. Kahn, *Successful Aging* (New York: Pantheon, 1998).

J. Walker Smith and Ann Clurman, *Rocking the Ages: The Yankelovich Report on Generational Marketing* (New York: HarperBusiness, 1997).

John Tierney, "The Optimists Are Right," *New York Times Magazine*, September 29, 1996.

U.S. Census Bureau, *65+ in the United States. Current Population Reports: Special Studies.* (Washington, DC: Government Printing Office, 1996).

The Long Gray Wave—and Responses

John Cassidy, "Spooking the Boomers," *New Yorker*, January 13, 1997.

Kenneth Chew et al., "Who Cares About Public Schools?" *American Demographics*, May 1991.

Lisa W. Foderaro, "Schools Appeal to Elderly for Support," *New York Times*, August 27, 1991.

James N. Gardner and Roger S. Ballentine, "Robbing America's Cradles," *State Government News*, March 1996.

Robert C. Johnston, "Schools Courting Vote of Nation's Burgeoning Population of Seniors," *Education Week*, September 25, 1996.

Robert Kuttner, *Everything for Sale: The Virtues and Limits of Markets* (New York: Alfred A. Knopf, 1997).

Phillip Longman, "Justice Between Generations," *Atlantic Monthly*, June 1985.

———, "The Global Aging Crisis: The World Turns Gray," *U.S. News & World Report*, March 11, 1999.

Richard Louv, "How Seniors Rescued the Schools of Dade County, Florida," in Richard Louv, *101 Things You Can Do for Our Children's Future* (New York: Anchor Books, 1994).

Nina Munk, "Finished at Forty," *Fortune*, February 1, 1999.

Peter G. Peterson, *Will America Grow up Before It Grows Old?* (New York: Random House, 1996).

———, "Will America Grow up Before It Grows Old?" *Atlantic Monthly*, May 1996.

———, *Gray Dawn: How the Coming Age Wave Will Transform America—and the World* (New York: Times Books, 1999).

Samuel H. Preston, "Children Will Pay," *New York Times Magazine*, September 29, 1996.

Theodore Roszak, *America the Wise* (Boston: Houghton Mifflin, 1998).

William Sterling and Stephen Waite, *Boomernomics: The Future of Your Money in the Upcoming Generational Warfare* (New York: Ballantine Books, 1998).

Lester C. Thurow, "The Birth of a Revolutionary Class: Today's Elderly Are Bringing Down the Social Welfare State and Threatening the Nation's Economic Future," *New York Times Magazine*, May 19, 1996.

———, *The Future of Capitalism* (New York: William Morrow, 1996).

Civil Society, Volunteering, and Later Life

Scott A. Bass, ed., *Older and Active: How Americans over 55 Are Contributing to Society* (New Haven: Yale University Press, 1995).

Susan M. Chambre, "Older Volunteers: Trends," *Leadership*, October–December 1993.

———, "Volunteerism by Elders: Past Trends and Future Prospects," *Gerontologist*, 1993.

The Commonwealth Fund, *The Untapped Resource: The Final Report of The Americans Over 55 At Work Program* (New York: Commonwealth Fund, 1993).

Kristin Goss, "Volunteering and the Long Civic Generation," unpublished paper, Department of Government, Harvard University, 1999.

Independent Sector, *Giving and Volunteering in the United States* (Washington, DC: Independent Sector, 1996).

Dominica Marchetti, "Retirees Seek Challenges, and Charities Struggle to Provide Them," *Chronicle of Philanthropy*, April 17, 1997.

Marriott Senior Volunteerism Study (Washington, DC: Marriott Senior Living Services, 1991).

Phillis Moen and Vivian Fields, "Retirement, Social Capital, and Well-Being: Does Community Participation Replace Paid Work?" unpublished paper, Department of Human Development and Family Studies, Cornell University, 1998.

Robert D. Putnam, "Bowling Alone: America's Declining Social Capital," *Journal of Democracy*, January 1995.

———, "The Prosperous Community," *American Prospect*, 1996.

———, "The Strange Disappearance of Civic America," *American Prospect*, 1997.

Wendy Schmelzer, "Many Older Americans Reap Benefits of Volunteering," *Morning Edition*, August 23, 1995.

Marianne Szegedy-Maszak, "Done with Work, Volunteers Move on to Giving Back," *New York Times*, March 20, 1999.

Robert Wuthnow, *Acts of Compassion: Caring for Others and Helping Ourselves* (Princeton, NJ: Princeton University Press, 1991).

The Time Bind and the Leisure Ideal

Dora Costa, *The Evolution of Retirement: An American Economic History, 1880–1990* (Chicago: University of Chicago Press, 1998).

David Galernter, "Why Mothers Should Stay Home," *Commentary*, February 1996.

Ellen Goodman, "A Perpetual Rush Hour for Baby Boomers," *Boston Globe*,
    September 4, 1995.

Arlie Hochschild, *The Second Shift: Working Parents and the Revolution at Home*
    (New York: Avon Books, 1989).

———, *The Time Bind: When Work Becomes Home and Home Becomes Work* (New
    York: Henry Holt/Metropolitan Books, 1997).

John Robinson and Geoffrey Godbey, *Time for Life: The Surprising Ways Ameri-
    cans Use Their Times* (State College: Pennsylvania State University Press,
    1997).

John Robinson, Perla Werner, and Geoffrey Godbey, "Freeing up the Golden
    Years," *American Demographics*, October 1997.

Juliet Schor, *The Overworked American* (New York: Basic Books, 1991).

Janny Scott, "Working Hard, More or Less," *New York Times*, July 10, 1999.

Chapter Two: A Year-Round Vacation

The title for this chapter comes from a press release of the Del Webb Corporation.

The History of Later Life and Retirement in America

This history of aging in America is distilled entirely from seven excellent
sources (and all the quotations in the historical section derive from these
texts):

W. Andrew Achenbaum, *Old Age in a New Land* (Baltimore: Johns Hopkins
    University Press, 1978).

Thomas R. Cole, *The Journey of Life: A Cultural History of Aging in America* (New
    York: Cambridge University Press, 1992).

Dora Costa, *The Evolution of Retirement: An American Economic History,
    1880–1990* (Chicago: University of Chicago Press, 1998).

David J. Ekerdt, "Retirement," in George Maddox, ed., *The Encyclopedia of Aging*
    (New York: Springer, 1995).

David Hackett Fischer, *Growing Old in America* (New York: Oxford University
    Press, 1978).

William Graebner, *A History of Retirement: The Meaning and Function of an
    American Institution, 1885–1978* (New Haven: Yale University Press, 1980).

Carole Haber and Brian Gratton, *Old Age and the Search for Security: An American Social History* (Bloomington: Indiana University Press, 1993).

Del Webb, Sun City, and the Origins of the Retirement Community Movement

The story of Webb and Sun City derives from numerous sources: papers and advertisements housed at the Sun Cities Area Historical Society in Sun City, Arizona; information provided by the Del Webb Company (largely through its Web site); interviews with individuals living in Sun City and Sun City West; and an array of secondary sources (from which the vast majority of quotations are drawn). These sources include the following:

Richard B. Calhoun, *In Search of the New Old: Redefining Old Age in America, 1945–1970* (New York: Elsevier, 1978).

Lawrence Davies, "The Retirement Village: A New Life Style," *New York Times*, January 18, 1970.

Del Webb Corporation, "Del Webb: The Man" (Phoenix: Del Webb Corporation, no date available).

Margaret Finnerty, *Del Webb: A Man, a Company*. (Flagstaff, AZ: Heritage Publishers, Inc., 1991).

Jane Freeman and Glenn Sanberg, *Jubilee: The 25th Anniversary of Sun City, Arizona* (Sun City: Sun City Historical Society, 1984).

Paul Friggens, "Where Life Begins at 65," *Reader's Digest*, January 1966.

Jerry Jacobs, *Fun City: An Ethnographic Study of a Retirement Community* (Prospect Heights, IL: Waveland Press, 1974).

Lewis Mumford, "For Older People—Not Segregation but Integration," *Architectural Record*, May 1956.

"Old Folks at Home," *Newsweek*, February 25, 1963.

Paul O'Neill, "You Make So Many Friends Here," *Life*, April 4, 1964.

———, "For the Retired: A World All Their Own," *Life*, May 14, 1970.

Leon A. Pastalan, ed., *The Retirement Community Movement: Contemporary Issues* (New York: Haworth Press, 1989).

Elizabeth Pillsbury, "Consuming Retirement: The Creation of the Recreational Retirement Community, Del Webb's Sun City 1960–Present," B.A. thesis, Kenyon College, 1998.

"A Place in the Sun," *Time*, August 3, 1962.

"Spreading Webb," *Time*, January 26, 1962.

Hubert B. Stroud, *The Promise of Paradise: Recreational and Retirement Communi-*

ties in the United States Since 1950 (Baltimore: Johns Hopkins University Press, 1995).

Calvin Trillin, "Wake up and Live," *New Yorker*, April 4, 1964.

Implications of Sun City and the Retirement Community Movement

Edward J. Blakely and Mary Gail Snyder, *Fortress America: Gated Communities in the United States* (Washington, DC: Brookings Institution Press, 1997).

James Brooke, "Young Unwelcome in Retirees' Haven," *New York Times*, February 16, 1997.

David J. Eckerdt, "The Busy Ethic: Moral Continuity Between Work and Retirement," *Gerontologist*, 1986.

Frances FitzGerald, *Cities on a Hill: A Journey Through Contemporary America Cultures* (New York: Simon and Schuster, 1986).

Verne Kopytoff, "For Metropolitan Phoenix, 6 Golf Courses a Year," *New York Times*, March 22, 1998.

Sue Ann Pressley, "School Fight in a Gray Area," *Washington Post*, January 13, 1997.

Steve Schatt, "Sun City Tries to Sell Seniors Not Only a Home But a Lifestyle," *Newsday*, November 8, 1996.

Mike Steere, "Ready When You Are," *Worth*, April 1998.

"Time Select Special Report: Age Is No Barrier," *Time*, September 22, 1997.

Chapter Three: The Quiet Revolution

Much of this chapter is based on interviews with Foster Grandparents beginning in the late 1980s and continuing for over a decade. In addition, numerous source materials were used to provide historical context and determine the contribution of the program. These include, by section:

Origins of the Foster Grandparent Program

Information in this section is drawn largely from interviews with Bernie Nash and Sargent Shriver, as well as Sandy Kravitz, John Keller, and others involved in the development and early years of the Foster Grandparent Program. In addition, the articles set out below were used in developing the story of the program's origins and are the source of many quotations in the chapter.

Before listing these sources, however, it is important to note that significant discrepancies exist in the recollections of key individuals involved in founding the Foster Grandparent Program, some of which I was able to sort out through the research for this book, others of which remain unresolved. Sandy Kravitz, a key figure in the creation of the program and an impeccable source of information about the War on Poverty, asserts that the basis for the program was not Sargent Shriver's experience in Cincinnati but rather a similar encounter by Dick Boone, the number two person in the Community Action Agency at Cook County Hospital in Chicago. Furthermore, according to Kravitz, the story about Shriver's wanting to lower the age of the Foster Grandparents is inaccurate; Kravitz recalls that Shriver was trying to raise the eligibility age for the program.

W. Andrew Achenbaum, *Shades of Gray: Old Age, American Values, and Federal Policies Since 1920* (Boston: Little, Brown, 1983).

Mark Arnold, "What About the Elderly Poor? Battle Brews over Program's Accent on Youth," *National Observer*, March 7, 1966.

"A Compilation of Materials Relevant to the Message of the President of the United States on Our Nation's Senior Citizens," *Special Committee on Aging*, U.S. Senate, June 1963.

"Developments in Aging, 1966," *A Report of the Special Committee on Aging*, U.S. Senate, February 17, 1966.

"Developments in Aging, 1967," *A Report of the Special Committee on Aging*, U.S. Senate, February 17, 1967.

"Developments in Aging, 1968," *A Report of the Special Committee on Aging*, U.S. Senate, February 17, 1968.

John W. Gardner, *No Easy Victories* (New York: Harper and Row, 1968).

Michael L. Gillette, *Launching the War on Poverty: An Oral History* (New York: Twayne Publishers, 1996).

Green Thumb: The Starting Point, History 1965–1982 (Washington, DC: Green Thumb, 1982).

Nicholas Lemann, *The Promised Land: The Great Black Migration and How It Changed America* (New York: Knopf, 1991).

Bernard E. Nash, "Foster Grandparents in Child-Care Settings," *Public Welfare*, October 1968.

"National Service Corps," testimony before the Subcommittee on the National

Service Corps of the Committee on Labor and Public Welfare, U.S. Senate, May 1963.

Nancy Reagan, *To Love a Child* (Indianapolis, IN: Bobbs-Merrill, 1982).

Janet S. Sainer and Mary L. Zander, *SERVE: Older Volunteers in Community Service—a New Role and a New Resource* (New York: Community Service Society, 1971).

"The Senior Community Service Employment Program: Its History and Evolution," *A Report by the National Sponsors of the Senior Community Service Employment Program*, Select Committee on Aging, House of Representatives, December 1988.

"White House Announces Older Citizen Program," *New York Times*, August 28, 1965.

"Wings of Silver: Twenty-five Years of Love, 1965–1990" (Portland, OR: Metropolitan Family Services, 1995).

Effectiveness and Implications of the Foster Grandparent (and Senior Companion) Programs

Mary Achatz, *Effective Practices of Foster Grandparents in Head Start Centers: Benefits for Children, Classrooms, and Centers* (Washington, DC: Westat, for the Corporation for National Service, 1998).

ACTION, *Volunteers in Criminal Justice* (Washington, DC: ACTION, 1976).

———, *The Effect of Foster Grandparents on Juvenile Offenders in Georgia Youth Development Centers* (Washington, DC: ACTION, 1984).

———, *Descriptive Evaluation of RSVP and FOP Volunteers Working with Head Start: Final Report* (Washington, DC: ACTION, 1984).

Alzheimer's Association, *Alzheimer Care Demonstration Evaluation Report* (Washington, DC: ACTION, 1991).

Booz, Allen, and Hamilton, *Senior Companion Program Study* (Washington, DC: ACTION, 1975).

Booz, Allen, Public Administration Services, Inc., *Cost–Benefit Study of the Foster Grandparent Program* (Washington, DC: ACTION, 1972).

Laura Carstensen, "Everything Old Is New Again: Myths and Realities of Aging in the '90s," *Stanford Today*, March/April 1998.

Marc Freedman, *Seniors in National and Community Service* (Philadelphia: Public/Private Ventures, 1994).

———, *The Kindness of Strangers: Adult Mentors, Urban Youth, and the New Voluntarism* (New York: Cambridge University Press, 1999).

Litigation Support Services, *Impact Evaluation of the Foster Grandparent Program on the Foster Grandparents* (Washington, DC: ACTION, 1984).

Pamela Margoshes, "For Many, Old Age Is the Prime of Life," *Monitor* (American Psychological Association), May 1995.

Merrill-Palmer Institute, *Further Analysis of Data Gathered 1966–1968 by Merrill-Palmer Foster Grandparent Research Project* (Washington, DC: ACTION, 1968).

Research Triangle Institute, *Senior Companion Program: Homebound Elderly Demonstration Projects* (Washington, DC: ACTION, 1988).

Rosalyn Saltz, "Aging Persons as Child-Care Workers in a Foster Grandparent Program: Psychosocial Effects and Work Performance," *Aging and Human Development*, vol. 2, 1971.

———, "Effects of Part-Time 'Mothering' on IQ and SQ of Young Institutionalized Children," *Child Development*, vol. 44, 1973.

———, "Research Evaluation of a Foster Grandparent Program," *Journal of Children in Contemporary Society*, vol. 20, 1989.

Essie Seck, *National Intergenerational Research and Dissemination Project* (Los Angeles: Andrus Gerontology Center, University of Southern California, 1983).

Henrietta Sherwin and Judith Whang, *Foster Grandparents Providing Care for New Populations of High-Risk Children: A Research Study* (New York: New York City Department for the Aging, 1990).

Sociometrics, Inc., *An Evaluation of Family Caregiver Services* (Washington, DC: ACTION, 1988).

SRA Technologies, *Senior Companion Program Impact Evaluation* (Washington, DC: ACTION, 1985).

Laura Wilson, *The Senior Companion Program and Visiting Nurse Associations of American Public/Private Partnership Program: An Evaluation Report* (College Park: Center on Aging, University of Maryland, 1994).

Chapter Four: Reinventing Retirement

Volunteers in Medicine

In addition to visiting Volunteers in Medicine clinics in Hilton Head, South Carolina, and Stuart, Florida, reviewing materials from these organizations, and conducting interviews in each of these locations, I drew on the following important secondary sources (and some of the quotations and stories in this section are taken from them):

Jeri Butler, "Stuart Doctor Leads the Path to Healing Ways," *Palm Beach Post*, November 20, 1996.

———, "Volunteers See Dream of Clinic Become Reality," *Palm Beach Post*, March 27, 1998.

Tom Graves, "Open Arms, Healing Hands," *Tennessee Alumnus*, Spring 1996.

Lindsey Gruson, "Free Clinic Provides Model for Nation," *New York Times*, December 25, 1993.

John Kasich, *Courage Is Contagious* (New York: Doubleday, 1998).

Jack B. McConnell, *Circle of Caring* (Englewood, CO: Estes Park Institute, 1998).

———, "Transforming Lives, Transforming Communities," *Celebration Journal*, issue unknown.

Ponchitta Pierce, "These Doctors Work for Free," *Parade Magazine*, January 8, 1995.

Samaritan House Clinic

Because very little has been written about the Samaritan House Clinic, most of the material in this section is from extensive interviews with the individuals involved in the project. However, of use in developing this story was an unpublished article: Clifford Sewell et al., "A Free Multispecialty Medical and Dental Clinic for Needy Residents in an Affluent Community."

The Clinic Movement and Changing Face of Medicine

Peter J. Kilborn, "The Uninsured Find Fewer Doctors in the House," *New York Times*, August 30, 1998.

Shannon McCaffrey, "Retired Doctors to Offer Care for Uninsured," Associated Press State and Local Wire, January 14, 1999.

"Retired, but Not from Medicine," *American Medical News*, August 21, 1995.

Jennifer Steinhauer, "Rebellion in White: Doctors Pulling Out of H.M.O. Systems," *New York Times*, January 10, 1999.

Harriet Webster, "How a Small Town Started a Free Clinic," *Parade Magazine*, July 21, 1996.

Nancy Weil, "Born 20 Years Ago, Free Clinics Reach Out to Growing Numbers of Uninsured," *American News Service*, April 19, 1997.

Abigail Zuger, "Are Doctors Losing Touch with Hands-On Medicine?" *New York Times*, July 13, 1999.

Social Entrepreneurs

All quotations and material in this section are from these secondary sources:

Susan Agrest, "The Give-Back Years," *Time Select: Second Careers*, December 14, 1998.

J. Gregory Dees, "The Meaning of 'Social Entrepreneurship,'" unpublished paper, Stanford University Graduate School of Business.

HOPE MEADOWS

Steven Covey, "Brenda Krause Eheart," in Steve Covey, *Living the 7 Habits* (New York: Simon and Schuster, 1999).

Mark Harris, "It Takes This Village," *HOPE*, January/February 1997.

Dirk Johnson, "Program Creates Community for Foster Care," *New York Times*, April 1, 1996.

TROOPS TO TEACHERS

Elena Cabral, "From Tactics to Textbooks: Ex-Soldiers Get a Second Chance on the Teaching Front," *Ford Foundation Report*, Summer/Fall 1996.

Gail Russell Chaddock, "Atten-Hut! Teacher on Deck and Ready for Duty," *Christian Science Monitor*, September 1, 1998.

Mike Feinsilber, "Retiree Helps Turn Drill Instructors into Teachers," *Los Angeles Times*, May 15, 1994.

Richard W. Lyman, "Hexter's Good Idea," *New York Times*, December 20, 1996.

John McCormick, "A Class Act for the Ghetto: The Urban Teacher Corps Confronts the Inner City," *Newsweek*, December 23, 1991.

Charles Peters, "Tilting at Windmills," *Washington Monthly*, April 1999.

Amy Pyle, "Idled Scientists, Engineers to be Retrained as Teachers," *Los Angeles Times*, December 21, 1994.

Jacques Steinberg, "The Changing Face of America's Teachers," *New York Times*, April 5, 1998.

A. Alfred Taubman, "An Untapped Pool of Teachers," *New York Times*, March 12, 1989.

Nicole Tsong, "Surveys Show U.S. Veterans Make High-Caliber Teachers,"
    Hearst News Service, August 30, 1998.
Victor Volland, "J. H. Hexter, Professor Emeritus at WU, Dies," *St. Louis Post-
    Dispatch*, December 10, 1996.

PRINCETON PROJECT '55

Aims McGuinness, "In the Public Service," *Princeton Alumni Weekly*, February
    19, 1992.
Ralph Nader, "Making a Difference," *White House Conference on Aging Materials*,
    1995.
Ralph Nader and R. Gordon Douglas, "An Ancient Marauder Looms Again,"
    Los Angeles Times, February 16, 1998.

Chapter Five: Leaving a Legacy

This section is based chiefly on several years of field research at various Experience Corps projects around the country. The following secondary sources were also used and are the source of some quotations in the chapter:

The Origins of Experience Corps

William F. Buckley, Jr., *Gratitude* (New York: Random House, 1990).
Richard Danzig and Peter Szanton, *National Service: What Would It Mean?* (Lex-
    ington, MA: Lexington Books, 1986).
Marc Freedman, *The Kindness of Strangers: Adult Mentors, Urban Youth, and the
    New Voluntarism* (New York: Cambridge University Pres, 1999).
Marc Freedman, C. Anne Harvey, and Catherine Ventura-Merkle, "The Quiet
    Revolution: Elder Service and Youth Development in an Aging Society," pa-
    per prepared for the Carnegie Council on Adolescent Development, 1993.
————, *Seniors in National and Community Service* (New York: The Common-
    wealth Fund, 1994).
John W. Gardner, *No Easy Victories* (New York: Harper and Row, 1968).
————, "The Experience Corps," concept paper, 1988.
————, "Reinventing Community," speech to the Carnegie Council on Adoles-
    cent Development, December 11, 1992.
Eugene M. Lang, "We Have a Dream: The Generations Working Together To-
    ward the Future," in Robert N. Butler and Kenzo Kiikuni, eds., *Who Is Re-
    sponsible for My Old Age?* (New York: Springer, 1993).

Joseph Michalak, "Father of Invention," *New York Times*, November 3, 1991.
"Record Number of Students Expected in Fall," Associated Press, August 21,
   1998.

Experience Corps and Its Implications

Most of the material describing Experience Corps and its implications
comes from direct interviews with individuals involved in the program, with
the exception of quotations from the articles (listed below) by Constance
Casey (from Laurie Chilcote and Alfreda Horn), Murray Dubin (regarding
the Philadelphia Experience Corps), and Marianne Szegedy-Maszak (from
Harold Allen and the Philadelphia program).

Elijah Anderson, *Code of the Street* (New York: W. W. Norton, 1999).
Governor George W. Bush, "The Crisis Now at Hand," State of the State Ad-
   dress, January 31, 1996.
Robert N. Butler, *Why Survive?* (New York: Harper Torchbooks, 1975).
————, "Living Longer, Contributing Longer," *JAMA*, October 22–29, 1997.
Constance Casey, "Growing Elderly Population Not a Crisis but an Opportu-
   nity," Newhouse News Service, March 10, 1999.
Murray Dubin, "Seasoned Mentors," *Philadelphia Inquirer*, June 12, 1997.
Mitchell Duneier, *Slim's Table* (Chicago: University of Chicago Press, 1990).
Ken Dychtwald, *Age Wave: How the Most Important Trend of Our Time Will
   Change Your Future* (New York: Bantam Books, 1990).
Marc Freedman, "The Aging Opportunity," *American Prospect*, Winter 1996.
Marc Freedman and Linda Fried, *Launching Experience Corps* (San Francisco:
   Civic Ventures, 1999).
Linda P. Fried et al., "Building Communities That Promote Successful Aging,"
   Western Journal of Medicine, October 1997.
Michael Lerner, *The Politics of Meaning* (Reading, MA: Addison-Wesley, 1996).
Richard Louv, *101 Things You Can Do for Our Children's Future* (New York: An-
   chor Books, 1994).
Laurel McFarland, "A Golden National Service," *Brookings Review*, Summer
   1993.
Marc Peyser, "Home of the Gray," *Newsweek*, March 1, 1999.
Carol Stack, *Call to Home: African Americans Reclaim the Rural South* (New York:
   Basic Books, 1996).
Marianne Szegedy-Maszak, "Done with Work, Volunteers Move on to Giving
   Back," *New York Times*, March 20, 1999.

Joseph P. Tierney and Jean Baldwin Grossman, *Making a Difference: An Impact Study of Big Brothers/Big Sisters* (Philadelphia: Public/Private Ventures, 1996).

Chapter Six: If We Build It . . .

The Shifting Context for Later Life

AARP Public Policy Institute, *Boomers Approaching Midlife: How Secure a Future?* (Washington, DC: AARP, 1998).

Jonathan Alter, "Eject Button on Cynicism," *Newsweek*, November 9, 1998.

Douglas Brinkley, *The Unfinished Presidency* (New York: Viking, 1998).

Dana Canedy, "Gadgets to Go Gentle into Age," *New York Times*, October 17, 1998.

Jimmy Carter, *The Virtues of Aging* (New York: Ballantine, 1998).

———, "The Best Years of Our Lives," *Business Week*, July 20, 1998.

Andrew Cassel, "We May Have to Retire the Idea of Retirement," *Philadelphia Inquirer*, June 7, 1998.

Peter D. Hart Research Associates, The New Face of Retirement (Washington, DC: Peter D. Hart Research Associates, September 1999).

Susan Crowley, "Auto Legend Back in Business: Iacocca Pedals Quickly Away from Retirement," *AARP Bulletin*, February 1999.

William A. Davis, "The New School of Retirement," *Boston Globe*, February 17, 1999.

Arlyn Tobias Gajilan, "A Golden Age on Campus," *Newsweek*, November 9, 1998.

William L. Hamilton, "You're Not Getting Older, Products Are Getting Better," *New York Times*, June 27, 1999.

Michelle Himmelberg, "Graying Work Force Redefines Tradition," *Orlando Sentinel*, March 17, 1999.

Ellen Hoffman, "States' New Cash Crop: Recent Retirees," *AARP Bulletin*, May 1999.

Albert R. Hunt, "Fundamental Shift in What It Means to Be a Senior," *Wall Street Journal*, March 11, 1999.

Jon Jeter, "Never Too Old to Learn," *Washington Post*, April 14, 1998.

"John Glenn: The Sky Proved No Limit for This Ageless Astronaut," *People*, January 4, 1999.

Dirk Johnson, "In the Frost Belt, a Place in the Sun," *New York Times*, February 6, 1999.

Connie Koenenn, "Intellectual Property," *Los Angeles Times*, July 15, 1997.

———, "The Second Half: Raising Vitality of Retirement Communities," *Los Angeles Times*, July 6, 1998.

Robert Lewis, "Boomers May Spend Their Retirement—Working," *AARP Bulletin*, June 1998.

Cindy Looke, "Retirees Going Back to School—to Live," *Washington Post*, November 11, 1998.

Edwin McDowell, "Travel Industry Finds Adventure Is Now Ageless," *New York Times*, February 20, 1999.

Paula Mergenhagen, "Sun City Gets Boomerized," *American Demographics*, August 1996.

Lyn Riddle, "The Formula for Sun City Moves East and North," *New York Times*, January 4, 1998.

Robert A. Rosenblatt, "The Hucksters See Gold in That Gray Hair," *Los Angeles Times*, April 14, 1999.

James Peter Rubin, "Is There a P.A. in the House?" *Wall Street Journal: Encore Retirement*, March 8, 1999.

Glenn Ruffenach, "So Long, Bingo: Forget the Old Image of Retirement Communities," *Wall Street Journal: Encore Retirement*, March 9, 1998.

David Schwartz, "Planned Community Aims to Keep Aging Brains Fit," *Dallas Morning News*, May 17, 1998.

J. Walker Smith and Ann Clurman, *Rocking the Ages: The Yankelovich Report on Generational Marketing* (New York: HarperBusiness, 1997).

Debora Vrana, "A New Wrinkle in Retirement: With Baby Boomers Expected to Redefine Aging, Builders Are Trying to Stay Ahead," *Los Angeles Times*, August 28, 1996.

Prescriptions for an Aging Society

Philippe Aries, *Centuries of Childhood: A Social History of Family Life* (New York: Vintage, 1962).

Bill Bradley, "Back to School," *Bill Bradley Listening, Third Age Media*, Web article, December 1997.

Lisa Falk, "Intergenerational Center: New Option for Working Single Parents," paper for Parents Without Partners, September 1991.

Marilyn Gardner, "A Generation Plans Earlier—and More Boldly," *Christian Science Monitor*, November 6, 1997.

Malcolm Johnson, "Slowness," paper delivered to the American Sociological Association meeting, San Francisco, August 1998.

Carl Jung, "The Stages of Life," in Carl Jung, *The Structure and Dynamics of the Psyche* (Princeton: Princeton University Press, 1969).

Tom Moroney, "Many Retirees Find Work Is Less Taxing," *Boston Globe*, December 11, 1994.

Betsy Morris, "The Future of Retirement," *Fortune*, August 19, 1996.

Holcomb B. Noble, "Secret of Health in Old Age: Muscles," *New York Times*, October 30, 1998.

Robert Samuelson, "Off Golden Pond: The Aging of America and the Reinvention of Retirement," *New Republic*, April 12, 1999.

————, "Youth Service America Seeks to Pave Way for New Breed of Social Entrepreneurs," *Education Week*, May 10, 1999.

Meg Sommerfeld, "New Generation of Activists Channels Their Idealism," *Education Week*, May 10, 1995.

Toward a New Third Age

Natalie Angier, "Theorists See Survival Value in Menopause," *New York Times*, September 16, 1997.

Benjamin R. Barber, *A Place for Us: How to Make Society Civil and Democracy Strong* (New York: Hill and Wang, 1998).

Stuart Brand, *The Clock of the Long Now*, (New York: Basic Books, 1999).

Horace Deets, "New Retirement Means New Opportunities," *Modern Maturity*, July–August 1998.

John W. Gardner, "The Experience Corps," *Modern Maturity*, May–June 1998.

Daniel Goleman, "Erikson, in His Own Old Age, Expands His View of Life," *New York Times*, June 14, 1988.

————, "Compassion and Comfort in Middle Age," *New York Times*, February 6, 1990.

David Gutmann, *Reclaimed Powers: Men and Women in Later Life* (New York: Basic Books, 1987).

Carolyn G. Heilbrun, *The Last Gift of Time: Life Beyond Sixty* (New York: Dial Press, 1997).

John Kotre, *Outliving the Self* (New York: W. W. Norton, 1996).

Christopher Lasch, "Aging in a Culture Without a Future," *Hastings Center Report*, August 1977.

David Nicholson-Lord, "Mass Leisure Class Is on the Way, Say Forecasters," *The Independent*, April 18, 1994.

"Remarkable Individuals Receive Legacy Awards," *AARP Bulletin*, June 1999.

Zalman Schachter-Shalomi and Ronald S. Miller, *From Age-Ing to Sage-Ing*, (New York: Warner Books, 1995).

In writing this book I have accumulated a vast intellectual and emotional debt, one that I will never be able to repay. I am grateful, at least, to be able to acknowledge the support I received from many individuals.

First, I wish to thank the two brilliant documentary photographers I was privileged to work with on this project, Alex Harris and Thomas Roma, whom I can now count as friends. Their photographs are so beautiful that I think the great contribution of this book may be as a vehicle for showing their pictures. Anna Roma also deserves thanks for her advice in selecting the photographs.

Second, I would like to recognize my colleagues present and past at Civic Ventures, who not only picked up the slack while I was struggling to finish the manuscript, but also contributed in a variety of important, substantive ways to this project: Christa Scharfenberg, Beth Allison, Monica Regan, Cara Rice, Andrew Robinson, Martha Diepenbrock, and Trudy Patch. Jennifer Seltz and Sarah Bailin contributed additional research assistance, and Sue Halpern, Jane Staw, and Martin Kramer provided skilled editorial advice.

I am equally grateful for unwavering support from Civic Ventures' distinguished Board of Directors, who encouraged me to pursue this project and see it through to completion—and who sparked many of the ideas in *Prime Time*: Bill Berkeley, Phyllis Moen, Lisbeth Schorr, Gary Walker, John Rother, Jim Gibbs, and John Gardner.

Gary Walker deserves special thanks. As President of Public/Private Ventures during many of my fourteen years working at that organization, he did everything imaginable to help give birth to this book, from introducing me to The Work Connection, to putting Public/Private Ventures' resources behind the creation of Experience Corps and Civic Ventures, to enabling me to take a sabbatical to begin the writing that culminated in this manuscript. . . . The list could go on for many more pages, but the message is the same: This book would not have ever been written without Gary Walker.

Or for that matter Mike Bailin, Gary's predecessor as President of Public/Private Ventures, and the person who not only raised the money to study The Work Connection, but who mentored me every step of the way from a summer internship in 1983 to the creation of Civic Ventures a decade and a half later. In addition to Gary and Mike and my other former colleagues at Public/Private Ventures, I would like to thank that organization's Board of Directors—who tolerated my forays into the realm of later life even as Public/Private Ventures remained focused principally on young people.

Alongside Civic Ventures and Public/Private Ventures, another set of Experience Corps colleagues deserve credit for their invaluable contribution to this project. First and foremost, I would like to acknowledge the staff at the Corporation for National Service, in particular my friend Tom Endres. I am also indebted to John Keller, the heart and soul of the Experience Corps, and to Harris Wofford, Jim Scheibel, and Tess Scannell. Many thanks also go to Dr. Linda Fried of Johns Hopkins, who played an essential role in the creation of Experience Corps.

The individual Experience Corps projects contributed key perspectives to this book, and helped arrange my interviews with many of the individuals profiled in *Prime Time*. I would like to extend my appreciation to: Nancy Henkin and Rob Tietz of the Center for Intergenerational Learning at Temple University; Marcia Gross of the Philadelphia RSVP project; Stefana Sardo at the Portland, Oregon Foster Grandparent Program; Roxanne Smith-Parks, Cindy Mabry, and Jane Quist of the Port Arthur, Texas Foster Grandparent and RSVP Programs; Jean Greener and Rick Devich of Senior Resources in Minneapolis; and Alina Molina and Becky Haase of the RSVP/Community Service Society of New York.

This project could not have been undertaken without the generous financial support to Civic Ventures, Public/Private Ventures, and Experience Corps by a set of exemplary funders. In particular, I would like to thank Jane Quinn and Pam Stevens of the DeWitt Wallace-Reader's Digest Fund; Carol Larson, Hugh Burroughs, Mark Valentine, and Lucy Carter at the David and Lucile Packard Foundation; Sylvia Robinson, Gene Wilson, Dave Lady, Mark Kenney, Bob Rogers, and Leon Franklin of the Ewing M. Kauffman Foundation; Joan Colello, Laurie Dien, and Chris Bell at the Pinkerton Foundation; Mike Bailin and Nancy Roob at the Edna McConnell Clark Foundation; Sylvia Yee and Diane Yamashiro-Omi at the Evelyn and Walter Haas, Jr. Fund; Gilda Wray and Andy Fisher at the Charles Hayden Foundation; Jane Englebardt at the Hasbro Children's Foundation; Marilyn Hennessey and Sharon Markham at the Retirement Research Foundation; Carol Guyer and Anne

Romasco at the James C. Penney Foundation; Joan Wylie, formerly of the Luke B. Hancock Foundation; Joan Lipsitz, formerly of the Lilly Endowment; and the Carnegie Council on Adolescent Development.

The Commonwealth Fund of New York deserves special thanks for their critical support of the work that would eventually lead to this book, first through providing a grant to study the role older Americans could play in the realm of national service, and for supporting—along with the Foreign and Commonwealth Office of the British Government—an Atlantic Fellowship in Public Policy that enabled me to study aging issues while living in London during 1995–1996. I owe a great debt of thanks to Karen Davis and Margaret Mahoney at the Fund.

During my year in the U.K. I benefited from the hospitality, friendship, and intelligence of: Enid Irving and Sally Greengross of AgeConcern; Janet Atfield and Elizabeth Hoodless of Community Service Volunteers; Professor Anthea Tinker of King's College, University of London; William Plowden and Keith Kirby of the Atlantic Fellowships; Sir Norman Warner, formerly of the Home Office; Geoff Mulghan and Helen Wilkinson of DEMOS; Peter Laslett of Trinity College, Cambridge University; and Penelope Leach.

Back home, I have been the lucky recipient of much sage advice about this manuscript. John Rother, Carol Larson, Judy Goggin, Bill Berkeley, Phyllis Moen, John Gardner, and Steve Weiner read the book at various stages and provided valuable feedback. Emmy Werner, Suzanne Aisenberg, Peter Edelman, Suzanne Goldsmith, Cathy Ventura-Merkel, Barbara Herzog, Dick Gunther, Amitai Etzioni, Thomas Cole, Richard Danzig, Sara Rimer, Nancy Henkin, Julia Hough, Joel Fleishman, Gene Burns, Rob Gurwitt, Robert Putnam, Kristin Goss, Rachel Baker, Isabel Bradburn, Alex Hoffinger, Dan Levitt, Nancy Florence, Sara Glaser, Tom Long, and many others provided suggestions that enriched this book. Thanks go, as well, to Paul Starr, Jonathan Cohn, and Scott Stoessel at *The American Prospect* for helping me to craft the article that became the basis for the first chapter.

Connie Casey, Murray Dubin, Rob Eure, and Marianne Szegedy-Maszak enlightened me through their articles about Experience Corps and community service by older Americans—which I drew upon particularly in Chapter Five. I also want to acknowledge considerable intellectual debt to the historians whose work provides the foundation for Chapter Two, most notably Carole Haber and Brian Gratton, Tom Cole, Andrew Achenbaum, David Hacket Fischer, and William Graebner. The Sun Cities Area Historical Society was a great help, particularly its President Phyllis Street.

The following individuals (many of them featured in this book) gave generously in explaining their important work to me: Tom Flood, Peter DiCicco, Nick Spaneas, John Prybil, Mary Flynn, Susan Lavigne, Linda Angel, Bernie Nash, Sandy Kravitz, Sargent Shriver, Jack McConnell, Diane Montella, Richard Aulwurm, Anand Mehta, Adriana Valdovinos-Campa, John Curtis, Patsy LaViolette, Cherry Hendrix, Jesse Davidson, Richard Russell, Martha Jones, Laurie Chilcote, Ed Blystone, Harry Nelson, Oliver Crawford, Jeanette and Norman Mayer, Yakov Gritchener, and Arnita Murray.

Steve Weiner, Harold Allen, Thea Glass, Marv Welt, Aggie Bennett, and Louise Casey, spent many hours working with me to develop the first-person narratives that appear between the book's chapters. I thank them also for their willingness to be photographed by Alex Harris and Tom Roma for this project. Immense gratitude goes, additionally, to Bill Schwartz, Scott Smyth, and the other volunteers at the Samaritan House Clinic who form the backbone of Chapter Four.

None of the vast support described in the preceding paragraphs would have been translated into a book were it not for PublicAffairs. Peter Osnos took a chance on this book for his new publishing initiative then proceeded, in a trio of remarkable meetings, to contribute many of the most important insights contained in *Prime Time*. Geoff Shandler came up with the title for this book. But the greatest appreciation of all is reserved for Robert Kimzey, a gifted and generous editor who stood by the project even as I failed to meet deadline after deadline. His patience was heroic, his editing unsurpassed, and his intellectual contribution to this book central. Thanks go as well to the rest of PublicAffairs' talented staff.

In addition, I want to recognize the contribution of my family. My father, Bud Freedman showed me directly through his "retirement" work teaching basketball to developmentally disabled adults just how mutually-beneficial the contribution of older Americans could be. My grandmother, Martha Kravitz, found new life through volunteering in the RSVP program and imparted a similar set of lessons. Thanks also go to Phyllis Freedman, and to Lisa, Bill, Melinn, Josie, and Veronica Phifer.

I would also like to thank Anne Cheung for her intellectual contributions to this project, and for her steadfast emotional support as I was struggling to finish the writing. The book would never have been completed were it not for her help.

Finally this book is dedicated to John Gardner. I want to thank him for all he has taught me. His thinking constitutes the intellectual underpinning for this book, and his kindness, sense of humor, and abiding friendship are the inspiration for it. John embodies, in the richest possible way, the kind of later-life this book has attempted to champion.

INDEX

ABOUT THE AUTHOR

MARC FREEDMAN is President of Civic Ventures, a nonprofit organization dedicated to expanding the contribution of older Americans to our society. A former visiting fellow of Kings College, University of London, he has served as advisor to a wide range of organizations, including AARP, the Pillsbury Corporation, the Carnegie Council on Adolescent Development, the Corporation for National Service, and the David and Lucile Packard Foundation. His earlier book, *The Kindness of Strangers*, was described by the *Los Angeles Times* as the "definitive book on the [mentoring] movement." A high honors graduate of Swarthmore College with an MBA from Yale University, recipient of the Atlantic Fellowship in Public Policy, and delegate to the White House Conference on Aging, Freedman has testified before the U.S. Senate and U.S. House of Representatives on aging, children in poverty, and volunteer service. He lives in San Francisco.

Readers are invited to contact the author at mfreedman@civicventures.org.

PublicAffairs is a new nonfiction publishing house and a tribute to the standards, values, and flair of three persons who have served as mentors to countless reporters, writers, editors, and book people of all kinds, including me.

I.F. Stone, proprietor of *I. F. Stone's Weekly*, combined a commitment to the First Amendment with entrepreneurial zeal and reporting skill and became one of the great independent journalists in American history. At the age of eighty, Izzy published *The Trial of Socrates*, which was a national bestseller. He wrote the book after he taught himself ancient Greek.

Benjamin C. Bradlee was for nearly thirty years the charismatic editorial leader of *The Washington Post*. It was Ben who gave the *Post* the range and courage to pursue such historic issues as Watergate. He supported his reporters with a tenacity that made them fearless, and it is no accident that so many became authors of influential, best-selling books.

Robert L. Bernstein, the chief executive of Random House for more than a quarter century, guided one of the nation's premier publishing houses. Bob was personally responsible for many books of political dissent and argument that challenged tyranny around the globe. He is also the founder and was the longtime chair of Human Rights Watch, one of the most respected human rights organizations in the world.

. . .

For fifty years, the banner of Public Affairs Press was carried by its owner Morris B. Schnapper, who published Gandhi, Nasser, Toynbee, Truman, and about 1,500 other authors. In 1983 Schnapper was described by *The Washington Post* as "a redoubtable gadfly." His legacy will endure in the books to come.

Peter Osnos, *Publisher*